Multi-level Governance

Multi-level Governance

Edited by

IAN BACHE

and

MATTHEW FLINDERS

OXFORD
UNIVERSITY PRESS

OXFORD
UNIVERSITY PRESS

Great Clarendon Street, Oxford OX2 6DP

Oxford University Press is a department of the University of Oxford.
It furthers the University's objective of excellence in research, scholarship,
and education by publishing worldwide in

Oxford New York

Auckland Cape Town Dar es Salaam Hong Kong Karachi
Kuala Lumpur Madrid Melbourne Mexico City Nairobi
New Delhi Shanghai Taipei Toronto

With Offices in

Argentina Austria Brazil Chile Czech Republic France Greece
Guatemala Hungary Italy Japan South Korea Poland Portugal
Singapore Switzerland Thailand Turkey Ukraine Vietnam

Oxford is a registered trade mark of Oxford University Press
in the UK and in certain other countries

Published in the United States
by Oxford University Press Inc., New York

British Library Cataloguing in Publication Data
Data available

Library of Congress Cataloging in Publication Data
Data available

ISBN 978-0-19-925925-0 (Hbk.)
ISBN 978-0-19-925926-7 (Pbk.)

Printed in Great Britain
on acid-free paper by
Biddles Ltd., King's Lynn, Norfolk

Foreword

Multi-level governance, as the contributions to this book make clear, is both one of the oldest and one of the newest concepts in the study of politics. It is new because it offers a way of thinking about politics that moves beyond the concentration on the formal institutions and policy-making processes of states and governments that had come to characterize a certain kind of political science. But it is also old, because the opposition between pluralist and monist conceptions of politics, and between bottom-up and top-down explanations, has been present as long as there has been systematic reflection on politics and the nature of the political world.

The changes of the last thirty years in the way in which politics is conducted and organized have been unusually rapid and wide-ranging, and have challenged many assumptions that had become taken for granted. In the first half of the twentieth century strong trends enhanced the position of the nation state. But since the 1970s these trends have gone into reverse, with implications for the role of the nation state, leading to talk of its 'hollowing out' and even of its demise.

The concept of multi-level governance has been so widely adopted because it raises important questions about the continuing importance of nation states and central governments, and focuses attention on other levels and other actors, including non-state actors, as well as on the many ways in which governing functions can be discharged by agencies other than central government itself. The manner in which societies and political systems are steered, authoritative decisions taken, and outcomes achieved becomes of primary interest. Governance becomes organized through multiple jurisdictions and can no longer be understood as a central state monopoly. As the editors of this book, Ian Bache and Matthew Flinders, put it, the concept of multi-level governance seeks to explain 'the dispersion of central government authority both vertically, to actors located at other territorial levels, and horizontally, to non-state actors'.

The need for a new concept came about through reflection first on the emerging experiment in multi-level governance represented by the European Union, and second on the broader implications of the changing position of the nation state in a post-Westphalian world. The different phases of European integration over the last fifty years have furnished rich material for social scientists. But the concept of multi-level governance grew from the recognition that the European Union was best studied as a political system in its own right, rather than as a set of arrangements between governments. As a novel form of political organization it cannot be fully understood using the old categories. Nation states were centrally involved in the setting-up of the first European

Communities, and remain key actors in the European Union, but the kind of cooperation that they established has created a highly complex political system, which has become increasingly differentiated. Alongside the nation states, the central institutions of the Union such as the European Commission, the European Parliament, and the European Court have constituted a supranational level, while at the same time encouraging the development of a subnational regional level, particularly in those countries with little tradition of regional government. This is a multi-level system but it is not a simple hierarchy—rather the point of the concept of multi-level governance is that there are multiple jurisdictions that in many respects are overlapping. The complex interdependence of the European political space can be interpreted and analysed in many different ways, but without a concept like multi-level governance it would be difficult to know where to begin. This complexity is shortly due to increase with the expansion of the Union to twenty-five members, and further expansion beyond that is planned. The problems of framing the rules to coordinate such an association will require ever more sophisticated forms of multi-level governance.

A second reason for the interest in multi-level governance is because, as James Rosenau explains, widespread contemporary dissatisfaction with the quality of government by existing nation states is combined with an explosion in new forms of governance, the proliferation of new sets of rules and steering mechanisms to achieve the outcomes that citizens desire. These steering mechanisms reflect both the decline in the monopoly of the central state, and the increasing dissociation of some territorial and functional aspects of the state from the centralized nation state, whether at subnational or at supranational level. It is this sense of politics escaping from the control of nation states and becoming located in other agencies and institutions that characterizes the notion of multi-level governance. The response to new forms of interdependence, as the example of the European Union makes clear, is not the emergence of a new breed of super-states—a United States of Europe, for example, which would take over all the functions of the nation states from which it is composed. Instead the pattern is for a fragmentation and reorganization of state functions, both horizontally and vertically. As European integration has proceeded, so its character as a system of multi-level governance has become more pronounced.

Multi-level governance helps social scientists grasp the contemporary forms of interdependence and cooperation in political systems, but, as several contributors to this book make clear, notably Guy Peters and Jon Pierre, it is best studied through institutions rather than processes. It sets up an important research agenda, but we are only at the beginning of understanding the complex relationships that multi-level governance identifies, and of thinking through its implications. Many of these implications are troubling, in particular for the legitimacy and transparency of politics. Whatever the faults of nation states, their aspiration to acquire a monopoly of governance functions within

a specified territory did permit relatively clear forms of democratic accountability and representation to emerge. In a multi-level governance world, the
complexity of governance makes such accountability harder to establish, and
therefore makes widespread governance failure more likely, as noted by
Bob Jessop, as well as potentially increasing disaffection from politics and the
political class, and the declining political participation that is such a feature of
contemporary politics.

This book follows on from a very successful conference held by the Political
Economy Research Centre in Sheffield in July 2001, which brought together
social scientists interested in multi-level governance from a number of different
disciplines. We hoped to stimulate exchanges between the different approaches
represented at the conference and were not disappointed. The first part of the
book sets up debates on multi-level governance, drawing on key contributions
to the conference. The remaining chapters were commissioned subsequently to
address themes and issues raised by these contributions that were identified by
the editors.

The Political Economy Research Centre (PERC) has always seen its role as
providing a space in which interdisciplinary work in the social sciences can
flourish, and in which social scientists from different traditions and with
different commitments can engage and learn from one another. This volume is
an excellent product of that tradition, and an important contribution to the
study of multi-level governance.

Andrew Gamble
Director of the Political Economy Research Centre

Acknowledgements

In recent years the concept of 'multi-level governance' has located itself at the centre of debates concerning the future of nation states and the reallocation of powers both upwards to supranational organizations and downwards to sub-national levels. Recognition of the broad appeal of multi-level governance emerged from discussions between members of the interdisciplinary Political Economy Research Centre (PERC) at the University of Sheffield. The result of these discussions was a three-day conference on Multi-Level Governance, organized by the PERC, which attracted papers on multi-level governance from over scholars working in diverse academic traditions. This collection draws on the keynote addresses to that conference (Part One). These contributions were revised and subsequent chapters were commissioned after the conference to respond to the key themes and issues identified by the editors.

We are grateful to the contributors to this volume and to all those who took part in the Sheffield Conference. We would also like to thank Dominic Byatt, Philip Catney, Rachael Chapman, Andrew Gamble, Stephen George, Mike Kenny, Liesbet Hooghe, Sylvia McColm, Tony Payne, Martin Smith, and Andrew Taylor for their assistance and support during this project.

Ian Bache
Matthew Flinders
University of Sheffield
September 2003

Contents

Abbreviations and Acronyms

ABI	Area Based Initiative
BEPG	Broad Economic Policy Guidelines
BIC	British/Irish Council
BIGC	British/Irish Governmental Conference
CEC	Commission of the European Communities
CEN	Committee for European Normalization
CI	Community Initiative
COSLA	Convention of Scottish Local Authorities
CPRE	Campaign to Protect Rural England
DCMS	Department for Culture, Media and Sport
DETR	Department of the Environment, Transport and the Regions
DoE	Department of the Environment
DTI	Department of Trade and Industry
EC	European Community
ECB	European Central Bank
ECJ	European Court of Justice
ECOFIN	Council of Economic and Finance Ministers
ECPR	European Consortium for Political Research
EEC	European Economic Community
EIA	Environmental Impact Assessment
EIS	Environmental Impact Statements
EMU	European Monetary Union
EMU	Economic and Monetary Union
EPI	Environmental Policy Integration
EPO	European Policy Office
ERDF	European Regional Development Fund
ESCB	European System of Central Banks
ESRC	Economic and Social Research Council
EU	European Union
FOCJ	Functional, Overlapping, Competing Jurisdictions
GATT	General Agreement on Tariffs and Trade
GNP	Gross National Product
GOEM	Government Office for the East Midlands
GOR	Government Office in the Region
GOYH	Government Office for Yorkshire and Humber
HL	House of Lords
IGC	Intergovernmental Conferences
IGO	International Governmental Organization

IICK	Independent International Commission on Kosovo
ILO	International Labour Organization
IMF	International Monetary Fund
INGO	International Not-For-Profit Organisations
IPE	International Political Economy
IR	International Relations
JMC	Joint-Ministerial Council
KWNS	Keynesian Welfare National State
LI	Liberal Intergovernmentalism
MAFF	Ministry of Agriculture, Fisheries and Food
MEP	Member of the European Parliament
MOU	Memorandum of Understanding
NATO	North Atlantic Treaty Organisation
NGO	Non-Governmental Organization
NPM	New Public Management
NUTS	Nomenclature des Unite's Statistiques Territoriales
ODPM	Office of the Deputy Prime Minister
OECD	Organization for Economic Coooperation and Development
OJ	Official Journal
OMC	Open Method of Coordination
PERC	Political Economy Research Centre
PIU	Performance and Innovation Unit
QMV	Qualified Majority Voting
QUANGO	Quasi-Autonomous Non-Governmental Organization
RCU	Regional Coordination Unit
RDA	Regional Development Agency
RECHAR	Community Initiative Programme for the Conversion of Coal Mining Areas
RSPB	Royal Society for the Protection of Birds
SEA	Single European Act
SEA	Strategic Environmental Assessment
SGP	Stability and Growth Pact
SNA	Subnational Authority
SOA	Sphere of Authority
SPA	Special Protection Area
SPD	Single Programme Document
SRA	Strategic-Relational Approach
SRB	Single Regeneration Budget
SWPR	Schumpetarian Workfare Post-National Regime
TBD	Trans-Atlantic Business Dialogue
TI	Transparency International
TNC	Transnational Corporation
UK	United Kingdom

UN	United Nations
UNHRC	United Nations Human Rights Commission
US	United States
WB	World Bank
WBCSD	World Business Council for Sustainable Development
WEF	World Economic Forum
WEPE	Welsh European Programme Executive
WM	Westminster Model
WMD	Weapons of Mass Destruction
WTO	World Trade Organization
WWF	World Wildlife Fund

Notes on Contributors

IAN BACHE is Senior Lecturer in Politics at the University of Sheffield.

JENNY FAIRBRASS is a Senior Research Associate at the Centre for Social and Economic Research on the Global Environment (CSERGE) at the University of East Anglia.

MATTHEW FLINDERS is Senior Lecturer in Politics at the University of Sheffield.

ANDREW GAMBLE is Professor of Politics at the University of Sheffield.

STEPHEN GEORGE is a Professor in the Department of Politics, University of Sheffield.

LIESBET HOOGHE is Associate Professor of Political Science at the University of North Carolina at Chapel Hill, and Research Professor of Political Science at the Free University of Amsterdam.

BOB JESSOP is Professor of Sociology at Lancaster University.

ANDREW JORDAN is a Manager of the ESRC Programme on Environmental Decision Making (PEDM) at the University of East Anglia.

CAROLINE KENNEDY-PIPE is Professor of International Relations in the Department of Politics at the University of Sheffield.

GARY MARKS is Professor of Political Science at the University of North Carolina at Chapel Hill and Director of the UNC Center for European Studies, and Research Professor of Political Science at the Free University of Amsterdam.

GUY PETERS is Maurice Falk Professor of Government at the University of Pittsburgh.

JON PIERRE is Professor of Political Science at the University of Gothenburg, Sweden and Adjunct Professor of Political Science, University of Pittsburgh.

JONATHAN PERRATON is Lecturer in Economics and Deputy Director of the Political Economy Research Centre, University of Sheffield.

JAMES N. ROSENAU is University Professor of International Affairs at the George Washington University.

STEPHEN WELCH is Lecturer in Politics at the University of Durham.

PETER WELLS is Principal Research Fellow at the Policy Research Institute, Leeds Metropolitan University.

1

Themes and Issues in Multi-level Governance

IAN BACHE AND MATTHEW FLINDERS

> a new stage in the development of the world economic and political system
> has commenced, a new kind of world order, which is characterised both by
> unprecedented unity and unprecedented fragmentation. Understanding
> this new world order will require new modes of analysis and new theories,
> and a readiness to tear down intellectual barriers and bring together many
> approaches, methods and disciplines which have for too long been apart.
>
> (Gamble et al. 1996: 5)

This book takes the view that a more coherent view of knowledge demands
greater collaboration and understanding across academic approaches than
presently exists. Following this, we seek to develop understanding of the notion
of multi-level governance through a critical exploration of its definitions and
applications by scholars with very different concerns within the broad discipline
of Political Studies. Increasingly, there is a consensus emerging amongst scholars
from different academic perspectives that multi-level governance may provide a
unique opportunity to foster and develop a deeper understanding of the
complementarity of a range of theoretical and empirical models and tools drawn
from a number of interrelated disciplines and subdisciplines. It is in this vein that
this book seeks to assess and develop the concept of multi-level governance.

One of the clearest examples of the problems associated with academic
boundaries is the traditional separation between domestic and international
politics. A critique of this false dichotomy forms a central component of the
notion of multi-level governance (Marks et al. 1996: 346–7) and has more
generally been accepted in academic approaches to understanding the
European Union (EU). As Scharpf (2001: 2) argued, 'the conceptual tools with
which the political science subdisciplines of international relations and comparative politics are approaching the study of European institutions are ill suited to
deal with multilevel interactions'. The argument put is that the EU neither
resembles domestic polities nor international organizations, and therefore
defies explanation from approaches applied either to politics within states or
politics between states. As such, these traditional disciplines must engage in

dialogue to facilitate understanding of a complex and unpredictable world. Increasingly, multi-level governance has been seen to capture the shifting and uncertain patterns of governance within which the EU is just one actor upon a contested stage. However, in advance of attempting to gauge the utility of multi-level governance it is important to appreciate the intellectual development of the approach.

The Origins of Multi-level Governance: European Union Studies

Gary Marks (1992) first used the phrase multi-level governance to capture developments in EU structural policy following its major reform in 1988. Subsequently, Marks and others developed the concept of multi-level governance to apply more broadly to EU decision making. In developing his approach, Marks drew on insights from both the study of domestic politics and of international politics. Before this, most of the theorizing about the EU had been dominated by approaches derived from the study of international relations (IR). From the IR tradition of pluralism, Haas (1958) and Lindberg (1963) developed neofunctionalism, while from state-centred realism, Hoffmann (1964, 1966) applied intergovernmentalism. The concern of these theorists was with explaining the nature and pace of European integration. Intergovernmentalists emphasized the centrality of states in the process, developing the concept of governments as 'gatekeepers' able to resist unwanted consequences of integration. Neofunctionalists claimed that governments were increasingly caught up in a web of interdependence that provided a role for supranational actors and organized interests in shaping integration. The development of multi-level governance was part of a new wave of thinking about the EU as a political system rather than seeking to explain the process of integration (for a discussion of this, see Hix 1994; George and Bache 2001: 3–31).

The 'new wave' of thinking followed swiftly from the accelerated deepening of the integration process in the mid to late 1980s. This deepening was symbolized by Member States' agreement to the Single European Act (SEA) in 1987. While the SEA was ostensibly important in formalizing governments' collective commitment to completing the internal market, which had been the aspiration of the 1957 Treaty of Rome, the less publicized reforms to the EU's decision-making processes contained provisions that stimulated the shift away from perceiving the European Union in the same way as other international organizations. In particular, agreement to the increased use of qualified majority voting in place of unanimity across a number of policy areas was the starting point for the treatment of the EU as something with characteristics more reflective of domestic political systems than international organizations. As such, theorizing the EU grew more concerned with issues of EU governance than with understanding it as an example of international cooperation.

In the context of moves to complete the single market, and to assimilate Greece, Portugal, and Spain into the Community, the Commission and its allies in the European Parliament won support from governments for a major reform of structural policy in 1988. As a side-payment to poorer member states for the anticipated consequences of the internal market programme, governments agreed to double allocations of structural funding to assist the development of disadvantaged regions. As part of the desire to ensure effective use of these funds, governments—some reluctantly—accepted the Commission's proposal that funds be administered through partnerships established within member states, consisting of representatives of national, regional (and/or local), and supranational actors (namely, the Commission). It was from a study of these developments in structural policy, and the partnership principle in particular, that Gary Marks (1992, 1993) developed the concept of multi-level governance.

In an early article on the subject, Marks defined multi-level governance as 'a system of continuous negotiation among nested governments at several territorial tiers' (1993: 392). In developing this definition, he drew on analysis of domestic politics, specifically the policy networks approach, in describing how within multi-level governance 'supranational, national, regional, and local governments are enmeshed in territorially overarching policy networks' (Marks 1993: 402–3). The multi-level governance concept thus contained both vertical and horizontal dimensions. 'Multi-level' referred to the increased interdependence of governments operating at different territorial levels, while 'governance' signalled the growing interdependence between governments and non-governmental actors at various territorial levels.

Although not a theory of integration, Marks's conception of multi-level governance shared with neofunctionalism the view that supranational actors and interest groups were significant in shaping EC decisions. In addition, Marks argued, subnational actors were increasingly influential in decision making, so EC decision making could be described as multi-level, whereas previously only two territorial levels—national and supranational—had been deemed worthy of serious analysis in the debate between neofunctionalists and intergovernmentalists. To this insight on the importance of the subnational tier, Marks added insights from the policy networks approach, which had gained much support from the late 1980s onwards. In Britain, the development of this approach owed much to the work of Rhodes (1988) and emphasized state fragmentation and the growing role of non-state actors in decision making. In short, therefore, the rise of the subnational level and acknowledgement of the significance of policy networks combined to stimulate the initial conception of multi-level governance in EU studies.

Multi-level Governance beyond European Union Studies

That multi-level governance drew on domestic and international approaches to politics in analysing the EU provided overlaps with the approaches of scholars working in other academic areas. The concept of governance in particular already had prominence in domestic and international studies, and the 'multi-level' aspect echoed the work of those studying intergovernmental relations within states. Increasingly though, scholars found the need for analysis across increasingly contested jurisdictional and territorial boundaries both within and beyond states. For example, academics seeking to explain developments in British politics increasingly acknowledged the importance of a multi-level framework to recognize not only the formal institutional levels of locality, region, state, and Europe, but also the 'steering role' of transnational organizations such as the World Trade Organization, International Monetary Fund and World Bank (Pierre and Stoker 2000: 29).

Of course, multi-level governance is not the only concept used to describe such developments. As Hooghe and Marks point out in Chapter 2 of this volume, terms such as multi-tiered governance, polycentric governance, multi-perspectival governance, FOCJ (functional, overlapping, competing jurisdictions), fragmegration, and SOAs (spheres of authority) have all been employed to capture developments. While these concepts have different aspects, they share a concern with explaining the dispersion of central government authority both vertically, to actors located at other territorial levels, and horizontally, to non-state actors. To date, however, none of these alternative conceptualizations has captured the imagination and thus seeped across academic boundaries in the way that multi-level governance has begun to do.

The Structure of the Book

From the chapters in the first part of the book we highlight here a number of themes that are addressed in subsequent contributions. Some of these themes are common to all of the chapters in Part 1; others emerge from specific contributions. According to their focus, contributors to Parts 2 and 3 of the book address different themes to different degrees. However, we return to address all seven themes directly in the concluding chapter.

Themes

The future of nation states vis-à-vis subnational and supranational organizations and the increasing fluidity of political power are fundamental issues for scholars of politics and government. While multi-level governance remains a contested concept, its broad appeal reflects a shared concern with understanding increased complexity, proliferating jurisdictions, the rise of non-state actors, and the related challenges to state power. Hooghe and Marks (Chapter 2, p.16) note:

A common element across these literatures is that the dispersion of governance across multiple jurisdictions is both more efficient than and normatively superior to the central state monopoly. Most important is the claim that governance must operate at multiple scales in order to capture variations in the territorial reach of policy externalities. Because externalities arising from the provision of public goods vary immensely—from planet-wide in the case of global warming to local in the case of most city services—so should the scale of governance.

That there are many concepts that seek to capture the changing context in which the state operates gives rise to the need for conceptual clarity. This provides the first two of our themes:

Theme One—How should we define multi-level governance?
Theme Two—How is multi-level governance utilised by scholars working in different academic fields?

In Chapter 2, Hooghe and Marks argue that an understanding of the dynamics of authoritative decision making requires a broader focus than the distribution of policy and fiscal responsibilities between jurisdictions. In most cases, it is necessary to consider how different jurisdictions interact with each other. This requires a focus on both formal and informal institutions to explain whether hierarchy, interdependence, or relative independence characterizes relationships. Beyond this, it is necessary to consider whether jurisdictions are general-purpose or specialized, mutually exclusive or overlapping, stable or fluctuating.

In seeking clarity, Hooghe and Marks distinguish between contrasting visions from various literatures, which they label Type I and Type II multi-level governance. Type I multi-level governance echoes federalist thought, conceiving the dispersion of authority as being limited to a 'limited number of non-overlapping jurisdictional boundaries at a limited number of levels'. In this view, authority is relatively stable and analysis is focused on individual governments rather than on specific policies. Type II multi-level governance provides a vision of governance that is 'a complex, fluid, patchwork of innumerable, overlapping jurisdictions'. Here, jurisdictions tend to be flexible as demands for governance change. Examining specific policies provides a way of exploring variations in the operation of multi-level governance and its validity as an analytical model. This leads us to our third theme:

Theme Three—How do the structures and processes of multi-level governance differ across policy sectors and how can these differences be explained?

In Chapter 3, James Rosenau considers whether multi-level governance can serve as a 'prime mechanism' to steer the tensions of 'fragmegration' in constructive directions. Fragmegration, a contraction of the terms 'fragmentation' and 'integration', refers to the 'diverse and contradictory forces that can be summarized in the clash between globalization, centralization, and integration on the one hand and localization, decentralization, and fragmentation on the other' (p.34). The process of fragmegration stimulates the need for new and relevant forms of governance.

For Rosenau, governance consists of 'rule systems'; these are 'steering mechanisms through which authority is exercised in order to enable the governed to preserve their coherence and move toward desired goals'. Rule systems have authority through a range of both formal and informal means. Formal means include constitutions and laws, while processes created informally can be regarded as authoritative through repeated practices, even where there is no constitutional or legal sanction. Both formal and informal rule systems constitute what Rosenau describes as 'spheres of authority' (SOAs) that 'define the range of their capacity to generate compliance on the part of those persons towards whom their directives are issued'. As Rosenau argues, 'compliance is the key to ascertaining the presence of a SOA'. Following this, Rosenau suggests that politics can be conceptualized as governed through a 'bifurcated system', one in which states and their national executives have long dominated events and the other as a 'multi-centric system' which contains a diverse array of collectivities that have emerged as rival sources of authority to states. These rival sources can both compete and cooperate with states in this multi-centric system.

Rosenau prefers the concept of SOAs, because he suggests the concept of multi-level governance, while having many virtues, can both be 'misleading and imprisoning' and 'does not allow for a full analysis of the complexity of the emergent political world'. In particular, 'its scope does not encompass the diverse arrays of SOAs that are crowding the global stage'. Rosenau's main criticism of multi-level governance is an important one and is worth quoting at length:

The notion of multi-levels suggests governmental hierarchies and explicitly posits the various levels as vertically structured in layers of authority, whereas the mushrooming demands for governance are also being met in a host of horizontal ways, through SOAs that may be widely dispersed and not necessarily linked to each other through layered hierarchies. Put differently, many of the demands for governance involve an insistence on autonomy that may or may not be operative within hierarchical structures. (Chapter 3, p.39)

Further:

Since governance involves the exercise of authority and the necessity of people looking 'up' to, and complying with, the authorities to which they are responsive, it is understandable that the multi-level governance concept connotes hierarchy. But once one broadens one's analytic antennae to encompass networking processes and a variety of dissimilar SOAs, it becomes clear that authority relations have to be reconceived. (Chapter 3, p.40).

This is a contentious issue, which, at this stage, we simply highlight as a theme for contributors to consider.

Theme Four—Does multi-level governance connote hierarchy? If so, is this a weakness in the approach?

In Chapter 4, Bob Jessop seeks to criticize the 'principal theoretical approaches to EU government and/or governance from the viewpoint of a strategic-relational approach to the state'. In particular, Jessop considers the rival approaches for understanding multi-level governance in the EU that can be conceptualized as 'state-centric' and 'simple governance' perspectives. The failure of these approaches leads him to propose an alternative account 'in terms of the strategic selectivity of the state as a social relation, issues of governance failure, meta governance, and meta governance failure'. Here we focus on Jessop's critique of governance approaches, of which there are three. First, he suggests that 'work on governance often tends to remain at the pre-theoretical stage of critique: it is much clearer what the notion of governance is against than what it is for' (p.61). Second, 'governance theories tend to be closely connected to problem-solving and crisis-management in a wide range of fields . . . this can easily lead to a neglect of problems of governance failure' (p.61). Third, 'because many studies of governance are concerned with specific problem fields or objects of governance, they tend to ignore questions of the relative compatibility or incompatibility of different governance regimes and their implications for the overall unity of the European project and European statehood. And . . . many empirical studies have overlooked (or, at least failed to theorize) the existence of meta-steering' (p.62).

From this critique, Jessop suggests that what we are perhaps witnessing is the 're-scaling of the sovereign state or the emergence of just one more arena in which national states pursue national interests' (p.63). In other words, the shift to governance is being countered by the increased role of governments in metagovernance: that is, in providing the 'ground rules' for governance. This emerging metagovernance role 'means that the forms of networking, negotiation, noise reduction, and negative coordination characteristic of governance take place ' "in the shadow of hierarchy" ' (p.65). This argument leads us to the fifth theme of the book:

Theme Five—What implications does multi-level governance have for the power, position and role of the nation state? Does multi-level governance indicate an erosion of the nation state, as is often assumed, or does it lead to a transformation or reorganisation of state power? In particular, what evidence is there of national governments attempting to increase their steering capacity in the context of multi-level governance?

Jessop argues that the changes taking place redefine the role of the nation state to that of coordination in the context of metagovernance. However, this redefinition does not exclude state executives from a 'continuing and central political role'. This remaining centrality of state executive power is ensured by its democratic credentials: 'Unless or until supranational political organization acquires not only governmental powers but also some measure of popular democratic legitimacy, the national state will remain a key political factor as the highest instance of bourgeois democratic political accountability' (p.66) Yet, there is no end metagovernance position in which subordinate forms of governance will be coordinated in stable equilibrium. As Jessop argues, 'this would re-introduce the principle of sovereignty or hierarchy which growing social complexity and globalization now rule out' (p.66).

In summary, and in accordance with the objectives of this book, Jessop suggests that 'the key issue for a research agenda into this new form of statehood becomes the manner and extent to which the multiplying levels, arenas, and regimes of politics, policy making, and policy implementation can be endowed with a certain apparatus and operational unity horizontally and vertically; and how this affects the overall operation of politics and the legitimacy of the new political arrangements'. This final point links well with the concern for democratic accountability in the context of multi-level governance outlined in Chapter 5.

In Chapter 5, Guy Peters and Jon Pierre argue that 'most of the analytical models and interpretations of multi-level governance that we have seen so far have fallen into the same trap as some analyses of governance, that is, a previously state-centric and constitutional perspective has been almost completely replaced by an image of governing in which institutions are largely irrelevant' (p.75). They suggest that multi-level governance 'lacks both a clear conceptual analysis as well as a critical discussion of multi-level governance as a democratic process' (p.76). They identify a particular danger in relation to the development of multi-level governance in that 'the absence of distinct legal frameworks and the reliance on sometimes quite informal negotiations between different institutional levels could well be a 'Faustian Bargain' where actors only see the attractions of the deal and choose to ignore the darker consequences of the arrangement' (p.76). Along the same lines as other authors in Part 1, Peters and Pierre suggest that the key question is that of the role of government in these emerging forms of governance (p.78).

Peters and Pierre address multi-level governance both as an analytic concept and as a system adopted by decision-makers for its capacity to address the complex governance demands of the modern epoch. In relation to this, they consider whether the problem-solving capacity of multi-level governance and the achievement of effective policy outcomes take precedence over democratic input and accountability. This leads to the argument that multi-level governance could be a 'Faustian bargain' in which, 'core values of democratic government are traded for accommodation, consensus and the purported efficiency in governance' (p.85), or put another way, where 'informal patterns of political coordination could in fact be a strategy for political interests to escape or bypass regulations put in place explicitly to prevent that from happening' (p.85). This argument leads us to our sixth theme.

Theme Six—What are the implications of multi-level governance for democratic accountability?

Peters and Pierre also point to some of the perceived problems of multi-level governance as a theoretical model. In particular, they suggest that 'multi-level governance appears incapable of providing clear predictions or even explanations (other than the most general) of outcomes in the governing process'. Following this argument, we present our final theme.

Theme Seven—What are the limitations of the multi-level governance model?

In Part two of the book the concept of multi-level governance is applied within what may be considered territorially defined sub-disciplines of politics. On one level, it appears contradictory to apply a model that explicitly challenges the notion of traditional territorial boundaries to the study of, say, British politics. Our purpose here though is to examine whether this model does have value within politics sub-disciplines that have been traditionally defined in this way.

In Chapter 6, Ian Bache and Matthew Flinders assess the value of multi-level governance in relation to British politics. A number of authors in this field have developed governance approaches, often in explicit counterpoint to the dominant framework for understanding British politics, the Westminster Model (WM). The governance literature points to challenges to state power in the context of the upwards, downwards, and sideways flows of competences discussed above. However, the related processes of devolution and decentralization have arguably given added resonance to the 'multi-level' dimension of governance *within* the territorial boundaries of the British State. In this context in particular, this chapter considers whether multi-level governance provides a useful framework of analysis.

In Chapter 7, Stephen George considers the application of multi-level governance to developments in the EU. While multi-level governance developed from and has been most often applied to studies of the EU, its capacity to explain developments remains strongly contested. This chapter outlines the main applications of the concept in a number of policy areas and evaluates the position of multi-level governance alongside competing approaches in the current 'state of the debate' on the EU.

In Chapter 8, Stephen Welch and Caroline Kennedy-Pipe consider the relevance of multi-level governance to developments in international relations (IR). In doing so, they provide a synoptic review of five issue areas in IR, where multi-level governance might be thought likely to arise, before coming to an assessment of the utility of the concept in this field. The areas discussed are: the *international system*; the role of *supranational organizations; international civil society; international civic norms*; and *transnational threats and risks*.

Part three of the book turns to policies. In Chapter 9, Jenny Fairbrass and Andrew Jordan examine the relevance of multi-level governance for understanding environmental policy-making. In doing so, their case studies of biodiversity and land use planning policy in the United Kingdom (UK) are seen as 'critical tests' for multi-level governance. This is partly because the UK is seen as an 'extreme case' of a unitary state and the government has traditionally approached European negotiations with great scepticism. Moreover, because environmental policy is regulatory, the costs are likely to fall most heavily on national actors rather than the EU. Drawing on a comparison with EU structural policy, they find that there are parallels in the governance of the two policy domains in that they both exhibit intricate, disputed, and unpredictable decision-making.

In Chapter 10, Ian Bache considers the utility of multi-level governance in relation to the implementation of EU regional policy. This chapter provides an examination of multi-level governance on its 'own ground': the concept was developed from a study of EC/EU regional policy and is said to be most prominent at the implementation stage of the policy process. However, in addition to discussing multi-level governance and EU regional policy across Member States, particular attention is given to its implementation in the UK: which, for reasons suggested above, presents a 'hard case' for multi-level governance theorists.

In Chapter 11, Jonathon Perraton and Peter Wells explore the relevance of multi-level governance for understanding economic policy-making. They note that three general trends can be seen in this policy area in the last 50 years: first, the ceding of power to supranational institutions in the field of economic policy-making, second, the creation of subnational regional infrastructures that can often have economic policy-making capacities, and third, the adoption of new policy instruments by national governments that commonly involve partnership arrangements with the private sector. Perraton and Wells explore the relevance of multi-level governance in relation to these trends and its relationship to approaches that are grounded in economics, notably fiscal federalism.

In the concluding chapter, we return to the issue of the challenges of and opportunities for multi-disciplinarity that multi-level governance provides. In this discussion, we reflect on the key themes developed above that we bring together below.

- How should we define multi-level governance?
- How is multi-level governance utilized by scholars working in different disciplinary traditions?
- How do the structures and processes of multi-level governance differ across policy sectors and how can these differences be explained?
- Does multi-level governance connote hierarchy? If so, is this a weakness in the approach?
- What implications does multi-level governance have for the power, position, and role of the nation state? Does multi-level governance indicate an erosion of the nation state, as is often assumed, or does it lead to a

transformation or reorganization of state power? In particular, what evidence is there of national governments attempting to increase their steering capacity in the context of multi-level governance?

- What are the implications of multi-level governance for democratic accountability?
- What are the limitations of the multi-level governance model?

Part One

Theory

2

Contrasting Visions of Multi-level Governance

GARY MARKS AND LIESBET HOOGHE

Centralized authority has given way to new forms of governing.[1] Formal authority has been dispersed from central states both up to supranational institutions and down to regional and local governments. A recent survey finds that sixty-three of seventy-five developing countries have been undergoing some decentralization of authority (Garman et al. 2001: 205). A detailed index drawn up by the authors of this paper finds that no EU country became more centralized since 1980, while half have decentralized authority to a regional tier of government (Hooghe and Marks 2001). The 1980s and 1990s have also seen the creation of a large number of transnational regimes, some of which exercise real supranational authority. At the same time, public/private networks of diverse kinds have multiplied from the local to the international level.

The diffusion of authority in new political forms has led to a profusion of new terms: multi-level governance, multi-tiered governance, polycentric governance, multi-perspectival governance, functional, overlapping, competing jurisdictions (FOCJ), fragmegration (or spheres of authority), and consortio and condominio, to name but a few. The evolution of similar ideas in different

Earlier versions of this chapter have been presented at the EU Studies Association, May 2001; a conference on 'Multi-Level Governance: Interdisciplinary perspectives', Sheffield University, June 2001; a conference on 'Multi-Level Governance and Federalism' at the University of North Carolina at Chapel Hill, March 2002; European Consortium for Political Research (ECPR) pan-European Conference on European Union Politics, Bordeaux, September 2002; and at the Free University of Amsterdam; Indiana University at Bloomington; University of Hanover; Harvard University; University of Mannheim; Humboldt University; Sciences Po, Paris; the Social Science Center, Berlin; and the Technical University of Munich. We wish to thank participants at these events for comments. Our special thanks go to Chris Ansell, Ian Bache, Arthur Benz, Tanja Börzel, Renaud Dehousse, Peter Hall, Matthew Flinders, Stephen George, Bob Jessop, Beate Kohler Koch, Hans Keman, David Lake, Patrick Le Galès, Richard Haesly, Christiane Lemke, David Lowery, Michael McGinnis, Andrew Moravcsik, Franz U. Pappi, Thomas Risse, James Rosenau, Elinor Ostrom, Alberta Sbragia, Philippe Schmitter, Christian Tusschoff, and the political science discussion group at the University of North Carolina. None of the above is responsible for errors.

[1] We define governance as binding decision making in the public sphere.

fields can be explained partly as diffusion from two literatures—federalism and public policy. But we suspect that this conceptual invention has independent sources. In this chapter, we do not summarize the particularities of the concepts that have been put forward, nor do we do justice to the intellectual history of the field. Instead we mine the relevant literatures for some conceptual benchmarks in order to facilitate empirical analysis.

These literatures agree that the dispersion of governance across multiple jurisdictions is both more efficient than, and normatively superior to, central state monopoly (Marks and Hooghe 2000). They claim that governance must operate at multiple scales in order to capture variations in the territorial reach of policy externalities. Because externalities arising from the provision of public goods vary immensely—from planet-wide in the case of global warming to local in the case of most city services—so should the scale of governance. To internalize externalities, governance must be multi-level. This is the core argument for multi-level governance, but there are several other perceived benefits. For example, more decentralized jurisdictions can better reflect heterogeneity of preferences among citizens.[2] Multiple jurisdictions can facilitate credible policy commitments (Pollack 1997; Majone 1998). Multiple jurisdictions allow for jurisdictional competition (Weingast 1995; Frey and Eichenberger 1999). And they facilitate innovation and experimentation (Gray 1973).

However, beyond the presumption that governance has become (and should be) multi-jurisdictional, there is no agreement about how multi-level governance should be organized. We detect two contrasting visions.

The first conceives of dispersion of authority to jurisdictions at a limited number of levels. These jurisdictions—international, national, regional, meso, local—are *general-purpose*. That is to say, they bundle together multiple functions, including a range of policy responsibilities, and in many instances, a court system and representative institutions. The membership boundaries of such jurisdictions do not intersect. This is the case for jurisdictions at any one level, and it is the case for jurisdictions across levels. In this form of governance, every citizen is located in a Russian Doll set of nested jurisdictions, where there is one and only one relevant jurisdiction at any particular territorial scale. Territorial jurisdictions are intended to be, and usually are, stable for several decades or more, though the allocation of policy competencies across levels is flexible.

A second vision of governance is distinctly different. It conceives of *specialized* jurisdictions that, for example, provide a particular local service, solve a

---

[2] Assuming that this heterogeneity can be jurisdictionally captured. For most purposes, this demands that heterogeneity is territorial, so that groups with distinct preferences have a separate territorial government, or that heterogeneity is socially pillarized, and thus amenable to consociational arrangements. Moreover, the greater the number of jurisdictions, the higher the informational demands on citizens who are assumed to fully understand the costs/benefits of alternative jurisdictional arrangements. This assumption is often unrealistic, as has been demonstrated even at the local level, where opportunities for accurate citizen information are greatest (Lowery et al. 1995; Hoogland DeHoog et al. 1990).

TABLE 2.1. Types of multi-level governance

Type I	Type II
General-purpose jurisdictions	Task-specific jurisdictions
Non-intersecting memberships	Intersecting memberships
Jurisdictions at a limited number of levels	No limit to the number of jurisdictional levels
System-wide architecture	Flexible design

common pool resource problem, select a product standard, monitor water quality in a particular river, or adjudicate international trade disputes. The number of such jurisdictions is potentially huge, and the scales at which they operate vary finely. And there is no great fixity in their existence. They tend to be lean and flexible—they come and go as demands for governance change.

Table 2.1 summarizes these visions of governance as logically consistent ideal-types. The first two attributes in Table 2.1 describe variation among individual jurisdictions, while the remainder describe systemic properties. We call these types simply Type I and Type II to avoid burdening readers with yet more jargon in an already jargon-laden field.[3]

Type I Multi-level Governance

The intellectual foundation for Type I multi-level governance is federalism, which is concerned with power sharing among governments operating at just a few levels. Federalism is chiefly concerned with the relationship between central government and a tier of non-intersecting subnational governments. The unit of analysis is the individual government, rather than the individual policy. In the words of Wallace Oates, dean of fiscal federalism, 'the traditional theory of fiscal federalism lays out a general normative framework for the assignment of functions to different levels of government and the appropriate fiscal instruments for carrying out these functions' (Oates 1999: 1121). The framework is system-wide; the functions are bundled; and the levels of government are multiple but limited in number.[4] Type I multi-level governance shares these basic characteristics, but is not confined to national states. We discuss these characteristics in turn.

---

[3] This and the following section are based on Hooghe and Marks 2003.

[4] Traditional federalism studies focused on constitutional federations, which reduced the universe to a handful of primarily western cases (e.g. Wheare 1953; Riker 1964; but not Daniel Elazar 1987, 1991). Contemporary work focuses more broadly on the benefits and costs of centralization versus decentralization of authority. This expands the universe of cases in two directions. First, it enables scholars to apply insights from federalism to all countries with some form of non-unitary rule.

General-purpose jurisdictions. Decision-making powers are dispersed across jurisdictions, but bundled in a small number of packages. Federalists and students of intergovernmental relations tend to emphasize the costs of decomposing authority. This concern is especially strong in Europe where local government usually exercises 'a wide spread of functions, reflecting the concept of general-purpose local authorities exercising comprehensive care for their communities' (Norton 1991: 22).

Non-intersecting memberships. Type I jurisdictions are characterized by non-intersecting memberships.[5] Membership is usually territorial, as in national states, regional, and local governments, but it can also be communal, as in consociational polities.[6] Such jurisdictions are defined by durable memberships that do not intersect at any particular level. Moreover, the memberships of jurisdictions at higher and lower tiers do not intersect. This extends the Westphalian principle of exclusivity into the domestic arena (Caporaso 2000: 10; see also Krasner 1999). The same principle is present in the international arena, where the United Nations, the World Trade Organization (WTO), and the European Union encompass national states.[7]

The key systemic characteristics of Type I multi-level governance are as follows:

Limited number of jurisdictional levels. Type I multi-level governance organizes jurisdictions at just a few levels. Among students of intergovernmental relations, it is common to distinguish a local, an intermediate, and a central level although, in practice, the number of levels varies. According to the European NUTS (Nomenclature des Unite's Statistiques Territoriales) classification, they vary between three in the case of Luxembourg and six for Finland, Greece, Portugal, and the United Kingdom. That count is on the high side; in some countries, not all NUTS tiers correspond to governmental organizations. For example, upon entry

---

Hence, the wave of studies on decentralization in former non-democratic countries (Prud'homme 1995; Inman and Rubinfeld 1997; Besley and Coates 1999; Panizza 1999; Treisman 1999). Second, relaxing federalism to include non-constitutional dispersion of authority has led students of federalism to examine diffusion of authority *beyond* the national state. Applying categories from American federalism, Inman and Rubinfeld have analysed the dynamics of fiscal federalism in the European Union (Scharpf 1988; Bureau and Champsaur 1992; Casella and Frey 1992; Inman and Rubinfeld 1992; Sbragia 1992, 1993; Vaubel 1994; Casella and Weingast 1995; see also Alesina and Wacziarg 1999; Weiler 2000). Yet the premises of this recent literature are the same: 'how many local and state governments there should be; how they will be represented in the central government; and how policy responsibilities should be allocated between the central government and the lower tiers' (Inman and Rubinfeld 1997: 43). The levels of jurisdictions are limited—usually two or three, and sometimes four; the number of jurisdictions is restricted; and policy competencies are bundled.

[5] While membership of Type I jurisdictions is non-intersecting, competencies are often shared or overlapping. There has, for example, been a secular trend away from compartmentalization in federal polities.

[6] Other examples of non-territorial Type I governance are the clan system in Somalia, communal self-governance in the Ottoman empire, and religious self-governance in India.

[7] There are a few exceptions. For example, Greenland and the Faeroe Islands, self-governing parts of Denmark, are not members of the European Union.

in the European Union, the Swedish government created eight larger regions (*riksområden*) at the NUTS 2 level to facilitate the implementation of EU cohesion policy. However, these are merely statistical constructs (Hooghe and Marks 2001).

System-wide, durable architecture. One does not arrive at general-purpose, non-intersecting, and nested jurisdictions by accident. Systemic institutional choice is written all over Type I multi-level governance. In modern democracies, Type I jurisdictions usually adopt the *trias politicas* structure of an elected legislature, an executive (with a professional civil service), and a court system. As one moves from smaller to larger jurisdictions, the institutions become more elaborate but the basic structure is similar. Though the institutions of the German federal government are far more complex than those of a French town, they resemble each other more than they do the Type II arrangements described below.

Type I jurisdictions are durable. Jurisdictional reform—that is, creating, abolishing, or radically adjusting new jurisdictions—is costly and unusual. Change normally consists of reallocating policy functions across existing levels of governance. The institutions responsible for governance are sticky, and they tend to outlive the conditions that brought them into being.

Type I multi-level governance is not limited to federalism and inter-governmental relations. It captures a notion of governance common among EU scholars. Elsewhere, we have described the reorganization of authority in the European Union as 'a polity-creating process in which authority and policy-making influence are shared across multiple levels of government—subnational, national, and supranational. While national governments [remain] formidable participants in EU policy making, control has slipped away from them' (Hooghe and Marks 2001: 2). Alberta Sbragia observes that, 'The decision-making process evolving in the Community gives a key role to governments—national government at the moment, and . . . subnational government increasingly in selected arenas' (Sbragia 1992: 289). European integration and regionalization are viewed as complementary processes in which central state authority is dispersed above and below the national state (Scharpf 1988, 1994; Sbragia 1993; Jeffery 1996; Marks et al. 1996; Le Galès and Lequesne 1997; Bache 1998; Bomberg and Peterson 1998; Keating 1998; Kohler-Koch 1998; Ansell 2000; Börzel and Risse 2000; Burgess 2000; Börzel 2001). Few observers expect the outcome to be as neat and orderly as a conventional federation. Yet even fewer believe that the final product will resemble an Escher-like polity characterized by territorially variable, functionally specific, overlapping, non-hierarchical networks. Governments, according to Sbragia, 'will continue to be central actors' because 'the territorial claims that national governments represent . . . are exceedingly strong. It is nearly impossible to overestimate the importance of national boundaries as key organizers of political power and economic wealth in the European Community' (Sbragia 1992: 274, 289; see also Peters and Pierre 2000).

Type I multi-level governance dominates thinking in international relations among those describing the modification—but not elimination—of the Westphalian state (Caporaso 2000). These scholars do not deny that transnational movements, public–private partnerships, and corporations play important roles in international regimes, but they highlight the staying power of national states. Robert Keohane and Joseph Nye argue that, 'Contrary to some prophetic views, the nation state is not about to be replaced as the primary instrument of domestic and global governance. . . . Instead, we believe that the nation state is being supplemented by other actors-private and third sector ... in a more complex geography' (Keohane and Nye 2000: 12).

Type II Multi-level Governance

An alternative form of multi-level governance is one in which jurisdictions are aligned not on just a few levels, but operate at numerous territorial scales; in which jurisdictions are task-specific rather than general-purpose; and where jurisdictions are intended to be flexible rather than durable. This conception is predominant among neoclassical political economists and public choice theorists, but it also summarizes the ideas of several scholars of federalism, local government, international relations, and European studies.

Task-specific jurisdictions. In Type II multi-level governance, multiple, independent jurisdictions fulfill distinct functions. '[E]ach citizen . . . is served not by "the" government, but by a variety of different public service industries . . . . We can then think of the public sector as being composed of many public service industries including the police industry, the fire protection industry, the welfare industry, the health services industry, the transportation industry, and so on' (Ostrom and Ostrom 1999: 88–9). In Switzerland, where Type II multi-level governance is quite common at the local level, these jurisdictions are aptly called *Zweckverbände*— goal-oriented/functional associations (Frey and Eichenberger 1999).

Intersecting memberships. 'There is generally no reason why the smaller jurisdictions should be neatly contained within the borders of the larger ones. On the contrary, borders will be crossed, and jurisdictions will partly overlap. The "nested," hierarchical structure of the nation state has no obvious economic rationale and is opposed by economic forces' (Casella and Weingast 1995: 13).

Frey and Eichenberger coined the acronym FOCJ for this form of governance (1999). 'Polycentricity' was initially used to describe metropolitan governance in the United States, which has historically been more fragmented than in Europe. It is now applied by Elinor and Vincent Ostrom as a generic term for the coexistence of 'many centers of decision-making that are formally independent of each other' (Ostrom et al. 1961: 831). Philippe Schmitter uses the term 'condominio' to describe 'dispersed overlapping domains' having 'incongruent memberships' that 'act autonomously to solve common problems and produce different public goods' (1996: 136).

Type II multi-level governance has the following key systemic characteristics:

Many jurisdictional levels. Type II multi-level governance is organized across a large number of levels. Instead of conceiving authority in neatly defined local, regional, national, and international layers, public choice students argue that each public good or service should be provided by the jurisdiction that effectively internalizes its benefits and costs. The result is jurisdictions at diverse scales—something akin to a marble cake. Students of Type II multi-level governance generally speak of 'multi' or 'poly' centred governance, which, they feel, have less of ring of hierarchy to them than the terms multi-level or multi-tiered governance.

Some scholars conceive of Type II multi-level governance in the international arena. A critic of the traditional statist view of governance describes this process as 'fragmegration'—a neologism suggesting,

the simultaneity and interaction of the fragmenting and integrating dynamics that are giving rise to new spheres of authority and transforming the old spheres. It is also a label that suggests the absence of clear-cut distinctions between domestic and foreign affairs, that local problems can become transnational in scope even as global challenges can have repercussions for neighbourhoods. (Rosenau 1997: 38)

In this conception, there is no up or down, no lower or higher, no dominant class of actor; rather, a wide range of public and private actors who collaborate and compete in shifting coalitions. The outcome is akin to Escher's famous lithograph of incongruously descending and ascending steps.

Flexible design. Type II jurisdictions are intended to respond flexibly to changing citizen preferences and functional requirements. The idea is rooted in Charles Tiebout's argument that mobility of citizens among multiple competing jurisdictions provides a functional equivalent to market competition (1956). In a subsequent article, Vincent Ostrom et al. (1961) describe a polity in which groups of citizens band together in 'collective consumption units' to procure public goods. Individual citizens can join or leave particular collective consumption units, and these units can acquire a public good in one of several alternative ways—for example, by producing it themselves, hiring private producers, subsidizing local community groups, or joining up with other jurisdictions (Ostrom et al. 1961; Ostrom and Ostrom 1999; for an assessment of the literature see Dowding et al. 1994). A defining characteristic of polycentric governance is 'the concurrence of multiple opportunities by which participants can forge or dissolve links among different collective entities' (McGinnis 1999: 6). In his advocacy of FOCJ, Frey and Eichenberger emphasize a similar jurisdictional flexibility: 'FOCJ . . . are flexible units which are established when needed . . . [And] FOCJ are discontinued when their services are no longer demanded as more citizens and communities exit and the tax base shrinks' (1999: 18). 'FOCJ are an institutional way to vary the size of public jurisdictions in order to minimize spillovers. A change in size is, therefore, a normal occurrence' (Frey and Eichenberger 1999: 41). Under Type II multi-level governance, the capacity to take collective decisions, and make them stick, is diffused among a wide variety of actors. As Elinor Ostrom and James Walker put it,

The choice that citizens face is not between an imperfect market, on the one hand, and an all-powerful, all-knowing, and public-interest-seeking institution on the other. The choice is, rather, from among an array of institutions—all of which are subject to weaknesses and failures . . . . These include families and clans, neighborhood associations, communal organizations, trade associations, buyers and producers' cooperatives, local voluntary associations and clubs, special districts, international regimes, public-service industries, arbitration and mediation associations, and charitable organizations. (Ostrom and Walker 1997: 36)

Type II multi-level governance comprises dispersed self-rule on the part of diverse voluntary groups. Collective action problems are dealt with in heterogeneous arenas mobilized by many kinds of groups.[8] Several writers point out that Type II multi-level governance resembles pre-modern governance. John Ruggie identifies commonalities between contemporary and medieval 'multiperspectival' governance (Ruggie 1993). Students of polycentric governance trace the prevalence of special districts and other forms of polycentric governance in the United States back to the conception of federalism anchored in the US constitution (Ostrom 1999). Analysts of multi-centred governance in Europe find inspiration in pre-modern theories of federalism. The father of societal federalism, Johannes Althusius, formulated his ideas against Jean Bodin's unitary conception of the state (Elazar 1987; Hueglin 1999a; Elazar and Kincaid 2000; Nicolaidis 2001).

Locating Type I Multi-level Governance

Type I multi-level governance predominates in conventional territorial government up to the national level. While measures of decentralization vary, cross-national analyses reveal a robust trend towards greater decentralization since the end of the Second World War. Decentralization has been particularly impressive in Europe, but it has permeated the developing world as well (Bird and Vaillancourt 1998; Manor 1999). Data on taxation and spending confirm this. *Government Finance Statistics* of the International Monetary Fund (IMF) show that the share of subnational expenditure in total government expenditure has risen from 20 per cent in 1978 to over 32 per cent by 1995. Fiscal decentralization has been most pronounced in Spain and Latin America (Rodden 2003). The same trend appears when one examines policy making. Vernon Henderson has traced the extent to which central government can override decisions of subnational governments. The proportion of countries in which central governments have this formal power has decreased from 79 per cent in 1975 to 40 per cent in 1995 (Henderson 2000). There has been a steep rise in political decentralization.

---

[8] James Rosenau distinguishes eight types of collectivities (Chapter 3, this volume).

Thirty per cent of local governments were directly elected in 1970; 86 per cent were directly elected in 1999. The proportion of regional governments that are elected has increased from 25 to 55 per cent in the same period (Henderson 2000; Rodden 2003).[9]

In Europe, Type I multi-level governance has been pressed forward by the simultaneous empowerment of supranational and subnational institutions (Keating and Hooghe 1996; Ansell et al. 1997; Bomberg and Peterson 1998; Goldsmith and Klausen 1997; Kohler-Koch 1998). An index summarizing the formal authority of regions, special territorial autonomy for minorities, the role of regions in central government, and whether the regional government is elected, reveals a deep and broad reallocation of authority from central states to regions in the European Union (Hooghe and Marks 2001: appendix 2). The greatest changes have been in France, Italy, Spain, and Belgium, but no EU country has become more centralized since 1950. This index does not capture decentralization to local government. Local empowerment has been particularly pronounced in northern Europe, although recent local government reforms in several southern European countries have begun to narrow the gap (Page and Goldsmith 1987; John 2001).

Subnational dispersion of authority follows the logic of Type I—not Type II. The overall structure in the European Union is relatively simple, even elegant. There are *few* rather than many tiers. The territorial scales of government across the EU range between three and six. This is a far cry from the near infinite jurisdictional dispersion conceived in Type II multi-level governance.

Once one reaches beyond the national state into the international arena, one finds very little Type I multi-level governance—with one major exception: the European Union. The European Union bundles together policy competencies that in other parts of the world are handled by numerous, overlapping, and functionally specific jurisdictions. Most EU policies, with the major exceptions of monetary policy and border controls, have a single unified jurisdiction.

However, some salient features of EU architecture are consistent with Type II multi-level governance: variable territorial jurisdictions as a result of treaty derogations; distinct governance systems or 'pillars' for different policies; the multiplication of independent European agencies; and the flexibility clause of the Amsterdam and Nice Treaties specifying the conditions under which a subset of member states can engage in greater integration. As Richard Balme and Didier Chabanet point out, 'the competencies of the European Union in different sectors (environment, agriculture, competition . . .) are very different . . . Even in the same policy area the decision rules are variable and ad hoc'

---

[9] Data limitations are a major constraint for this kind of analysis. For example, the IMF has very incomplete time series data on fiscal decentralization; the results here are based on twenty-nine countries for which IMF has complete, and credible, data for 1970–1995. Henderson's data are primarily self-collected, and concern forty-three developed and developing countries. For a thoughtful discussion of data collection problems, see Rodden 2003.

(Balme and Chabanet 2002: 44). Philippe Schmitter regards these characteristics as defining features of the European polity: 'The core of the emerging Euro-polity's novelty lies in the growing dissociation between territorial constituencies and functional competencies' (Schmitter 2000: 15).

Locating Type II Multi-level Governance

Type II multi-level governance tends to be embedded in legal frameworks determined by Type I jurisdictions. The result is a large number of relatively self-contained, functionally differentiated Type II jurisdictions alongside a smaller number of general-purpose, nested Type I jurisdictions.

The National/International Frontier

Type II multi-level governance is ubiquitous in efforts to internalize transnational spillovers in the absence of authoritative coordination. Most target specific policy problems ranging from ozone layer protection, to shipment of hazardous waste, to migratory species. Task-specificity is a common feature of international regimes.

Type II jurisdictions at the national/international frontier are more fluid than Type I jurisdictions. A count of international governmental organizations shows steep growth over the past half century, but also sizeable fluctuation. For example, of 1063 organizations existing in 1981, only 723 survived a decade later, while an additional 400 or so came into being (Shanks et al. 1996: 143). The mortality rate for international governmental organizations is estimated to be five times higher than for Type I organizations, such as American federal bureaucracies (Kaufman 1976, cited in Shanks et al. 1996: 594).

While public–private partnerships are found in Type I jurisdictions, they are more common in Type II.[10] The role of public–private partnerships in the international arena is contested. In some cases, private actors negotiate on an equal basis with governmental actors, or bypass states altogether (Rosenau 1997, and Chapter 3, in this volume; Hocking 1999; Young 1999). However, many Type II transnational jurisdictions coordinate governments—not private parties, or they open up public decision making to private actors to different degrees. Tanja Börzel and Thomas Risse distinguish five types of public–private partnerships. In the first type, private groups are merely consulted or coopted by public actors. This is the case for the WTO, the IMF, and the World Bank, all of which have recently reached out to civil society representatives (O'Brien et al. 2000). A second form includes private actors as negotiating partners next to public actors, as in the Transatlantic Business Dialogue, which brings together business and government representatives from both sides of the Atlantic. Public actors may also delegate functions to private

---

[10] Neocorporatism is an example of a Type I public–private partnership.

actors, as is the case for many standardization bodies, for example, the Committee for European Normalization (CEN). A fourth form authorizes self-regulation among firms in the shadow of hierarchy (e.g. the World Business Council for Sustainable Development). The final type of public–private partnership is one in which private actors predominate and in which the role of government is restricted to adopting, *post-hoc*, privately negotiated regimes. An example is the regulation of domain names on the Internet. Börzel and Risse conclude that '[P]rivate regimes appear to be confined to one issue-area: international political economy. In all other areas, states seem reluctant to provide private actors with true governance authority outside their control' (Börzel and Risse 2002: 5).

At the national/international frontier, Type II multi-level governance tends to predominate. The European Union, which is mainly a Type I jurisdiction, is an exception that proves the rule. It is extremely difficult to tie national states into authoritative transnational jurisdictions that are general-purpose, rather than designed around particular policy problems. Type II jurisdictions are instrumental arrangements that do not directly challenge state authority, nor do they demand a strong sense of identity on the part of their members. Most successful international regimes focus on Pareto optimality and avoid explicit redistribution. As we discuss below, this is both a virtue and a limitation of Type II multi-level governance.

Cross-border Regions

Type II jurisdictions are common in cross-border regions, especially in North America and Western Europe. *Ad hoc*, problem-driven jurisdictions in the form of inter regional commissions, task forces, and inter-city agencies have mushroomed over the past three decades. In the Upper Rhine Valley, for example, the Swiss cantons of Basel-Land and Basel-Stadt, the French department Haut Rhin, and the German region Baden have created a web of trans-national jurisdictions, involving meetings of regional government leaders, a regional council of parliamentary representatives, a conference of city mayors, boards of regional planners, associations of local authorities, agricultural associations, chambers of commerce, cooperation projects among universities, joint research projects on regional climate change and biotechnology, teacher exchange programmes, and school partnerships (Weyand 1996; Perkmann 1999). Dense cross-border cooperation has also emerged along the Californian/Mexican border and the US/Canadian border (Blatter 2001).

Governance arrangements that straddle national borders are usually functionally specific, and overlap with existing jurisdictions in order to solve particular collective action problems. Such jurisdictions operate within Type I architecture. Cooperation is difficult when regions and local authorities in different countries have dissimilar competencies or resources. This has constrained one of the Commission's best-known programmes, Interreg, which aims to facilitate inter-regional networks along the European Union's internal and external borders

(Perkmann 1999). Contrasting Type I architectures in Europe and the United States help explain why cross-border cooperation has evolved differently (Blatter 2001). Joachim Blatter notes that in Europe, cross-border arrangements show a tendency to evolve in a Type I direction—under the influence of relatively resource-rich, general-purpose local and regional governments. In contrast, cross-border cooperation in North America has remained task-specific, territorially overlapping, and dominated by non-governmental actors, and thus complements uncoordinated, relatively resource-poor, Type I governments (Blatter 2001).

Local Level

Type II multi-level governance is widespread at the local level. In Switzerland, Frey and Eichenberger identified six types of FOCJ that complement or compete with general-purpose local governments. According to the authors' calculations, in 1994, 178 Type II associations provided specialized services such as local schooling, electricity, or street lighting, in the canton of Zurich alone (Frey and Eichenberger 1999: 49–53). The closest functional equivalent in the United States consists of 'special districts', which, as in Switzerland, have intersecting territorial boundaries and perform specific tasks. Special district governance is particularly dense in metropolitan areas: in 1992, the metropolitan area of Houston had 665 special districts, Denver 358, and Chicago 357 (Foster 1997: 122). Overall, the number of special districts has risen threefold from 12,340 in 1952 to 35,356 in 2002. Ninety-one per cent of these districts perform a single function concerned with natural resources, fire protection, water supply, housing, sewerage, cemeteries, libraries, parks and recreation, highways, hospitals, airports, electric power or gas supply, or public transit. These figures do not include several interstate special districts, such as the New York and New Jersey Port Authority; nor do they include independent school districts, of which there were over 13,500 in 2002 (US Bureau of the Census 1999, 2002; Foster 1997: 1–22). Type II multi-level governance at the local level is more common in Switzerland and the United States than in Europe, though 'partnership between a whole variety of service providers and levels of [local] government is the normal practice in most West European countries' (Batley 1991: 225).

Type II special districts are generally embedded in Type I local government, but the way this works varies. There is no general blueprint. The legal context is decisive for the density of special districts in the United States. A tally of district-enabling laws in California in the early 1980s counted 206 state statutes enabling 55 varieties of special districts for 30 government functions (Foster 1997: 11). No less than 200 pages of the most recent US Census of Government were devoted to 'a summary description' of local government variation across US states (US Bureau of the Census 1999: 73–277). Some districts are created by state legislatures, others are set up by one or more counties or municipalities, while others are initiated by a citizen petition. Special districts may be governed by appointed or elected boards; for some elected boards, only property owners rather than residents can vote. Some special districts levy taxes or fees, while others do not. The geographical scope varies from interstate, to regional and submunicipal, but the majority of special districts are smaller than the county *and* overlap with other local governments (Foster 1997: 9–15). The result is a baroque patchwork of Type II jurisdictions overlaying a nested pattern of Type I jurisdictions.

Type II multi-level governance may also appear where local communities are faced with local common pool resource problems, that is, where scarce, renewable resources—for example, a water basin, a lake, an irrigation system, fishing grounds, forests, hunting grounds, or common meadows—are subject to depletion because it is difficult to restrict access. As Elinor Ostrom has argued, diversity of ecological systems is an important source of multi-level governance (Ostrom and Janssen 2002). Around the world, communities have developed task-specific governance structures, often self-generated, to cope with locally specific common pool resource problems (Ostrom 1990; also Keohane and Ostrom 1995).

Biases of Multi-level Governance

The types of governance that we outline in this chapter frame basic political choices. Type I and Type II multi-level governance are not merely different ways of doing the same thing. Their contrasting institutional arrangements give rise to contrasting virtues and vices. We list these in Table 2.2, and describe them below.

Biases of Type I Multi-level Governance

Intrinsic community. Type I jurisdictions express citizens' identities with a particular community. Intrinsic communities represented in Type I jurisdictions are often based in national, regional, and/or local identity, but they may also reflect religion, tribe, or ethnicity. Such jurisdictions satisfy a preference for collective self-government, a good that is independent of citizens' preferences for efficiency or for any particular policy output.

TABLE 2.2. Biases of Type I and Type II multi-level governance

Type I	Type II
Intrinsic community	Extrinsic community
Voice	Exit
Conflict articulation	Conflict avoidance

Voice. Type I multi-level governance is biased towards voice, that is, political deliberation in conventional liberal democratic institutions. Type I jurisdictions are determined in a deliberative multi-issue process in which conflicts are highly structured and articulated. Rules about rules (*Kompetenz-Kompetenz*) are decided consciously, collectively, and comprehensively. Conversely, barriers to exit are relatively high. Exit in a Type I world usually means moving from one locality, region, or country to another. Where jurisdictions are designed around religion or group membership, exit demands that one change one's identity.

Conflict articulation. Bundling issues in a limited number of jurisdictions facilitates party competition and the articulation of dimensions that structure political contestation, first and foremost a left/right dimension tapping greater versus less government regulation of market outcomes and, in many communities, a new politics dimension tapping communal, environmental, and cultural issues. This promotes meaningful choice for citizens. Type I multi-level governance is well suited to deal with zero-sum issues, that is, distributional bargaining, because it facilitates logrolling and cross-issue trading. And because barriers to exit are high, it is also well suited to provide non-excludable public goods.

Biases of Type II Multi-level Governance

Extrinsic community. Type II jurisdictions are instrumental arrangements. They solve *ad hoc* coordination problems among individuals sharing the same geographical or functional space. Individuals relate to jurisdictions as members of fluid, intersecting communities—for example, as professionals, women, parents, homeowners, nature lovers, sports fans, shoppers, and so forth.

Exit. Type II multi-level governance is biased towards exit. Voluntary membership allows citizens, or the collective units of which they are members, to exit jurisdictions when these no longer serve their needs. To the extent that they facilitate entry and exit, Type II jurisdictions approximate markets. Jurisdictions may be created, deleted, or adjusted through inter-jurisdictional competition for citizens' participation or dues. Constitutional engineering is, therefore, a spontaneous process rather than a collective enterprise. Voice is secondary. The narrow focus of Type II jurisdictions concentrates the costs of liberal democratic institutions within small constituencies. Deliberation is focused on the production of a particular public good rather than on broader value choices.[11]

Conflict avoidance. By decomposing decision making into jurisdictions with limited externalities, Type II multi-level governance insulates decision making

---

[11] In *Governing the Commons* Elinor Ostrom describes several common pool resource arrangements with deliberative-democratic decision making. As Ostrom observes, such jurisdictions tend to become magnets for solving a wide range of community problems. Once such institutions are in place, it may be more efficient to add governance functions to an existing jurisdiction than to create a new one.

from other, potentially contradictory, issues. This jurisdictional fragmentation raises the bar for articulating ideological conflict, but it concentrates the mind on improving efficiency within existing jurisdictional bounds. Type II jurisdictions are well suited for decisions characterized by a search for Pareto-optimality.

Type I and Type II multi-level governance are not just different means to the same end. They embody contrasting visions of collective decision making. Type I jurisdictions are suited to political deliberation about basic value choices in a society: who gets what, when, and how. Because Type I multi-level governance bundles decision making in a limited number of jurisdictions at a few levels, it reaps economies of scale in translating citizen preferences into policy. Type I jurisdictions are at the heart of democratic elections, party systems, legislatures, and executives. Type I jurisdictions sustain a class of professional politicians who mediate citizen preferences into law.

Type II jurisdictions, in contrast, emphasize problem solving. How can citizens obtain public goods that they are unable to create individually? What are the most efficient means to public ends? How can market efficiency, based on consumer choice and competition among producers, be translated into the provision of public goods? The assumption underlying Type II jurisdictions is that externalities among jurisdictions are sufficiently limited to sustain compartmentalized decision making.

Conclusion

How should multi-level governance be organized? Who should be included in a jurisdiction, and what should that jurisdiction do? What criteria are relevant to these choices, and what are the implications of such choices?

The main benefit of multi-level governance lies in its scale flexibility. Multi-level governance allows jurisdictions to be custom-designed in response to externalities, economies of scale, ecological niches, and preferences. Both Type I and Type II multi-level governance deliver scale flexibility. But they do so in contrasting ways. Type I multi-level governance does so by creating general-purpose jurisdictions with non-intersecting memberships. Jurisdictions at lower tiers are nested neatly into higher ones. Type II multi-level governance, by contrast, consists of special-purpose jurisdictions that tailor membership, rules of operation, and functions to a particular policy problems.

Each type has distinctive virtues. Type I multi-level governance is oriented to intrinsic communities and to their demands for self-rule. It is predisposed to the articulation and resolution of conflict, including conflict on redistributive issues. Type II jurisdictions are well suited to achieve Pareto-optimality when redistribution is not salient. Yet, despite these differences—or more accurately, because of them—Type I and Type II multi-level governance are complementary.

As the European Union expands to the east and becomes yet more diverse, pressures for jurisdictional flexibility will intensify. Will it be possible to stretch a Type I jurisdiction over a European Union of twenty-five countries? Will there be more variable geometry—in our terms, Type II multi-level governance—in the European Union? These questions take us beyond the scope of this chapter, but the conceptual framework presented here appears to be relevant to their resolution.

3

Strong Demand, Huge Supply: Governance in an Emerging Epoch

JAMES N. ROSENAU

In a world where groups, organizations, and countries are simultaneously fragmenting and integrating, where the two contrary forces are pervasive, interactive, and feed on each other, are the resulting tensions subject to governance? If the deaths of time, distance, and sequentiality are taken seriously, can they operate as stimuli to a renewal of creative thought about what governance may mean in the twenty-first century? Can multi-level governance serve as a prime mechanism to steer the tensions in constructive directions? Except for qualifying the 'multi-level' concept, the ensuing chapter answers these questions in the affirmative and addresses them in the context of continuing processes that are disaggregating authority, rendering traditional boundaries increasingly obsolete, and fostering strong and widespread demands for governance.

To understand the extensive demands for governance one needs to appreciate the distinction between governance and government. Both governance and government consist of rule systems, of steering mechanisms through which authority is exercised in order to enable the governed to preserve their coherence and move towards desired goals. The rule systems of governments (local, regional, national, and international) can be thought of as formal structures, as institutions for addressing diverse issues that confront the people within their purview. Governance, on the other hand, is a broader concept. It refers to any collectivity, private or public, that employs informal as well as formal steering mechanisms to make demands, frame goals, issue directives, pursue policies, and generate compliance (Rosenau 1997). Thus governance consists of rule systems that perform or implement social functions or processes in a variety of ways at different times and places (or even at the same time) by a wide variety of organizations. Unlike governments, governance is not obliged to range across a wide variety of issues; often it does, but there are many governance processes that are single-issue in scope—as emphasized by Hooghe and Marks (Chapter 2, this volume). Viewing the government–governance distinction in this way, and influenced by the example of the European Union (EU), my qualification of the concept of multi-level governance is to regard it as referring exclusively to governmental levels. Such a conception precludes treating multi-level governance as a form or precursor of transnational civil society.

To govern, whether as structure or function, is to exercise authority. To have authority is to be recognized as having the right to govern, to issuing directives or requests that are heeded by those to whom they are addressed. Rule systems acquire authority in a variety of ways. These range from steering mechanisms that are structures endowed with authority through constitutions, by-laws, and other formally adopted instruments of rule to those that are processes informally created through repeated practices that are regarded as authoritative even though they may not be constitutionally sanctioned. Both the formal and the informal rule systems consist of what I call 'spheres of authority' (SOAs) (see Rosenau 2003) that define the range of their capacity to generate compliance on the part of those persons towards whom their directives are issued. Compliance is the key to ascertaining the presence of an SOA.

Viewed in terms of their compliance-generating capacities, the steering mechanisms that undertake governance may be just as effective (or ineffective) as those of governments. While governments generate compliance through formal prerogatives such as sovereignty and constitutional legitimacy, the effectiveness of governance rule systems derives from traditional norms and habits, informal agreements, shared premises, successful negotiations, and a host of other practices that lead people to comply with their directives. Thus, as the demand for governance increases with the proliferation of complex interdependencies, rule systems can be found in non-governmental organizations, corporations, professional societies, business associations, advocacy groups, and many other types of collectivities that are not considered to be governments.

It follows that world affairs can be conceptualized as governed through a bifurcated system, what can be called the two worlds of world politics, one a system of states and their national governments that has long dominated the course of events and the other a multi-centric system of diverse types of other collectivities that have lately emerged as rival sources of authority that sometimes cooperate with, often compete with, and endlessly interact with the state-centric system (Rosenau 1990). Viewed in the context of proliferating centers of authority, the global stage is thus dense with actors, large and small, formal and informal, economic and social, political and cultural, national and transnational, international and subnational, aggressive and peaceful, liberal and authoritarian, who collectively form a highly complex system of governance on a global scale.

Does the advent of a bifurcated system imply that states are in a process of disintegration? Not at all. Doubtless the interstate system will continue to be central to world affairs for decades and centuries to come. To stress that collectivities other than states have emerged as important SOAs is not in any way to suggest that states are headed for demise. Analysts differ over the degree to which the national state has been weakened by the dynamics of present-day transformations, but few contend that the weakening amounts to a trend line that will culminate in total collapse. States are still among the main players on the global stage, but they are no longer the only main players. Many of them are ensconced in paralysing authority crises that inhibit their governing capacities. This is not to refer to those states plagued with internal wars (e.g. Columbia) or to rioting protesters in the streets of national capitals. Some do experience such moments on occasion (e.g. Yugoslavia or the Philippines), but more often than not authority crises involve stalemate, an inability to frame, implement, and realize goals, an avoidance of decisions that would at least address the challenges posed by a world undergoing vast and continuous changes. Many governments, from Russia to Israel, from Peru to China, from the Congo to Indonesia, from the United States to Belgium, are torn by deep divisions and thus often have difficulty raising taxes, preserving societal harmony, ameliorating deep-seated conflicts, expanding their economies, recruiting or retaining members of their armed forces, or otherwise maintaining a level of compliance that sustains their effectiveness. Despite their difficulties, however, most states still control their banking systems and maintain legitimate monopoly over the use of force. Yes, states have undergone transformation into managerial entities and are thus still able to exercise a measure of control over the course of events. And yes, the aspiration to statehood is still shared widely in many parts of the world. But for all its continuing authority and legitimacy, key dimensions of the power of the modern state have undergone considerable diminution. In the words of Evans (1997: 65), 'As wealth and power are increasingly generated by private transactions that take place across the borders of states rather than within them, it has become harder to sustain the image of states as the preeminent actors at the global level.'

While present-day demands for both government and governance are extensive in the bifurcated system, they differ in one key respect. The demands for government are qualitative, while those for governance are quantitative as well as qualitative. People throughout the world are restless and unhappy over the quality of their governments, cynical about, and often alienated from, the effectiveness and integrity of the procedures whereby government frame and implement their policies. Except in those rare cases where statehood is sought, their demands are not for more governments; rather they want their governmental rule systems to be less corrupt, more streamlined, more ready to serve their needs. Indeed, in those instances where classical economic policies have come to prevail, some of the demands are for a diminution of government, for less intrusiveness in the marketplace and other routines of daily life.

The demands for governance, on the other hand, are also quantitative: innumerable rule systems are sought where none existed before because steering mechanisms have not previously operated to perform the desired social processes. Only recently, for example, an International Accounting Standards

Board was created to coordinate what previously had been unregulated practices by diverse accounting firms (see *New York Times* 26 January 2001: C1). As will be seen, this is only one example of literally millions that could be cited. It is the vast proliferation of SOAs in the multi-centric world that underlies the conception of our emergent epoch as marked by both a strong demand for and a huge supply of governance.

The Sources of Strong Demands

There are several compelling reasons why the demand for governance is so strong and pervasive. One is essentially normative: we live in a messy world. There are far too many people who survive on or below the poverty line. There are far too many societies paralyzed by division. There is too much violence within and between countries. In many places there is too little water and too many overly populated, pollution-ridden cities. And, most conspicuously, there is all too little effective governance capable of ameliorating, if not resolving, these and numerous other problems that crowd high on the global agenda. As David Ignatius forcefully noted in the *Washington Post* (28 January 2001: B7),

Global warming is getting worse. The destitute countries of Africa are becoming poorer and more disease-ridden. The digital gap between the wired 'haves' and the unwired 'have-nots' is growing . . . Not only are the problems getting worse, but it's increasingly clear that the mechanisms traditionally advanced for solving them won't work. Environmental treaties, multilateral organizations, U.N. agencies—none of them stands a prayer.

Hardly less troubling, the demands for governance are accompanied by a generational lack: even the most thoughtful analysts today are short of the orientations necessary to sound assessments of how the authority of governance can be brought to bear on the challenges posed by the prevailing disarray. Wendt (1999: 308) provides a succinct statement of this limitation:

So dominant in contemporary consciousness is the assumption that authority must be centralized that scholars are just beginning to grapple with how decentralized authority might be understood . . . [T]he question of how to think about a world that is becoming 'domesticated' but not centralized, about a world after 'anarchy', is one of the most important questions today facing not only students of international relations but of political theory as well.

A second source of the swelling demands for governance derives from the extent to which the emergent epoch has unleashed simultaneous, diverse, and contradictory forces that can be summarized in the clash between globalization, centralization, and integration on the one hand and localization, decentralization, and fragmentation on the other. The clashes between these forces—what I call 'fragmegration' in order to capture the intricate links between the polarities (see Rosenau 1997)—underlie the many huge challenges to humankind's capacity to lessen the messiness unfolding throughout the world and to meet the intensifying demands for new and relevant forms of governance that can exercise authority over the proliferating fragmegrative dynamics. Indeed, one way to understand any issue on governance agendas is to assess it through fragmegrative lenses and trace how the local and global forces that interactively sustain it both generate and complicate the need for new and more extensive governance.

Another source of the demands for more governance stems from the aforementioned changing capacities of states. Beset by the acceleration of fragmegrative dynamics and committed to neoliberal economic policies that highlight the centrality of markets, states are less and less able to control the flows of goods, money, pollution, people, ideas, drugs, and crime across their borders. And most important for present purposes, the lessened ability to control the course of societal and international life has reduced the capacity of governments to keep abreast of the proliferating SOAs and to cope with the new and myriad social functions to which the multiplying interdependencies of the fragmegrative epoch is heir. It could well be said that the burgeoning demands for governance bear an inverse relationship to the competence of governments.

Still another reason for the mushrooming of demands for governance concerns the ever-greater interdependence and complexity that new electronic and transportation technologies have induced and that marks the emergent epoch. What happens in one part of the world can now have consequences in remote places, thus leading to the rapid shrinking of time and distance and to what has been called a relationship revolution.[1] Today people are so fully and frequently in contact with like-minded others, and their interests so fully and frequently overlap, as to engage in organization building and networking processes that call for at least a modicum of governance.[2] The relationship revolution is founded on an organizational explosion that is staggering in its scope. In all parts of the world and at every level of community, people, ordinary folk as well as elites and activists, are coming together to concert their efforts on behalf of shared needs and goals. In addition, SOAs proliferate because increasingly people are capable of shouldering and managing multiple identities that lessen their allegiance to their states. As they get involved in more and more networks in the multi-centric world, so may their loyalties fractionate and become issue- and object-specific.

---

[1] Michael Schrage, 'The Relationship Revolution', Merrill Lynch Forum, www.ml.com/woml/forum/relation.htm.

[2] For an elaboration of forms of governance that are 'non-spatial in essence . . . and populated by people who share a strong affinity with each other', see Bruce E. Tonn and David Feldman (1999). 'Non-Spatial Government', *Futures*, Vol. 27, No. 1 (1995), pp. 11–38.

Exact statistics on the extent of the organizational explosion do not exist (largely because so much of it occurs at local levels and goes unreported), but few would argue with the proposition that the pace at which new associations are formed and old ones enlarged is enormous, so much so that to call it an explosion is almost to understate the scale of growth. It has been calculated, for example, that Indonesia had only one independent environmental organization 20 years ago, whereas now there are more than 2000 linked to an environmental network based in Jakarta. Likewise, registered non-profit organizations in the Philippines grew from 18,000 to 58,000 between 1989 and 1996; in Slovakia the figure went from a handful in the 1980s to more than 10,000 today; and in the United States 70 per cent of the non-profit organizations, not counting religious groups and private foundations, filing tax returns with the Treasury Department are less than 30 years old and a third are less than 15 years old (*New York Times* 10 July 1999: B7).

The links between the organizational explosion and the relationship revolution is easily explained by the shifting balance between hierarchical and network forms of organization, between vertical and horizontal flows of authority. Greatly facilitated by the Internet, people now converge electronically as equals, or at least not as superiors and subordinates. They make plans, recruit members, mobilize support, raise money, debate issues, frame agendas, and undertake collective action that amount to steering mechanisms founded on horizontal rather than hierarchical channels of authority. Indeed, it has been argued by Arquilla and Ronfeldt (1997: 5), with reason, that

The rise of network forms of organization—particularly 'all channel networks', in which every node can communicate with every other node—is one of the single most important effects of the information revolution for all realms: political, economic, social, and military. It means that power is migrating to small, nonstate actors who can organize into sprawling networks more readily than can traditionally hierarchical nation-state actors. It means that conflicts will increasingly be waged by 'networks', rather than by 'hierarchies'. It means that whoever masters the network form stands to gain major advantages in the new epoch.

In other words, not only has the advent of network forms of organization undermined the authority of states, but in the context of our concern with increasing demands for governance, it has also had even more important consequences. Most notably, networks have contributed to the disaggregation of authority as well as the formation of new collectivities not founded on hierarchical principles.

If the notion that new rule systems can be founded on horizontal as well as vertical structures of authority seems awkward, it warrants reiterating that the core of effective authority lies in the compliance of those towards whom it is directed. If people ignore, avoid, or otherwise do not heed the compliance sought by 'the' authorities, then it can be said that for all practical purposes the latter are authorities in name only, that their authority is more fiction than fact. Authority, in short, is profoundly relational. It links, or fails to do so, or does so somewhat, those who issue directives and those for whom the directives are intended. Stated more elaborately, authority needs to be treated as a continuum wherein at one extreme full compliance is evoked and at the other extreme it is not. The viability of all collectivities can be assessed by ascertaining where they are located on the continuum. The closer they are to the compliance extreme, the greater will be their viability and effectiveness, just as the nearer they are to the noncompliance extreme, the greater is the likelihood that they will be ineffective and falter. Accordingly, it becomes possible to conceive of collectivities held together through horizontal flows of authority, exercised through either face-to-face or electronic messages that initiate bargaining and culminate in compliance resulting from negotiated requests rather than authorized directives (see Hock 1999), and it is precisely the possibility of nonhierarchical authority that underlies the bifurcation of global structures into state- and multi-centric worlds, the proliferation of SOAs, the growing relevance of non-governmental organization (NGO), and the widespread demands for governance.

In sum, reinforced by the collapse of time and distance, the weaknesses of states, the vast movements of people, the proliferation of networks, and the ever-greater complexities of modern life, the question of how to infuse a modicum of order, a measure of effective authority and governance into the course of events looms as increasingly urgent. It is being asked within and among states as well as within and among associations and organizations at every level of community and in every walk of life as fragmegrative tensions intensify and as citizens and leaders alike ponder how to better govern their affairs in the face of transformative dynamics that are often bewildering and seemingly out of control.

Much of the bewilderment derives from the fast-paced dynamics of fragmegration. As suggested by linking, in a single phrase, the interactions between worldwide forces pressing for fragmentation and those exerting pressure for integration, fragmegrative dynamics are pervaded with contradictions and tensions. They tug people and institutions in opposite directions, often forcing choices between localizing or globalizing goals. Indeed, it is almost as if every increment of fragmentation gives rise to an increment of integration, and vice versa. This pervasiveness of fragmegrative dynamics is readily traceable in a wide variety of situations, from cultural sensitivities to inroads from abroad to fears of jobs lost through the lowering of trade barriers, from linguistic distortions fostered by the internet to environmental degradation generated by expanded productive facilities, and so on across all the situations that mark our transformative epoch. To repeat, there is considerable clarity to be had in viewing all the issues of modern life through fragmegrative lenses.

The Consequences of Strong Demands

In view of the foregoing analysis, it is hardly surprising that the major consequence of the unceasing demands for more governance is a vast disaggregation of authority. At every level of community and in every issue area that comprise their agendas, SOAs have come into being, some highly effective and some only nascent in their ability to evoke compliance, but altogether the world's population of SOAs is so great as to render the global stage extremely crowded and dense. Indeed, it is difficult to underestimate how crowded the global stage has become as the world undergoes a multiplication of all kinds of governance, from centralized to multi-level governments, from formally sanctioned entities such as arbitration boards to informal SOAs, from emergent supranational entities such as the European Union to emergent issue regimes, from regional bodies to international governmental organizations (IGOs), from transnational corporations to neighbourhood associations, from humanitarian groups to *ad hoc* coalitions, from certifying agencies to social movements, from truth commissions to private regulatory agencies, and so on across an ever-widening array of activities and concerns.

In short, the strong demand for governance has been and is being met. The supply of governance has been huge. But has the supply been adequate? Is the quality of disaggregated governance and proliferating SOAs sufficient for the needs of a fragmegrative epoch? Is the balance of supply and demand different for governance than it is in the marketplace? Is there a possibility that our messy world will become increasingly messier? Or is there reason to hope that the sheer number of SOAs will foster a trend towards coherence through multi-level governments within and among states and multi-level governance within and among organizations and associations in the diverse walks of life that comprise the private worlds of people? Does the bifurcation of global structures and processes contain the seeds of a sane and decent adaptation to our fragmegrative epoch?

Time and space do not permit an attempt to respond to such questions. But raising them has the advantage of more precisely specifying the normative and empirical concerns on which inquiries into governance and governability need to focus. The questions highlight the dangers of conventional analysis and the need for renewal in the ways we think about governance. For it is not a simple matter to grasp governance as congeries of diverse collectivities in the two worlds of world politics, as rooted in a vast array of private as well as public SOAs. Such a perspective requires one to wrench free of the long-standing and unquestioned premise that the boundaries separating countries are firm and impassable without permission of the states that preside over them. It also necessitates straining to overcome the premise that governments are the prime source of governance.

These wrenching tasks are not easily accomplished. Our analytic capacities are rooted in methodological territorialism (see Scholte 2000: 56–58), in a long-standing, virtually unconscious habit of probing problems in a broad, geographic framework. This habit poses an acute problem because of the ever-growing porosity of domestic-foreign boundaries that has rendered territoriality much less pervasive than it used to be even as all the social sciences continue to construct their inquiries, develop their concepts, formulate their hypotheses, and frame their evidence-gathering procedures in spatial contexts. Nor are officials free to think in alternative contexts: as Reinicke (2000: 45) noted, 'Trapped by the territoriality of their power, policy makers in traditional settings often have little choice but to address the symptoms rather than the causes of public problems.'

Yet, breaking out of the conceptual jail imposed by methodological territorialism is imperative because prime characteristics of fragmegration are that its processes readily span foreign–domestic boundaries and that its structures are not confined to governments. Fragmegrative dynamics: the microelectronic technologies that have rendered what used to be remote ever more proximate; the continuing proliferation of networked organizations; the variety of incentives that lead huge numbers of people, everyone from the tourist to the terrorist, to move widely around the world; the globalization of national economies and the neoliberal economic policies that have enhanced the relevance of markets and the power of multinational corporations; the skill revolution that has everywhere linked people ever more closely to the course of events; and, the divisive politics that have fostered authority crises, which inhibit many states from framing and implementing goals appropriate to the dilemmas they face (see Rosenau 2003), have greatly increased transborder flows and rendered domestic–foreign boundaries ever more porous. With the death of time and distance, subnational organizations and governments that once operated within the confines of national boundaries are now so inextricably connected to far-off parts of the world that the legal and geographic jurisdictions in which they are located matter less and less. What matters, instead, are the spheres of authority to which their members are responsive.

The immediate need for a jailbreak involves recognizing that the concept of multi-level governance can also be misleading and imprisoning. For all its virtues in capturing the complexities of modern-day governance, and I do not underestimate the clarity and utility inherent in the concept (for an elucidating discussion see Courchene 1995), multi-level governance does not allow for a full analysis of the complexity of the emergent political world. Most notably, its scope does not encompass the diverse array of SOAs that are crowding the global stage. The notion of multi-levels suggests governmental hierarchies and explicitly posits the various levels as vertically structured in layers of authority, whereas the mushrooming demands for governance are also being met in a host of horizontal ways, through SOAs that may be widely dispersed and not necessarily linked to each other through layered hierarchies. Put differently, many of the demands for governance involve an insistence on autonomy that may or may not be operative within hierarchical structures.

Since governance involves the exercise of authority and the necessity of people looking 'up' to, and complying with, the authorities to which they are responsive, it is understandable that the multi-level governance concept connotes hierarchy. But once one broadens one's analytic antennae to encompass networking processes and a variety of dissimilar SOAs, it becomes clear that authority relations have to be reconceived. As noted above, at the very least requests for compliance within effective SOAs have to be treated as exercises of authority in the same way directives and commands are seen as authoritative. 'That's not possible', some might say, 'behind every request under such circumstances is an appreciation that at some higher level there are authorities who have the ultimate sanctions even if compliance at lower levels is achieved through negotiated requests couched in harmonious language'. Such reasoning is as faulty as that which posits sovereignty as dichotomous and does not allow for variation within the extremes of having and not having sovereignty. SOAs can rule through requests if the consensus of those within their realm is extensive. Such an expansion of the authority concept ought not be difficult for those who analyse harmonious multi-level governance phenomena inasmuch as the interlinked and negotiated harmony across the levels reflects a consensual understanding of the responsibilities and obligations of officials at the several levels. Stated differently, 'authority cannot always be equated with domination'. Rather, it can be

rational-voluntaristic authority . . . in which fundamentally equal individuals reach collective decisions through rational deliberations that are open to all . . . [This conception] assumes that the interests of the individuals involved are not ultimately irreconcilable, that the rational process itself can lead to a shared understanding of the coincidence of interests once the latter are properly conceived (Boli 1999: 273).

A Six-governance Typological Scheme

The vast proliferation of rule systems calls for a sorting out, for typological clarification that will enable us to more clearly trace multi-level governance in the welter of SOAs. While the great number and variety of governance entities suggests parsimonious classification is a daunting task, more than a few analysts have undertaken to develop simplifying typologies. Indeed, the very concept of multi-level governance rests on a typological foundation. Unfortunately, none of the classifying efforts fully breaks with the practice of locating the state at the centre of the scheme. Different levels of government and different types of issues, for example, have been offered as typological schemes,[3] but in each case

---

[3] For example, the levels-of-government typology—'called the ladder of governance'—traces the movement of issues onto and around the various rungs of the ladder as they arrest the attention of officials and publics, thereby highlighting the prospect that multi-level governance will prevail in the future. This scheme has been developed by the Workshop on Globalization and the Comprehensive

they are amplified in the context of states. In order to account for the diversity, the horizontality, and the sheer number of steering mechanisms in addition to states that now crowd the global stage, here the typological focus is on the structures and processes that sustain the flows of authority, whether they be in the form of commands or requests for compliance.

For analytic purposes such a focus points to six general forms of transnational governance. Three of these reflect the complex and extensive non-linear feedback processes that have accompanied the advent of fragmegration: one can be called 'network' governance, another labelled 'side-by-side' governance, and still another designated as 'mobius-web' governance. These three can, in turn, be distinguished from three other, more straightforward forms that are less complex and more linear and familiar sources of governance: those that can be traced so fully to the cajoling, shaming, noisy pressures, or other activities of NGOs and transnational advocacy groups that the governments of states are, in effect, mere policy ratifiers at the receiving end of the flow of authority (the governance-without-government or bottom-up model); those that derive from the downward flow of authority originating within corporations or among national states and their bureaucracies (the governance-by-government or top-down model); and those that stem from the informal horizontal flows whereby economic exchanges occur in the framework of formal regulatory mechanisms (the governance-by-market model).

These six forms of governance come more fully into focus if a key structural attribute of the governance system (the degree to which authority is formally established) and a key process attribute (the degree to which authority flows in vertical or horizontal directions) serve as analytic bases for classifying the various collectivities active on the global stage. More precisely, the structural attribute can usefully be trichotomized, with governance arrangements consisting of (1a) formal, (1b) informal, or (1c) both formal and informal (mixed) structures, while the process attribute can be dichotomized in terms of whether authority flows in a (2a) single direction (up or down) or (2b) multiple directions (both up and down as well as back and forth horizontally). The resulting 3 × 2 matrix (see Fig. 3.1) serves to distinguish the six forms of global governance.

Before differentiating more fully among the forms of governance, let us specify the eight types of collectivities that crowd the global stage. These consist of (1) public subnational and national governments founded on hierarchical

Governance of Water, sponsored by the Commission on Economic, Environmental, and Social Policy of the World Conservation Union (Gland, Switzerland). Similarly, another state-based typology seeks 'to capture a rather complex reality' through five models that 'constitute a continuum ranging from the [societies] most dominated by the State and those in which the State plays the least role and indeed one in which there is argued to be governance without government' (Guy Peters and Jon Pierre (2000). 'Is There A Governance Theory?' a paper presented at the International Political Science Association. Quebec City: August 1–5, pp. 4, 5).

Processes	
Unidirectional (vertical or horizontal)	Multidirectional (vertical and horizontal)
(Type of collectivities involved in this form of governance)	

Structures			
	Formal	**Top-down governance** (governments, TNCs, IGOs)	**Network governance** (governments, IGOs, NGOs, INGOs— e.g. business alliances)
	Informal	**Bottom-up governance** (mass publics, NGOs, INGOs)	**Side-by-side governance** (NGO and INGO, governments)
	Mixed formal and informal	**Market governance** (governments, IGOs, elites, markets, masspublics, TNCs)	**Mobius-web governance** (governments, elites, mass publics, TNCs, IGOs, NGOs, INGOs)

FIGURE 3.1   Six forms of transnational governance

structures formally adopted in constitutions; (2) for-profit private transnational corporations (TNCs) formally and hierarchically structured by articles of incorporation; (3) IGOs based on formal treaties and charters; (4) subnational and national not-for-profit NGOs sustained by either formal by-laws or informal, undocumented arrangements; (5) international or transnational not-for-profit non-governmental organizations (INGOs) either formally structured as organizations or informally linked together as associations or social movements; and (6) markets that have both formal and informal structures which steer horizontal exchanges between buyers and sellers, producers and consumers. In addition to the variety introduced by different degrees of formal or informal organization, note needs to be taken of unorganized (7) elite groups or (8) mass publics that form briefly in response to specific issues and then disband when the issue is settled.

Unlike top-down, bottom-up, and market governance, the other three forms are not marked by processes that flow in essentially one direction. The fourth form (the governance-by-network model) involves bargaining among equal (i.e. nonhierarchical), formally organized collectivities, between governments, within business alliances, or between NGOs and INGOs, that ensues when the impetus for governance stems from common concerns about particular problems. The fifth form (the side-by-side model) arises not out of the noisy pressures, internal deliberations, or horizontal bargaining that respectively mark bottom-up, top-down, or network governance, but out of cooperative interchanges among transnational non-governmental elites and state officials, interchanges that are so thorough and effective that the distinction between formal and informal inputs breaks down and the two become fully intertwined and indistinguishable. The sixth form (the mobius-web model) occurs when the impetus to steer a course of events derives from networked interactions across levels of aggregation among TNCs, INGOs, NGOs, IGOs, states, elites, and mass publics, interactions that are elaborate and diverse enough to constitute a hybrid structure in which the dynamics of governance are so overlapping among the several levels as to form a singular, web-like process that, like a mobius, neither begins nor culminates at any level or at any point in time.

It is important to reiterate that all six models involve governance and government on a transnational or global scale. One cannot rely upon the literature on state–society relationships to distinguish these models, since this literature focuses on national governance and does not allow for transnational processes and structures of governance that transcend societal and state boundaries. National and subnational actors may be participants in any or all of the six processes, but their participation stems from their interdependence with issues and developments that unfold beyond their national or subnational jurisdictions.

It should also be stressed that while the labels used to designate the different forms of governance are descriptive of hierarchy or its absence, they do not preclude occasional fluctuations and reversals in the patterns of interaction. The labels are shorthand ways of referring to central tendencies, to the nature and essential direction of the paths along which authority and the impetus for governance flows. But they also allow for nuance. Top-down governance, for example, originates mainly within the halls of state governments, but corporations that dominate an industry can also initiate it. The campaign to get Yugoslavia to desist from ethnic cleansing in Kosovo is illustrative in this regard. Both during its diplomatic and military phases, the campaign was sustained exclusively by governments. To be sure, NATO's efforts were energized and supported by public shock over the scenes of cleansing depicted by the television media, but the origins and impetus for governance in that situation can be traced readily to the authority exercised by governments. On the other hand, bottom-up governance refers to policies that may be ratified by governments but that are propelled and sustained mainly outside the halls of governments. The processes in which governments eventually yielded to pressures from NGOs to approve a land-mine treaty are a quintessential example of bottom-up governance. The setting of standards for commodities and productive processes is no less a striking example of bottom-up governance. Thousands of standards were authorized for thousands of commodities and productive processes by autonomous and NGO well before quasi-state bodies became involved in monitoring and implementing the standards (e.g. see Loya and Boli 1999; Mattli forthcoming). As for market governance, its processes are horizontal in the sense that they involve the day-to-day interactions of traders and investors, and they are both formal and informal in the sense that governments and market officials exercise a modicum of formal regulation over the informal flows of trade and investment. In contrast to the three unidirectional types of governance, the network, side-by-side, and mobius-web forms of governance are pervaded with nuance, by interactive and multiple flows of influence in which authority may be exercised horizontally as well as vertically. The three types of governance in the right-hand column of Fig. 3.1 are too complex and overlapping to justify an essentially unidirectional presumption.

The existence of six discernible and meaningful forms of transnational governance speaks to the continuing expansion of complexity in the evolving fragmegrative epoch. If the statics of continuity rather than the dynamics of transformation prevailed today, it would be unnecessary to enlarge our analytic antennae beyond the long-standing conceptions in which the boundaries between domestic and foreign affairs are firmly in place and top-down and bottom-up governance serve as the prime means for framing and implementing policies both at home and abroad. As stressed throughout, however, such conceptions are no longer sufficient. More often than not, the global stage is witness to situations unfolding in ways that call for supplementing linear models with models rooted in non-linear feedback and network processes.

The non-linearity of network, side-by-side and mobius-web governance derives from the nature of the issues that each, respectively, undertakes to resolve. In the case of network governance, it occurs when interactions take place exclusively among formal actors such as states, NGOs, or business alliances (as distinguished from informal aggregations such as social movements) that form feedback loops to address and solve common problems. The 1992 summit meeting on the environment and the parallel and simultaneous, down-the-street meeting of established INGOs and NGOs was marked by extensive feedback loops between leaders at the two meetings, as also occurred at subsequent meetings on human rights, population, habitat, and women's rights, and exemplify network governance in the sense that all the participants who interacted at the meetings held posts in either governmental or non-governmental organizations (see Frank et al. 1999).

Side-by-side governance, on the other hand, emerges and is sustained in issue areas where the loci of action are so widely dispersed, unrelated, and situation-specific that neither the relevant governmental officials nor their non-governmental counterparts can usefully resort to mass mobilization and, instead, must rely on nonconfrontational cooperation to achieve control over the diverse and unrelated situations. The global effort to combat corruption is a classic example in this regard. A major INGO devoted to waging this fight, Transparency International (TI), has self-consciously avoided provoking mass publics and confined its efforts to working closely with the officials of both states and IGOs in the hope of persuading them to adopt anti-corruption policies. The efforts would appear to have been successful: 8 years of TI's short life has witnessed the World Bank, the OECD, the International Monetary Fund (IMF), several regional IGOs, and many states formally explicate goals and strategies for reducing corrupt practices within their realms of authority (see Wang and Rosenau 2001).

In a sense mobius-web governance would seem to amount to a vast elaboration of side-by-side governance. The major difference involves resort to mass mobilization. As noted, such processes are unlikely to occur in side-by-side governance. In the case of mobius-web governance, however, the relevant actors are closely linked and neither widely dispersed nor situation-specific, with the result that the relevant agencies are prone to cross the private–public divide by mobilizing mass publics as well as elites on behalf of the values at stake. The human-rights issue area is illustrative. It encompasses intricate networks of actors at subnational, national, transnational, and international levels who interact in such diverse ways as to render difficult, perhaps even fruitless, any attempt to tease out the direction of causal processes. That is, IGOs and most states tend to yield to the pressures of NGOs and INGOs on issues pertaining to human rights and, in so doing, have cooperatively formed both formal and informal networks through which the spreading norms get translated into mechanisms of governance. Indeed, mobius-web governance may be marked by a cumulative sequencing in which the pressures generated by bottom-up governance give rise to top-down and side-by-side governance that, in turn, becomes a vast network encompassing all levels of governance and diverse flows of authority. Given the ever-greater complexity of our fragmegrative epoch, mobius-web governance may well supersede the other five forms and become the dominant form of governance in the future.[4] Presumably it would also embrace multi-level governance, however that form may be defined.

Admittedly this six-governance typology is complicated and not lacking in overlaps among the types. Given the diversity of new forms of horizontal governance, however, the typology helps bring a modicum of order to the subject even as it highlights the complexity of our fragmegrative epoch. No less important, the typology allows for seemingly similar types of collectivities to be analysed differently to the extent their structures and processes vary. Indeed,

---

[4] One analyst estimates, however, that in the course of these complex sequences the governance of issues will become more formalized under IGOs and states, thereby 'eating into the realms of the INGOs/NGOs'. John Boli, personal correspondence (30 April 1999).

as indicated in Fig. 3.1, each of the various types of collectivities involved in governance can engage in more than one form of governance if different situations evoke their participation and authority in different ways. In other words, conceived on a global scale, governance is much too convoluted for there to be a perfect fit between the six forms of governance and the eight types of collectivities.

Conclusions

Of course, typologies are only aides to organizing thought. They do not in any way come close to resolving the problems of legitimacy, accountability, transparency, and effectiveness that loom large in the conduct of multi-level governance. To a large degree, however, much depends on one's temperament; on whether one pessimistically stresses the disarray inherent in weakened states or optimistically focuses on humankind's capacities for innovation and adaptation. Will the proliferation of rule systems, the disaggregation of authority, and the greater density of the global stage enhance or diminish the effectiveness of the various systems of governance? While there doubtless will be pockets of ineffectiveness and breakdown, will the emergent system, on balance, make for more humane and sensitive governance? Are the tensions and conflicts fostered by the deleterious aspects of fragmegration likely to prove ungovernable? If it is the case, as previously indicated, that none of the extant governmental mechanisms 'stand a prayer' of solving such global problems as environmental degradation, spreading poverty, and a widening digital gap, can a renewal of creative thought yield the outlines of new solutions?

As an optimist, I am inclined to note four aspects of an upbeat response if one is willing to look beyond the immediate. In the first place, more than a little truth attaches to the aphorism that there is safety in numbers. That is, the more pluralistic and crowded the global stage gets with SOAs and their diverse steering mechanisms, the less can any one of them, or any coalition of them, dominate the course of events and the more will all of them have to be sensitive to how sheer numbers limit their influence. As is the case in multi-level systems of governance, every rule system will be hemmed in by all the others, thus conducing to a growing awareness of the virtues of cooperation and the need to contain the worst effects of deleterious fragmegration.

Second, there is a consciousness of and intelligence about the proliferation of SOAs that is spreading widely to every corner of the earth. What has been designated as 'reflexivity' (Giddens and Pierson 1998: 115–17) and what I call 'the globalization of globalization' (Rosenau 2000) is accelerating at an extraordinary rate, from the ivory towers of academe to the halls of government, from the conference rooms of corporations to the peasant homes of China (where the impact of the WTO is an intense preoccupation), people in all walks of life have begun to appreciate their interdependence with others as time and distance shrink. For some, maybe even many, the processes underlying ever-greater complexity may be regrettable, but few are unaware that they live in a time of change and thus there is likely to be a growing understanding of the necessity to confront the challenges of fragmegration and of being open to new ways of meeting them. Put even more positively, an endlessly explosive literature on governance and globalization reflects substantial evidence that good minds in government, academe, journalism, and the business community in all parts of the world are turning, each in their own way, to the task of addressing and constructively answering the questions raised above. It is difficult to recall another period of history when so many thoughtful people concentrated their talents on the human condition from a worldwide perspective.

Third, the advent of networks and the flow of horizontal communications has brought many more people into one or another aspect of the ongoing dialogue. The conditions for the emergence of a series of consenses within and between societies never existed to quite the extent they do today. The skills of individuals and the orientations of the organizations they support are increasingly conducive to convergence around shared values. To be sure, the 'Battle of Seattle' and subsequent skirmishes between advocates and critics of globalization—quintessential instances of fragmegration—point to a polarization around two competing consensesus, but aside from those moments when their conflicts turn violent, the very competition between the opposing camps highlights a potential for dialogue that may lead to compromises and syntheses. There are signs already, for example, that the attention of international institutions such as the World Bank, the World Economic Forum, the WTO, and the IMF has been arrested by the complaints of their critics and that they are pondering the challenges posed by the growing gap between rich and poor people and nations.

Lastly, the aforementioned likelihood that mobius-web governance will become the dominant mode through which rule systems generate compliance in the years ahead points to opportunities for creative solutions to both local and global problems. It is a form of governance that can cope with deepening complexity, that in its lack of chains of command facilitates innovative feedback mechanisms for addressing the deeply entrenched problems that have long resisted solution, that enables the poor and the digitally deprived to seek redress through horizontal channels, that provides all the diverse actors that crowd the global stage access to governance processes, that allows for coalitions within and among public and private collectivities, and that is rooted in the interdependencies that mark life in our fragmegrative era.

For example, one creative solution to many of the challenges of our time closely resembles the formulation here of mobius-web governance and highlights its potential. It has been proposed by Jean-Francois Rischard, who is

Vice-President for Europe of the World Bank. He suggests that

The only models that have a chance in the 21 century will be ones that share the network effects of the New Economy. They'll be coalitions of interested nations, private companies and non-governmental organizations. They'll use online polling to speed their work along. And they'll focus on setting standards or norms—much like the informal bodies that built out the Internet without treaties or legislated rules and regulations.

Rischard calls them 'Global Issues Networks'. And he hopes that, over time, they'll issue ratings that measure how well countries and private businesses are doing in meeting specified norms on the environment and other issues that affect the welfare of the planet. The process will be quick and non-bureaucratic. The premise will be that if you do not meet the agreed-upon norms, you will be exposed as a rogue player in the global economy. Evidence that this approach can work comes from the recent success of the Group of Seven nations against money laundering. All it took was publishing a list of countries that are havens for global criminals—and threatening to 'blacklist' these countries from the process of international financial transfers that runs the global economy. Within 6 months, some of the most notorious offshore havens had rewritten their laws (*Washington Post*, 28 January 2001: B7).

To express a measure of optimism, however, is not to assert that nirvana lies ahead. Surely it does not. Surely fragmegration will be with us for a long time and surely many of its tensions will intensify and disrupt the balance between the strong demand and huge supply that presently sustains the conduct of governance. But the collective will to preserve and use new horizontal forms of authority is not lacking and that is not a trivial conclusion.

4

Multi-level Governance and Multi-level Metagovernance

Changes in the European Union as Integral
Moments in the Transformation and
Reorientation of Contemporary Statehood

BOB JESSOP

This chapter develops a strategic-relational approach (SRA) to the European
Union as a key point of intersection in the transformation of statehood. The
argument unfolds in four steps. It first introduces the SRA and its implications
for the study of government and governance. This approach gives equal attention in principle to the structural and strategic features of the state as a social
relation and also provides a basis to periodize state formation. Second, interest
turns to competing theoretical accounts of the European Union as an emerging
state form or political regime. Thus, I distinguish state- and governance-centric
approaches, consider two variants of each, and offer three criticisms of each
main approach. The two statist approaches are liberal intergovernmentalism
and supranationalism (a super-state); and the two governance accounts comprise multi-level governance and the 'network polity' (or, sometimes, network
state). A third section develops a strategic-relational account of the emergence,
restructuring, and strategic reorientation of the European Union and the
development of new forms of metagovernance such as the open method of
coordination. A key element of my critique and reformulation of other analyses
is a distinctive, ironic approach to market, state, and governance failures and the
correlative need for sophisticated forms of reflexive meta-steering of state
development.

The arguments on governance in this chapter have benefited from discussions at various times with
Henrik Bang, Ulrich Beck, Frank Deppe, Edgar Grande, Liesbet Hooghe, Beate Kohler-Koch, Gary
Marks, Markus Perkmann, Rod Rhodes, and Gerry Stoker. I also learnt much from the Sheffield conference. Given the idiosyncrasies of its approach to governance as well as many other matters, it is
especially important that the usual disclaimers apply.

A Strategic-Relational Approach to the State and Governance

The SRA is a general theoretical framework for addressing structure and strategy at various scales of social life from its micro-foundations to its most general macrostructural dynamics. Applied to the state (and, *a fortiori*, to its role in governance), it regards the state neither as a unitary political subject nor as a passive, instrumentalizable thing but as *a complex social relation* (cf. Poulantzas 1979). It treats the state as a relatively unified ensemble of socially embedded, socially regularized, and strategically selective institutions, organizations, social forces, and activities organized around (or at least involved in) making collectively binding decisions for an imagined political community. While it certainly accepts that there are material and discursive lines of demarcation between the state *qua* institutional ensemble and other institutional orders and the lifeworld (or civil society), the SRA also emphasizes the material interdependence of the state apparatus and state practices with other institutional orders and social practices. In this sense it is socially embedded. Moreover, as Tim Mitchell argues,

[t]he state should be addressed as an effect of detailed processes of spatial organization, temporal arrangement, functional specification, and supervision and surveillance, which create the appearance of a world fundamentally divided into state and society. The essence of modern politics is not policies formed on one side of this division being applied to or shaped by the other, but the producing and reproducing of this line of difference. (1991: 95)

These detailed processes also divide the globe fundamentally into *different* states and societies and thereby create a more or less complex interstate system. The manner in which these divisions are drawn and reproduced has specific effects on the political process and the effectivity of state power. This is why the SRA emphasizes the heuristic concept of strategic selectivity. This refers to the ways in which the state considered as a social ensemble has a specific, differential impact on the ability of various political forces to pursue particular interests and strategies in specific spatio-temporal contexts through their access to and/or control over given state capacities—capacities that always depend for their effectiveness on links to forces and powers that exist and operate beyond the state's formal boundaries. This means that analysts must look beyond the state to examine its embedding within a wider political system, its relationship to other institutional orders and functional systems, and to the lifeworld. In turn the attempted exercise of state power (or, better, state powers in the plural) will reflect the prevailing balance of forces as this is institutionally mediated through the state apparatus with its structurally inscribed strategic selectivity.

The SRA's main methodological conclusion is that state power must be studied not only in terms of the state's basic structure, institutional architecture, and specific organizational forms but also from the viewpoint of its strategic capacities both within the political system more generally and vis-à-vis the wider nexus of functional systems and the lifeworld. In this sense, the SRA is incompatible with a purely state-centred approach insofar as the latter assumes that the state can be examined in isolation and treated as an independent variable. In contrast, the SRA examines the state in terms of its structural coupling and co-evolution with a wider set of institutions and social practices. Putting the state in its place in this way does not exclude (and, indeed, presupposes) specifically state-engendered and state-mediated processes; but it does require that these be considered in their broader social context and that their effects are related to the strategic choices and conduct of particular actors within and beyond the state (see Poulantzas 1979; Jessop 1990).

It follows that to talk of state managers, let alone of the state itself, exercising power is at best to perpetrate a convenient fiction that masks a far more complex set of social relations that extend far beyond the state apparatus and its distinctive capacities. Interestingly, this is reflected in the practices and discourses of state managers themselves. For, whilst they sometimes proudly claim the credit for having initiated and carried through a general strategic line or a specific policy, at other times they happily seek to offload responsibility for state actions and/or outcomes to other social forces (or to *force majeure*) at one or more points elsewhere in the ongoing struggle over power. While the constitutionalization and centralization of state power enable responsibility to be formally attributed to named officials and bodies, this should not lead us to fetishize the fixing of formal political responsibility at specific points and/or in specific personages. We should always seek to trace the circulation of power through wider and more complex sets of social relations both within and beyond the state. This is especially important where the growing complexity and mass mediatization of the exercise of state power lead to a search for charismatic leaders who can simplify political realities and promise to resolve them. For charisma actually serves to hide complex, if not chaotic, behind-the-scenes practices which would be hard to explain or defend in public (Grande 2000). Attention to the circulation of power also matters where state power is undergoing major transformations and losing some of its formal constitutional and hierarchical aspects—as is the case with recent developments in the emerging Europolity as part of a more general reorganization of the interstate system (see below).

Studying the state from a strategic-relational perspective requires attention to at least six interrelated dimensions. Three dimensions primarily concern formal institutional aspects of the state regarded as a social relation. They are modes of political representation and their articulation, the internal articulation of the state apparatus, and modes of intervention and their articulation. Each of these dimensions has its own structurally inscribed strategic selectivities and, while analytically distinct, all three typically overlap empirically. They can be studied at different levels of abstraction and complexity, ranging from the most basic state forms through to specific regimes in particular conjunctures.

The other three dimensions concern the discursive and action-oriented aspects of the state *qua* social relation and give the first three dimensions their strategic meaning. These aspects give content to the more formal features of the state and it is the contest among social forces over their definition, articulation, and implementation that mediates structural and strategic changes in the state in given conjunctures. These three aspects comprise, first, the political projects articulated by different social forces that are represented within the state system, seek such representation, or contest its current forms, functions, and activities; second, the prevailing state project with its *raison d'état*—or governmental rationality—and statecraft[1] that seeks to impose an always relative unity on the various activities of different branches, departments and scales of the state system and that also defines the boundaries between the state and its environment as a precondition of the ongoing attempts to build such an improbable internal unity; and, third, the hegemonic projects that seek to reconcile the particular and the universal by linking the nature and purposes of the state into a broader—but always selective—political, intellectual, and moral vision of the public interest, the good society, the commonweal, or some analogous principle of societalization. These six aspects also provide one basis for periodization of state formation and transformation.

The forms of intervention associated with the state and statecraft are not confined to imperative coordination, that is, centralized planning or top-down intervention. Paraphrasing Gramsci (1971), who analysed the state apparatus in its inclusive sense as 'political society + civil society' and saw state power as involving 'hegemony armoured by coercion', we could also describe the state apparatus as based on 'government + governance' and as exercising 'governance in the shadow of hierarchy'. Studies of governance treat it as a general phenomenon concerned with issues of strategic coordination rather than as a state-specific matter. In broad terms, governance refers to mechanisms and strategies of coordination adopted in the face of complex reciprocal interdependence among operationally autonomous actors, organizations, and functional systems. Thus, governance occurs in all social fields and its students have examined a wide range of such mechanisms and strategies, including markets, clans, networks, alliances, partnerships, cartels, associations, and states. But governance is sometimes identified more narrowly with one specific mode of coordination: reflexive self-organization based on continuing dialogue and resource-sharing among independent actors to develop mutually beneficial joint projects and to manage the contradictions and dilemmas inevitably involved in such situations. In these terms, governance can be contrasted with *ex post* coordination based on the formally rational pursuit of self-interest by individual

---

[1] Statecraft (the art of government) can be considered as a repertoire of skilled, discursive practices that reflexively monitor events and activities beyond as well as within the state and thereby inform state projects and attempts to exercise state power.

agents, and with various forms of *ex ante* imperative coordination concerned with the pursuit of substantive goals established from above. This definition is the primary one adopted below in my discussion of multi-level governance. Such heterarchic mechanisms (as contrasted to market anarchy or bureaucratic hierarchy) have long been used in coordinating complex organizations and systems. They are especially suited for systems (non-political as well as political) that are resistant to top-down internal management and/or direct external control and that co-evolve with other (complex) sets of social relations with which their various decisions, operations, and aims are reciprocally interdependent.

State-centric Perspectives

State-centred approaches tend to adopt, albeit implicitly more than explicitly, the ideal-typical late nineteenth-century sovereign national state as their reference point and examine the European Union in one of two ways. Some commentators note the emergence of an increasingly important *new supranational arena* in which sovereign national states attempt to pursue their own national interests. This new arena is a site of intergovernmental (here, international) relations rather than a site to which important sovereign powers have been transferred and so, however important it has become for the joint pursuit of intergovernmental interests, it does not culminate in a new state form. This approach is often termed liberal intergovernmentalism (see especially Hoffman 1995; Moravcsik 1998). Other commentators identify a tendential, emergent, upward *re-scaling* of the traditional form of the sovereign state from the national to the supranational level. This is expected to culminate sooner or later in a new form of supranational statehood. They suggest that the associated re-allocation of formal decision-making powers is leading to a more or less complex form of multi-level government under the overall authority of a supranational super-state (see Taylor 1975; Weiler 1981; Pinder 1991). Whether the joint decision making that characterizes this emerging super-state is a transitional feature or will remain once the super-state is consolidated is still uncertain.

For liberal intergovernmentalists, on the one hand, national states are, and will necessarily remain, the key players in the emerging European political space. States abandon little or none of their sovereign authority and retain a comprehensive constitutional mandate in contrast to the limited powers of the European Union. Thus interstate interactions overwhelmingly take the form of international relations oriented to the pursuit of national interests, involving at best the provisional pooling of sovereignty for the pursuit of joint interests. For some this provides a new means to enhance the power and authority of the national state (e.g. Moravcsik 1998). More generally, rather than the leading to the transcendence of the national state, intergovernmental cooperation is said at most to produce a set of interlocking international arrangements among a self-selected group of national states. While this may eventually lead to a *Staatenbund* or confederation (e.g. a United Europe of National States), it could be blocked at any stage if one or more national states feel that their respective national interests would be hurt if the process continued.

Supranationalists, on the other hand, must posit a paradoxical transitional process in which national states conspire in their own transcendence (*Aufhebung*) as they promote supranational state formation. This involves a re-territorialization of political power as the three key features of the modern sovereign state are re-scaled upwards and re-differentiated vertically: *Staatsgewalt* (organized coercion), *Staatsgebiet* (a clearly demarcated territorial domain of state authority), and *Staatsvolk* (state subjects). This is linked to the re-scaling (and, perhaps, reorganization) of mechanisms for constitutionalizing and legitimating state authority in the expanded territory. Two factors distinguish the emergence of the supranational state (or super-state) from the simple territorial expansion of a single national state that absorbs all (or some) of the territories occupied by other relevant national states. First, it emerges from an agreement among independent national states to surrender their sovereignty and transfer it to a higher authority. Second, each of the affected national states becomes a subordinate unit of the new state whilst keeping the same territorial boundaries. Thus, the new super-state is a multi-tiered state apparatus.

What do these two approaches imply for the analysis of multi-level political relations? First, in the case of the upward re-scaling (or re-territorialization) of state sovereignty, the development of multi-level government could be seen as a transitional effect of the transition. In other words, it would take the form of relations between an emergent, but still incompletely realized, supranational state and existing, not yet transcended, national states. Moreover, if the emergent, but still incomplete, supranational state were to assume the form of a bi- or multi-tiered federal super-state (*Bundesstaat*), there would also be scope for analysing the relations between the different tiers of government with the tools previously used for analysing the dynamics of other federal states. Second, in the case of international relations, multi-level government could be interpreted in terms of distinctive features of the intergovernmental institutional arrangements established by national states and/or the specific governance strategies that they pursue from time to time. In terms of the language introduced by Collinge (1999) to analyse the relativization of scale, while the EU level becomes an increasingly important *nodal* scale in the overall exercise of state power, national states continue to form the *dominant* scale. Given the complexities of state power in such circumstances, it might be more appropriate, then, to call this *multi-level governance in the shadow of national government(s)*.

While liberal intergovernmentalism appears more persuasive than supranationalism, especially for the earlier stages of European economic and political integration, the statist approach as a whole errs on three main grounds: it adopts a restricted account of the state as a sovereign territorial apparatus, employs an anachronistic reference point, and is marred by its very state-centrism. First, although the essence of the state may well consist in the *territorialization of political power*, political power can nonetheless be territorialized in different ways. Yet, analyses of the European Union as an emerging supranational state tend to focus on three features of the state apparatus: (a) its monopoly of organized coercion; (b) the constitutionalization of state power through the rule of law and a clear allocation of authority; and (c) control over its own money, taxes, and state budget. This implies that the most significant criteria for assessing whether a European super-state has emerged are the development of a European *Kriegs- und Friedensgemeinschaft* (a War- and Peace-Community, complete with a European army subject to supranational control, a European police force for internal security, and a European foreign and security policy oriented to the pursuit of distinctively European interests in the wider world system of states), an explicit European constitution (which locates sovereign power at the apex of a multi-tiered political system, defines the relationship between a jointly sovereign European executive, legislature, and judicial system, and determines the division of powers and competencies between the different tiers of government), and a European monetary system, fisco-financial system, and a large, centralized budget. Anti-federalists already claim that the European Union has developed these features or, at least, will soon do so. Liberal intergovernmentalists note the absence of all or most of these same features and conclude that the European Union is primarily an arena in which traditional national territorial sovereign states compete to influence European policies, politics, and political regimes. Despite these disagreements, however, both sides fetishize formal constitutional and juridical features and ignore de facto state capacities and the modalities of the exercise of state power. They also focus excessively on territoriality at the expense of extra-territorial and non-territorial features.

Second, state-centred theorists overlook the successive historical transformations of the modern territorial state forms from the mid-to-late nineteenth-century onwards. This means that they adopt an *anachronistic* model of the national territorial state as their criterion for judging whether and how far a European super-state has emerged. This claim can be illustrated from Willke's periodization of the modern state. He distinguishes four stages: the *Sicherheitsstaat*, which is concerned to defend its territorial integrity at home and abroad; the *Rechtsstaat*, which provides legal security for its subjects; the *Sozialstaat*, which establishes and extends welfare rights to its subjects; and the *Risikostaat*, which protects its citizens from a wide range of unexpected and uncontrollable risks. These stages are associated with the primacy of different state resources, namely, *Gewalt* (organized coercion), *Recht* (law grounded in a constitution), *Geld* (national money and state budgets), and *Wissen* (organized intelligence) (Willke 1992). Although I do not accept that the 'risk state' is the most useful concept for the contemporary state, Willke's approach does highlight changes in the relative primacy of state resources. This suggests that the absence of a European army-police, constitution, and massive budgets may be less important than the presence of the EU's ability to mobilize organized intelligence and other forms of soft intervention that shape how national and regional states deploy their respective capacities (cf. Sbragia 2000). Overall, this suggests, first, that the key resources in today's *Staatenwelt* (world of states)—at least as far as relations among advanced bourgeois democratic states are concerned—are not so much coercion or money but soft law and intelligence; and, second, that the appropriate model for analysing EU state building is not an idealized nineteenth-century liberal state but the actually existing late twentieth-century state—whether this be a competition state, the regulatory state, or the Schumpeterian workfare post-national regime.

A related aspect of this second problem is the adoption of anachronistic normative assumptions about European political democracy. We should compare the still emergent EU polity with actually existing national democracies rather than earlier democratic systems—whether nineteenth-century liberal nightwatchman states, interwar interventionist states, or postwar Keynesian welfare national states with catchall governing parties. Contemporary western states tend towards authoritarian statism, with strong executives, mass-mediatized plebiscitary democracy, and authoritarian mass parties (cf. Poulantzas 1979). Thus, if there is a democratic deficit in the European Union, it may be linked to the contemporary form of statehood more generally, with deficits on different scales reinforcing each other. This, in turn, suggests that attempts to develop more democratic forms of representation and greater democratic accountability must be oriented to a different understanding of the nature and feasibility of democracy.

The third problem with state-centric analyses is precisely their state-centrism. In particular, they tend to naturalize the state–society distinction. Yet, the boundary between state and society is socially constructed, internal to the political system, and liable to change. Thus, to adequately interpret changes in the European Union as moments in the reorganization and reorientation of contemporary statehood, we must consider how the wider political system is organized and how changes in its territorial boundaries may contribute to the more general reorganization of state power (see below). The latter must also be related to the changing patterns of strategic selectivity linked to a changing institutional architecture and new forms of political mobilization. This implies in turn that the European Union is not a fixed form of state (apparatus) but an aspect, a path-shaping as well as path-dependent institutional materialization of a new balance of forces that is expressed, *inter alia*, in state building.

Governance-centric Approaches

Simple governance-centric approaches hold that the constitutionalized monopoly of violence and top-down modes of intervention associated with modern states are irrelevant or even harmful in an increasingly complex global social order. Thus they focus on the tendential *de-statization of politics (or de-hierarchization of the state)* rather than the *de-nationalization of statehood*; and they emphasize the enhanced role of reflexive self-organization in solving complex coordination problems that involve a wide range of partners or stakeholders beyond as well as within the state. This provides two bases on which to analytically distinguish de-centred forms of governance from the activities of centralized sovereign states. On the one hand, the sovereign state can be seen as the quintessential expression of hierarchy (imperative coordination) because it is, by definition, the political unit that governs but is not itself governed. Hence, beyond the sovereign state, we find the anarchy of interstate relations and/or the heterarchy of a self-organizing international society. And, on the other hand, it is primarily concerned with governing activities in its own territorial domain and defending its territorial integrity against other states. In contrast, governance is based on reflexive self-organization (networks, negotiation, negative coordination, positive concerted action) rather than imperative coordination. And it is concerned in the first instance with managing functional interdependencies, whatever their scope (and perhaps with variable geometries), rather than with activities occurring in a defined and delimited territory.

Adopting this approach leads to the view that the European Union is a major emerging site of governance that involves a plurality of state and *non-state actors* on different levels who attempt to coordinate activities around a series of functional problems. Without reference to non-state as well as state actors and to functional as well as territorial issues, the multi-level governance approach would be hard to distinguish from intergovernmentalism. Thus, the key question becomes how state and non-state actors manage, if at all, to organize their common interests across several territorial levels and/or across a range of functional domains. In this respect there are two main approaches: the self-described multi-level governance approach with its primary stress on the vertical dimension of multi-level governance and a parallel body of work that puts more emphasis on its horizontal dimension through the notion of the 'network polity' (sometimes referred to, less fortunately, as the 'network state').

In the present context, multi-level governance involves the institutionalization of reflexive self-organization among multiple stakeholders across several scales of state territorial organization. This has two implications. First, state actors would cooperate as negotiating partners in a complex network, pooling their sovereign authority and other distinctive capacities to help realize collectively agreed aims and objectives on behalf of the network as a whole. They would operate at best as *primus inter pares* in a complex and heterogeneous network rather than as immediate holders of sovereign authority in a single hierarchical command structure. Thus, the formal sovereignty of states is better seen as one symbolic and/or material resource among others rather than as the dominant resource. Indeed, from a multi-level governance perspective, sovereignty is better interpreted as a series of specific state capacities (e.g. legislative, fiscal, coercive, or other state powers) rather than as one overarching and defining feature of the state. Thus, states will supply other resources too that are not directly tied to their sovereign control over a national territory with its monopoly of organized coercion, its control over the national money, and its monopoly over taxation (Krätke 1984; Willke 1992). State involvement would therefore become less hierarchical, less centralized, and less directive in character. Other stakeholders in turn contribute other symbolic and/or material resources (e.g. private money, legitimacy, information, expertise, organizational capacities, or power of numbers) to advance collectively agreed aims and objectives. Second, in contrast to the clear hierarchy of territorial powers associated in theory with the sovereign state, multi-level governance typically involves tangled hierarchies and complex interdependence. Thus the European Union functions less as a re-scaled, supranational sovereign state apparatus than as a nodal point in an extensive and tangled web of governance operations concerned to orchestrate economic and social policy in and across many different scales of action with the participation of a wide range of official, quasi-official, private economic interests, and representatives of civil society.

The network polity (or state) provides a complementary account of the nature of the European state political system. Three variants can be noted: Castells' ambiguous claims about the European network state, a Foucauldian view that interprets recent patterns of European governance as a shift to an advanced (neo-) liberal form of governmentality, and governance-theoretical accounts of the network polity. The third variant is the most widespread but I will comment briefly on each.

Castells has gained attention in some circles for his recent extension of the overworked 'network' metaphor from the economy and society to the state. But his brief account of European governance is rendered ambiguous by his confused and confusing attachment to the concept of 'network state'. Castells claims that the European Union is organized essentially as a network that pools and shares sovereignty. As such, rather than involving the transfer of authority up to a European state that thereby supplants existing European nation states, the European Union *as a whole* tends to operate as a network state. He defines the latter as a state that shares authority (i.e. in the last resort, the capacity to impose legitimized violence) along a network. Here, Castells retains the conventional Weberian notion of the state as an apparatus possessing a legitimate monopoly of violence over a given territorial area, implying that the authority of the European Union corresponds to a specific territorial domain. But he adds that, by definition, a network has nodes, not a centre, thereby implying that control over this monopoly is more or less dispersed rather than centralized. This is particularly likely because nodes may vary in size and be connected to the network by asymmetrical ties. Indeed, the nodes formed by member states do differ in their respective powers and capacities; and even the three largest member states have different strengths (technological, industrial, financial, military).[2] This dispersion of authority and influence among nodes in the European 'network state' is reflected in the complex, variable, and changing geometry of European institutions. Thus, Castells notes that the European Union combines control of decision making by national governments (the European Council, its rotating presidency, and regular meetings of the Council of Ministers); management of common European business by a Euro-technocracy, directed by the politically appointed European Commission; and symbolic legitimacy vested in the European Parliament, the Court of Justice and the Court of Auditors. The endless negotiations in this set of institutions, and among the national actors pursuing their strategies, may, argues Castells, look cumbersome and inefficient. But it is exactly this indeterminacy and complexity that enable the European Union to muddle through, accommodating various interests and changing policies, not only from different countries, but from the different political orientations of parties elected to government (Castells 2000: 2, 5). From this brief summary, it can be seen that Castells' account is still strongly imprinted by state-theoretical assumptions and that his major innovation relative to their usual expression in liberal intergovernmentalism and/ or supranationalism is to use the idea of 'network' to reveal some (but far from all) of the complexity of the linkages between national states and European institutions.

A useful overview of the Foucauldian approach to the changing 'arts of inter-national government' (distinguishing between imperialism, developmentalism, and the 'new regionalism') is presented in Larner and Wallace (2002). Whilst referring in general terms to the European Union as the most advanced form of the 'new regionalism' considered as a form of liberal governmentality, they enumerate several key distinguishing features of this new art of international governmentality drawing on developments in North America and the Asian Pacific as well as Europe. Haahr (2002) provides a parallel Foucauldian study focused primarily on the emerging 'open method of coordination' (OMC) that was formally announced during the 1999 Portuguese Presidency.[3] The OMC is a 'soft' form of governance that differs from traditional top-down 'positive government' and the previous trend towards a European 'regulatory state' based on a neo-liberal *Ordnungspolitik* (on which, see Majone 1997). As such, it involves concerted, centralized formulation of objectives, quantification of indicators for measuring progress towards such objectives, decentralized implementation, and systematic monitoring of different member states'

---

[2] Castells argues, for example, that Germany is the hegemonic economic power, Britain and France have greater military power, and all three have at least equal technological capacity compared with other member states (2000: 5).

[3] For an alternative Anglo-Foucauldian account of Europe as a 'network state' that is also inspired by actor-network theory, see Barry 2001.

progress. It thereby enables member states to address problems at the European level without ceding new juridical competencies to the European Union (Haahr 2002: 7–8). In this sense, argues Haahr, the OMC reflects advanced liberal forms of government. These embody a notion of structured and conditioned freedom: they are 'practices of liberty' that establish and facilitate liberty but also discipline it and constrain its exercise. They govern through the manipulation of techniques and mechanisms rather than more directly through a classical liberal and/or Keynesian welfarist manipulation of processes. Thus, while these new techniques of rule involve contracts, consultation, negotiation, partnerships, empowerment, and activation, they also set norms, standards, benchmarks, performance indicators, quality controls and best practice standards. In short, '[a]dvanced liberal rule operates through our freedom, through the way this freedom is structured, shaped, predicted and made calculable' (Haahr 2002: 9). Re-scaled from national states to the European level, this is seen in the declared role of the OMC to help member states evolve their own policies in new and major areas in line with the constitutional principle of subsidiarity and in consultation with relevant regional and local political authorities as well as with the social partners and civil society. By developing strategies, setting and monitoring targets, and forming partnerships, such 'advanced liberal' forms of governmentality can both mobilize and discipline the energies of civil society. In this way, while member states appear as agents capable of devising strategies and achieving objectives without being directly subject to EU diktat, the European Commission can appear as the institution empowered to assess their relative performance in attaining the consensually determined agreed objectives (Haahr 2002: 10–14).

More conventional governance-theoretical analyses of the emerging European network polity start out from the difficulties of relying on rigid hierarchical coordination in contexts characterized by complex reciprocal interdependence among different fields across different scales (Pitschas 1995; Ladeur 1997). Ansell (2000: 311) provides a good overview of this approach and summarizes his (and other) findings as follows:

the networked polity is a structure of governance in which both state and societal organization is vertically and horizontally disaggregated (as in pluralism) but linked together by cooperative exchange (as in pluralism). Organizational structures in the networked polity are organic rather than mechanistic, which means that both knowledge and initiative are decentralized and widely distributed. Horizontal relationships within and across organizations are at least as important as vertical relationships, and organizational relationships in general follow a pattern of many-to-many (heterarchy) rather than many-to-one (hierarchy). Exchange is diffuse and/or social rather [than] discrete and/or impersonal. The logic of governance emphasizes the bringing together of unique configurations of actors around specific projects oriented toward integrative solutions rather than dedicated programs. These project teams will criss-cross organizational turf and the boundary between public and private. State actors with a high degree of centrality in the web of interorganizational linkages will be in a position to provide facilitative leadership in constructing or steering these project teams.

Three main criticisms can be levelled at the main governance-centred approaches, excluding for present purposes Castells and the Foucauldians (I will return to Haahr's analysis in my comments on 'multi-level metagovernance'). First, reflecting its different disciplinary roots and wide range of applications, work on governance often remains at a largely pre-theoretical stage: it is much clearer what the notion of governance excludes than what it contains. This is reflected in a proliferation of typologies of governance mechanisms constructed for different purposes and a large measure of (often unspoken) disagreement about what is included and excluded, from the overall concept. Thus, many early analyses served to establish that the EU political system cannot easily be assimilated to, or studied in terms of, a traditional conception of government; but it was unclear exactly how multi-level governance operates to produce the European polity, how objects of governance are defined in this context, and how stakeholders are defined. Later work has begun to address these problems but often does so for specific policy areas or policy networks, leaving open the issue of how different multi-level governance regimes are connected, let alone how, if at all, they may acquire a relative unity. Related to this comparative underdevelopment of the governance concept are marked ambiguities in the referents of multi-level governance. For the term is used to capture several trends in the development of the contemporary state—the de-nationalization of statehood, the de-statization of politics, and the re-articulation of territorial and functional powers. The fact that it is used to describe the interaction of three analytically distinct trends (each with its own counter-trend) or, at least, to characterize their combined impact, suggests that the concept may obscure as much as it clarifies about recent changes.

Second, governance theories tend to be closely connected to concerns about problem-solving and crisis management in a wide range of fields. This has led some governance theorists to focus on specific collective decision making or goal-attainment issues in relation to specific (socially and discursively constituted) problems and to investigate how governance contributes to problem solving (for a belated self-criticism on this score, see Mayntz 2001). But this can easily lead to a neglect of problems of governance failure, that is, the tendency for governance to fail to achieve its declared objectives; and, *a fortiori*, neglect of the various responses of different agents or subjects of governance to such failures as they attempt to engage in different forms of metagovernance (on governance failure and metagovernance, see Jessop 1998, 2002b). Two aspects of metagovernance are relevant here. On the one hand, because many studies of governance are concerned with specific problem fields or objects of governance, they tend to ignore questions of the relative compatibility or incompatibility of different governance regimes and their implications for the overall unity of the European project and European statehood. And, on the other hand, many empirical studies have overlooked (or, at least failed to theorize) the existence of meta-steering. This complicated process, which Dunsire (1996) has aptly termed 'collibration', involves attempts to modify the relative weight and targets of exchange, hierarchy, and networking in the overall coordination of relations of complex interdependence. Yet, such meta-steering is central to many of the disputes over European integration and / or state formation and has long been a key issue on the agenda of the European Union itself, especially regarding the different steps in integration. This is reflected in the increasing resort to partnerships, comitology, social dialogue, and the mobilization of non-governmental organizations (NGO) and social movements as additional elements in the attempts to guide European integration and to steer EU policy making and implementation (cf. Scott and Trubek 2002). The 'Lisbon Strategy', with its advocacy of the extension of the 'open method of co-ordination', and the recent White Paper on Governance (COM 2001: 428) are the latest phases in this search for appropriate mechanisms of metagovernance (see below).

Third, work on multi-level governance and the network polity poses fundamental issues about the extent to which a network polity will remain tightly anchored in territorial terms (as opposed to being necessarily territorially embedded) despite its highly pluralistic functional concerns and its equally variable geometries. Schmitter raised just such issues in another context, when he identified four possible, ideal-typical future scenarios for the emerging Europolity. These scenarios were generated in true sociological fashion through the formation of a two-by-two property space based on two dichotomized dimensions of political regime formation: (1) an essentially Westphalian versus 'neo-medieval' form of territorial organization; and (2) heterogeneous and flexible versus tightly ordered and highly stable functional representation.[4] The most interesting (and, he suggested, more plausible) scenarios both involved flexibility on the second dimension. They are a *condominio* (a neo-medieval state system with flexible functional representation and policy making) and a *consortio* (a largely intergovernmental *Europe des patries* with polycentric, incongruent flexible functional representation and policy making). A Westphalian state re-scaled to the European level with a well-ordered and congruent European system of functional representation (to produce a *stato*, which could be considered equivalent to a supranational European super-state) was deemed unlikely; and a *confederatio* (a neo-medieval territorial arrangement with tightly organized and stable functional representation) was judged even more implausible (Schmitter 1992).

As an open-ended thought experiment only loosely linked to empirical analysis, Schmitter's typological exercise is not directly relevant to my main

---

[4] I have simplified and renamed the dichotomies on Schmitter's two axes for the sake of brevity; see his text for the complete version, expressed, as usual, inimitably.

objectives in this chapter. But it does serve two purposes in the present context. For it suggests, first, that studies of multi-level governance and/or network forms of political organization should not ignore issues of territorial organization; and, second, once both sets of issues are posed together, issues of multi-level metagovernance become central both in practice and in theory. To these twin conclusions we might add a third, namely, the need to question how far analyses of the political actors in the European Union can be confined territorially to its member states (and, perhaps, candidate states) and functionally to organized interests and movements that are anchored primarily within the political space directly organized and controlled by the European Union and its Member States. For the forms, pace, and extent of European integration are also relevant to other states and to a wide range of non-state forces with strong roots outside the European Union.

Each of these problems has severe implications for an adequate analysis of multi-level governance. In particular, they have produced a situation described by Weiler and Wessels as comprising 'too many case studies, *ad hoc* lessons from limited experiences and organizational description [and] too little theoretical mediation' (1998: 230n). In part, of course, this *ad hoccery* reflects the real complexities of the emerging European polity. Indeed, it would be surprising if no such complexities existed. For national states also involve heterogeneous patterns of government and/or governance, with patterns varying with the objects of state intervention, the nature of policy fields, the changing balance of forces in and beyond the state, and so on. In this sense, perhaps, we may be witnessing a re-scaling of the complexities of government and governance rather than a re-scaling of the sovereign state or the emergence of just one more arena in which national states pursue national interests. It is to these complexities at the national scale that I now turn in order to provide some insights into how we might rethink the emerging EU polity.

Changes in Statehood in Advanced Capitalist Societies

Here, I advance three interrelated propositions about recent trends in national states to provide just one possible approach to the 'theoretical mediation' called for by Weiler and Wessels. These three trends are derived from theoretically informed observation of developments in developed capitalist economies in all triad regions rather than Europe alone. In this sense, their generality across these regions (and, hence, their occurrence elsewhere) suggests they are not generated by processes peculiar to the European region. For this reason they can help to contextualize and interpret recent trends in the development of European statehood (cf. Ziltener 1999). But it must also be recognized that these trends have many different causes. They should not be treated as singular causal mechanisms in their own right, which would mean neglecting their essentially descriptive, synthetic, and generalized nature. Nor should they be thought to entail unidirectional movement or multilateral convergence across all national or triadic regimes. Instead, they can, and do, take different empirical forms (e.g. on the differing dynamics of cross-border regions in North America and Europe, see Blatter 2001).

First, there is a general trend towards the *de-nationalization* of territorial statehood. This trend should not be mistaken, *pace* Shaw (2000), for the rise of a 'global state'—at least if the concept of state is to retain its core meaning of the territorialization of a centralized political authority so that a 'global state' amounts to a single 'world state'. Instead it represents a re-articulation of different levels of the territorial organization of power within the global political system. As such it is reflected empirically in the 'hollowing out' of the national state apparatus with old and new state capacities being reorganized territorially on subnational, national, supranational, and translocal levels. State powers are moved upwards, downwards, and sideways as state managers on different scales attempt to enhance their respective operational autonomies and strategic capacities. One aspect of this is the gradual loss of the *de jure* sovereignty of national states in certain respects as rule- and/or decision-making powers are transferred upwards to supranational bodies and the resulting rules and decisions are held to bind national states. Another aspect is the devolution of authority to subordinate levels of territorial organization and the development of transnational but inter-local policy making. The overall result is the proliferation of institutionalized scales of political decision making, the increasing complexity of inter-scalar articulation, and a bewildering variety of transnational relations.

Countering this trend is the enhanced role of national states in managing inter-scalar relations. That is, national states seek to control what powers or competencies go up, down, or sideways and to exercise this control so as to enhance their capacities to realize their current state projects; and they also seek, as far as possible, to retain the competence to revoke such transfers of powers and/or to implement them in ways that do least damage to their capacity to secure institutional integration and social cohesion with their corresponding territories. In this sense, even if state powers and competencies are no longer exercised in the framework of the national state *qua* 'power container', the advanced states still retain considerable autonomy in regard to how to organize and re-scale state powers to promote state projects. The key question then becomes how far the movement of competencies or powers away from the national state is irreversible either constitutionally (such that attempted repatriation of powers would be subject to legal sanction or a constitutional use of armed force) or informally (such that attempts to repatriate powers would be regarded as politically illegitimate and/or economically infeasible). This said, it is generally easier for national states to reclaim powers and competencies devolved downwards or sideways than those that are shifted upwards (but see below).

Second, there is a trend towards the *de-statization* of the political system. This involves a shift from govern*ment* to govern*ance* on various territorial scales and across various functional domains. There is a movement from the central role of the official state apparatus in securing state-sponsored projects and political hegemony towards an emphasis on partnerships between governmental, para-governmental, and NGOs in which the state apparatus is often only first among equals. Governance involves the complex art of steering multiple agencies, institutions, and systems that are both operationally autonomous from one another and structurally coupled through various forms of reciprocal interdependence. Governments have always relied on other agencies to assist them in realizing state objectives or projecting state power beyond the formally defined state apparatus. But this familiar reliance on government *and* governance has been increased and reordered. This is reflected in the proliferation of public–private partnerships in various guises to supplement and sometimes to replace more traditional forms of corporatism and concertation. The relative weight of governance has also increased on all levels—including horizontal cross-border transactions as well as coordination across different vertical scales from the local through the triads to the global level. Nonetheless this need not mean the loss of state capacity. Indeed a shift to governance can enhance the capacity to project state power and achieve state objectives by mobilizing knowledge and power resources from influential non-governmental partners or stakeholders.

Countering this shift is government's increased role in *metagovernance*. For political authorities (on and across all levels) are becoming more involved in all aspects of metagovernance: they get involved in redesigning markets, in constitutional change and the juridical re-regulation of organizational forms and objectives, in organizing the conditions for self-organization, and, most importantly, in the overall process of collibration. In this last respect, they provide the ground rules for governance and the regulatory order in and through which governance partners can pursue their aims; ensure the compatibility or coherence of different governance mechanisms and regimes; act as the primary organizer of the dialogue among policy communities; deploy a relative monopoly of organizational intelligence and information with which to shape cognitive expectations; serve as a 'court of appeal' for disputes arising within and over governance; seek to re-balance power differentials by strengthening weaker forces or systems in the interests of system integration and/or social cohesion; try to modify the self-understanding of identities, strategic capacities, and interests of individual and collective actors in different strategic contexts and hence alter their implications for preferred strategies and tactics; and also assume political responsibility in the event of governance failure. These emerging metagovernance roles mean that different forms of coordination (markets, hierarchies, networks, and solidarities) and the different forms of self-organization characteristic of governance take place 'in the shadow of hierarchy' (cf. Scharpf 1994: 40).

Third, there is a complex trend towards the internationalization of policy regimes. The international context of domestic state action has extended to include a widening range of extra-territorial or transnational factors and processes; it has become more significant strategically for domestic policy; the key players in policy regimes have also expanded to include foreign agents and institutions as sources of policy ideas, policy design, and implementation; and there is an increasing number of increasingly influential international regimes across a growing range of policy fields. This trend is reflected in economic and social policies as states become more concerned with 'international competitiveness' in the widest sense and with the transnational constraints, consequences, and conditions of state action. It is also reflected in the development of global public policy networks and increasingly ambitious plans for the harmonization (not standardization) of policy regimes across many policy fields. Somewhat ambiguously countering yet reinforcing this trend is a growing 'interiorization' of international constraints as the latter become integrated into the policy paradigms and cognitive models of domestic policy makers. And, more clearly representing a counter-trend, we find that states (on all levels) are now increasingly active in attempting to shape the nature of international regimes, their interrelations, and their local implementation. Currently, it is again the national state that generally has the key role in these struggles to shape international regimes and to shape their local implementation, using whatever arenas are available to this end. This is because the national state is generally the only political organization that is empowered to bind its citizens to international commitments. The European Union is an increasingly important exception to this rule, however, differing significantly from the supranational organization of the other triad regions in this regard.

In short, these three changes do not exclude a continuing and central political role for national states. But it is a role that is necessarily redefined as a result of the more general re-articulation of the local, regional, national, and supranational levels of economic and political organization. Unless or until supranational political organization acquires not only governmental powers but also some measure of popular-democratic legitimacy, the national state will remain a key political factor as the highest instance of bourgeois democratic political accountability. How it plays this role will depend on the changing institutional matrix and shifts in the balance of forces as globalization, triadization, regionalization, and resurgent local governance proceed apace. Possibly the most important role for the national state here is in metagovernance, that is, coordinating different forms of governance and ensuring a minimal coherence among them. In this sense Shaw (2000) is right to claim that the national state core to governance will not go away. But this will be less governmental and more oriented to issues of metagovernance. But there is no point at which a final metagovernance instance can be established to coordinate the myriad subordinate forms of governance—this would re-introduce the principle of sovereignty or hierarchy that growing social complexity and globalization now rule out.

I have introduced these three trends for one major reason. If the national state can no longer be understood in terms of the received notion of the sovereign national state, then perhaps this notion is also inadequate for studying the evolving European Union as a state form. Indeed, we can go further: if the national state is changing in the ways that I have suggested, then the future position and activities of the European Union within a re-territorialized, de-statized, and internationalized *Staatenwelt* must be very carefully reconsidered. What we are witnessing is the re-scaling of the complexities of government and *governance* rather than the re-scaling of the sovereign state or the emergence of just one more arena in which national states pursue national interests.

Much the same point can be made through changes in the state's form and functions regarding capital accumulation. These can be studied along four key dimensions. The first concerns the state's distinctive roles in securing conditions for profitable private business. This is the broad field of economic policy and matters because market forces alone cannot secure these conditions. The second dimension refers to the state's distinctive roles in reproducing labour power individually and collectively over various time spans from quotidian routines via individual lifecycles to intergenerational reproduction. This is the broad field of social policy and matters because market forces and civil society alone cannot fully secure these conditions in contemporary conditions. The third dimension refers to the main scale, if any, on which economic and social policies are decided—even if underpinned or implemented on other scales. This is important as economic and social policies are politically mediated and the scales of political organization may not coincide with those of economic and social life. The fourth concerns the relative weight of the mechanisms deployed in the effort to maintain private profitability and reproduce labour-power by compensating for market failures and inadequacies. Top-down state intervention is just one of these mechanisms and, as is well known, states as well as markets can fail. This suggests the need for additional governance mechanisms and, *a fortiori*, for an active collibrating role for the state (see above).

Referring to these four dimensions, the postwar state in northwestern Europe can be described ideal-typically as a Keynesian welfare national state (KWNS). First, the state was distinctively *Keynesian* insofar as it aimed to secure full employment in a relatively closed national economy and did so mainly through demand-side management and national infrastructural provision. Second, social policy had a distinctive *welfare* orientation insofar as it (a) instituted economic and social rights for all citizens so that they could share in growing prosperity (and contribute to high levels of demand) even if they were not employed in the high-wage, high-growth economic sectors; and (b) promoted forms of collective consumption favourable to the Fordist growth dynamic based on mass production and mass consumption. Third, the KWNS was *national* insofar as these economic and social policies were pursued within the historically specific (and socially constructed) matrix of a national economy, a national state, and a society composed of national citizens. Within this matrix, the national territorial state was mainly responsible for developing and guiding Keynesian welfare policies. Local and regional states acted mainly as relays for these policies; and, in addition, the leading international regimes established after the Second World War were mainly intended to restore stability to national economies and national states. And, fourth, the KWNS was *statist* insofar as state institutions (on different levels) were the chief supplement and corrective to market forces in a 'mixed economy' concerned with economic growth and social integration.

For reasons explored elsewhere (Jessop 2002b), the KWNS experienced a major and multiple crisis in the late 1970s and early 1980s. It has since been tendentially replaced by a new form of state with new functions on these four dimensions. I have termed this the Schumpeterian workfare post-national regime (SWPR). It can be described in ideal-typical terms as follows. First, it is *Schumpeterian* insofar as it tries to promote permanent innovation and flexibility in relatively open economies by intervening on the supply-side and to strengthen as far as possible their overall competitiveness.[5] Second, as a *workfare* regime, the SWPR subordinates social policy to the demands of labour market flexibility and employability and to the demands of economic competition. This includes putting downward pressure on the social wage *qua* cost of international production but, given the economic and political limits to welfare cuts, it is especially concerned with the re-functionalization of the inherited welfare state to serve economic interests. The state also attempts to create subjects to serve as partners in the innovative, knowledge-driven, entrepreneurial, flexible economy and its accompanying self-reliant, autonomous, empowered workfare regime. Third, the SWPR is *post-national* insofar as the national territory has become less important as an economic, political, and cultural 'power container'. This is associated with a transfer of economic and social policy-making functions upwards, downwards, and sideways and with an increasing role for supranational non-governmental bodies and quangos in policy advocacy and policy transfer. And, fourth, given the growing recognition of state as well as market failure, the SWPR is associated, as we have seen, with a dual shift from government to governance and, just as importantly, from government to metagovernance.

This account of the three trends and counter-trends in statehood and the distinction between the KWNS and SWPR also applies, of course, to the emerging Europolity. For the latter is an integral moment in the de-nationalization of the state, the de-statization of politics, and the internationalization of regimes—without being the highest level to which national state powers are shifted upwards, at which new forms of partnership are being organized, or on which the internationalization of policy regimes is occurring. Likewise, the

---

[5] This first term in the SWPR ideal type invokes Schumpeter, the theorist of innovation, entrepreneurship, and competition, rather than Keynes, the theorist of money, employment, and national demand, as its emblematic economist.

changes in the dominant strategies used to build the Europolity, however ineffective, the forms it assumes, however impure, the functions that it exercises, however imperfectly, and the theoretical paradigms used to interpret it, however flawed, are all related to the periodization of the state in the advanced capitalist economies. Thus, to narrate rather breathlessly the phases of Europolity development detailed at length by Ziltener (1999), the initial steps towards Western European integration were initiated through a transatlantic coalition aiming to promote a postwar reconstruction that would integrate Western Europe into the economic and political circuits of Atlantic Fordism (cf. van der Pijl 1984). During the boom years of Atlantic Fordism, the 'Monnet mode of integration' was concerned to create a 'Keynesian-corporatist' (sic) form of statehood on the European level that could secure the conditions for different national Fordist modes of development (cf. Ruigrok and van Tulder 1996) but developed crisis symptoms as the member states pursued divergent strategies in response to the interconnected economic and political crises in/of Fordism. The resulting crisis in European integration prompted the search for a new mode of integration and led to the internal market project—with important conflicts between neo-liberal, neo-corporatist, and neo-statist currents—and the development of new modes of economic and political coordination (cf. van Apeldoorn 2002). After a period of experimentation with new modes of coordination, the provisional outcome of these conflicts can be discerned in a new 'Schumpeterian workfare' mode of integration and coordination concerned to promote the structural competitiveness of Europe in a globalizing knowledge-based economy (cf. Telò 2002). Ziltener also suggests that the dominant line of conflict regarding Europolity construction during the Monnet period of Keynesian-corporatism was supranationalism versus intergovernmentalism and that the Delors project could be seen as a failed supranational attempt to re-scale the Keynesian welfare state to the European level (1999: 129–30, 18–184). To this we might add that the shift towards a European SWPR is clearly associated with a shift in the dominant line of conflict around appropriate forms of multi-level governance and the 'network polity'. This story is too brief, of course, to do justice to the complexities of European integration, the complexities of modes of coordination, their intended functions, their variation with the objects of coordination, and the complexities of competing paradigms and paradigm shifts within and across different disciplines. But it does illustrate the need to periodize the Europolity and, indeed, to locate it in a broader context concerned with the reorganization of statehood on a still more global scale.

The European Union and Multi-level Metagovernance

I now apply the preceding arguments on metagovernance to the European Union as part of the more general change in the forms of statehood. There are at least two levels of failure—the failure of particular attempts at governance using a particular governance mechanism and the more general failure of a mode of governance. Thus, corresponding to the three basic modes of governance (or coordination) distinguished above, we can differentiate three basic modes of metagovernance and one umbrella mode. First, there is the reflexive redesign of individual markets and/or the reflexive reordering of relations among two or more markets by modifying their operation, nesting, articulation, embedding, disembedding, or re-embedding. There are also 'markets in markets'. This can lead to 'regime shopping', competitive 'races to the bottom', or, in certain conditions, 'races to the top'. Moreover, because markets function in the shadow of hierarchy and/or heterarchy, attempts are also made by non-market agents to modify markets, their institutional supports, and their agents to improve their efficiency and/or compensate for market failures and inadequacies. Second, there is the reflexive redesign of organizations, the creation of intermediating organizations, the reordering of interorganizational relations, and the management of organizational ecologies (i.e. the organization of the conditions of organizational evolution in conditions where many organizations coexist, compete, cooperate, and co-evolve). This is reflected in the continuing redesign, re-scaling, and adaptation of the state apparatus, sometimes more ruptural, sometimes more continuous, and the manner in which it is embedded within the wider political system. And, third, there is the reflexive organization of the conditions of self-organization through dialogue and deliberation. There are many activities involved here from organizing opportunities for spontaneous sociability through various measures to promote networking and negotiation to the facilitation of 'institutional thickness'. Fourth, and finally, there is collibration or 'metagovernance' proper (see above). This involves managing the complexity, plurality, and tangled hierarchies found in prevailing modes of coordination. It is the organization of the conditions for governance and involves the judicious mixing of market, hierarchy, and networks to achieve the best possible outcomes from the viewpoint of those engaged in metagovernance. In this sense it also means the organization of the conditions of governance in terms of their structurally inscribed strategic selectivity, that is, in terms of their asymmetrical privileging of some outcomes over others. Unfortunately, since every practice is prone to failure, metagovernance and collibration are also likely to fail. This implies that there is no Archimedean point from which governance or collibration can be guaranteed to succeed and that there will always be an element of irony in attempts to engage in collibration in the face of likely failure.

Governments play a major and increasing role in all aspects of metagovernance: they get involved in redesigning markets, in constitutional change and the juridical re-regulation of organizational forms and objectives, in organizing the conditions for self-organization, and, most importantly, in collibration. Thus metagovernance does not eliminate other modes of co-ordination.

Markets, hierarchies, and heterarchies still exist, but they operate in a context of 'negotiated decision making'. On the one hand, market competition will be balanced by cooperation, the invisible hand will be combined with a visible handshake. On the other hand, the state is no longer the sovereign authority. It becomes just one participant among others in the pluralistic guidance system and contributes its own distinctive resources to the negotiation process. As the range of networks, partnerships, and other models of economic and political governance expand, official apparatuses remain at best first among equals.

It is in this context that we can best interpret the continuities and discontinuities in the development of the European Union as a moment in the structural transformation and strategic reorientation of statehood in a world of states that is not limited to Europe but extends to the global polity (cf. Hettne 1997; Shaw 2000; Sørensen 2001). For the European Union can be seen as a major and, indeed, increasingly important, supranational instance of *multi-level metagovernance* in relation to a wide range of complex and interrelated problems. While the sources and reach of these problems go well beyond the territorial space occupied by its member states, the EU is an important, if complex, point of intersection (or node) in the emerging, hypercomplex, and chaotic system of global governance (or, better, metagovernance) and is seeking to develop its own long-term 'Grand Strategy' for Europe (Telò 2002: 266). But it is still one node among several within this emerging system of global metagovernance and cannot be fully understood without taking account of its complex relations with other nodes located above, below, and transversal to the European Union.

It is clearly premature at a time when the European Union is conducting yet another debate on its future governance to predict the eventual shape of what is bound to be a complex and compromise-based form of multi-level metagovernance in the shadow of a post-national form of statehood. This underlines that the development of multi-level metagovernance is a reflexive process, involving intergovernmental conferences and other modes of metaconstitutional conversation (Walker 2000). But there can be little doubt that the overall movement is towards metagovernance rather than a re-scaling of the traditional form of sovereign statehood or a revamped form of intergovernmentalism inherited from earlier rounds of European integration. As an institutionalized form of metagovernance, emphasis falls on efforts at collibration in an unstable equilibrium of compromise rather than on a systematic, consistent resort to one dominant method of coordination of complex interdependence. Apparent inconsistencies may be part of an overall self-organizing, self-adjusting practice of metagovernance within a complex division of government and governance powers. Seen as a form of metagovernance, the emphasis is on a combination of 'super-vision' and 'supervision', that is, a relative monopoly of organized intelligence and overall monitoring of adherence to benchmarks. But in this evolving framework, there is also a synergetic division of metagovernance labour between the European Council, the specialized Councils, and the European Commission. The European Council is the political metagovernance network of prime ministers that decides on the overall political dynamic around economic and social objectives, providing a 'centripetal orientation of subsidiarity' (Telò 2002: 253), acting by qualified majority, and playing a key intergovernmental and monitoring role. The European Commission plays a key metagovernance role in organizing parallel power networks, providing expertise and recommendations, developing benchmarks, monitoring progress, exchanging best practice, promoting mutual learning, and ensuring continuity and coherence across presidencies. This is associated with increasing networking across old and new policy fields at the European level as well as with a widening range of economic, political, and social forces that are being drawn into multi-level consultation, policy formulation, and policy implementation.

New methods of multi-level metagovernance are being developed and combined in a complex system of metagovernance (cf. Scott and Trubek 2002) that is 'being made more precise and applied (with adaptations as for its intensity) to other fundamental policy fields, traditionally under the competence of national and sub-national authorities: education, structural reform and internal market, technological innovation and knowledge-based society, research and social protection' (Telò 2002: 253).[6] From a strategic-relational perspective, this clearly implies a shift in the strategic selectivities of the modes of governance and metagovernance in the European Union. For, while it builds on past patterns of liberal intergovernmentalism and neo-functionalist spillover, it has its own distinctive momentum and will weaken more hierarchical forms of coordination (whether intergovernmental or supranational). It also entails complementary changes in the strategic selectivities of national states and subordinate levels of government and governance, calling for new forms of strategic coordination and new forms of (meta-)governance in and across a wide range of policy fields.

The pattern of multi-level metagovernance in the European Union is still evolving and, given the inherent tendencies towards failure typical of all major forms of governance (market, hierarchy, network, etc.) as well as metagovernance itself (Jessop 2002a,b), continuing experimentation, improvization, and adaptation is only to be expected. Nonetheless:

the perspective would be that of a new system of democratic legitimacy and governance: multi-level (international, national, supranational, transnational), multi-faced (territorial, functional, modern and post-modern) and with a multitude of actors (social, economic, political and cultural; institutional and extra-institutional), rather

---

[6] Telò is commenting on the open method of coordination but his comment can be generalized to other forms of metagovernance, including partnership, comitology, social dialogue, and so forth.

than that of a classical democratic normative model—federal/constitutional or democrat/republican. (Telò 2002: 266; cf. Schmitter 1992)

Thus the key issue for a research agenda into this new form of statehood becomes the manner and extent to which the multiplying levels, arenas, and regimes of politics, policy making, and policy implementation can be endowed with a certain apparatus and operational unity horizontally and vertically; and how this affects the overall operation of politics and the legitimacy of the new political arrangements.

Concluding Remarks

I have argued that neither the state- nor the governance-centric perspective is adequate for analysing the complexities of multi-level governance in Europe. Each approach is flawed theoretically in its own distinctive ways; nor can their respective deficits be overcome by combining them to produce a more coherent account. Each approach is also plagued to different degrees by anachronistic views about the contemporary world—whether about the state or about the objects and subjects of governance. This means that neither approach can capture the novelty of the emerging European polity as a 'political machine' for multi-level metagovernance (cf. Barry 2001). The alternative approach offered here draws on the SRA and its application to the more general transformation of contemporary political economy as a means to contextualize and 'theoretically mediate' recent changes in statehood. This has two sets of implications for future research.

First, regarding the more immediate questions of governance and metagovernance, the SRA emphasizes the strategic selectivity of institutional arrangements. Multi-level government, multi-level governance, and multi-level metagovernance arrangements will all have their own distinctive strategic selectivities, that is, they are never neutral among actors, interests, spatio-temporal horizons, alliances, strategies, tactics, etc. They also have their own distinctive modalities of success, failure, tension, crisis, reflexivity, and crisis management. These selectivities and modalities depend on specific institutional, organizational, and practical contexts and few generalizations are possible about them (for further discussion, including some possibly hubristic generalizations, see Jessop 2002b). Nonetheless, one generalization that can safely be hazarded is that the belief that multi-level governance can solve old problems without creating new ones is wishful thinking (cf. Mayntz 2001). In turn this implies the need for an ironic, experimental approach to multi-level metagovernance that is concerned to ensure requisite variety in available modes of coordination as well as appropriate levels of reflexivity, super-vision, and supervision in their combination and implementation.

Second, and perhaps more importantly, it is only by situating the changing political forms of the European Union as part of the ongoing transformation and attempted re-regulation of global capitalism as well as part of the more general transformation of statehood in response to major socio-cultural as well as politico-economic changes that one can adequately understand what is at stake in these changes. Among other interesting results, this approach reinforces the importance of examining not only *multi-level governance* but also *multi-level metagovernance*. For the development of the European Union can be seen as part of continuing efforts (often at cross-purposes) by key economic and political actors to produce an appropriate balance between different modes of economic and political coordination across functional and territorial divides and to ensure, under the primacy of the political, a measure of apparatus unity and political legitimacy for the European Union. This has taken different forms at different periods in the pursuit of the European project, especially as this has been shaped at different times by shifts in the relative weight of Atlanticist and European economic and political strategies, by shifts in the relative weight of liberal and neo-liberal *échangiste* (money capital) perspectives and neo-corporatist and neo-mercantilist productivist projects, and by the tendential shift from a KWNS approach concerned to create a single market to realize economies of scale to a SWPR approach concerned to transform the European Union into the most competitive and dynamic knowledge-based economy and to 'modernize' the European social model. In addition, of course, this European-wide multi-level metagovernance project is being conducted in conditions of successive rounds of expansion (which have increased the heterogeneity of the growth dynamics and modes of regulation of different regional and national economies as well as the forms and extent of uneven development and inequalities) and in conditions where national economies and national states have been subject to their own individual structural problems and crises as well as the shared crisis-tendencies derived from their integration into the circuits of Atlantic Fordism and into the emerging globalizing knowledge-based economy. And, finally, this multi-level metagovernance project is part of a broader post-Westphalian 'meta-constitutional conversation' that is occurring between non-state and state actors (including meta-states such as the European Union) as they struggle to develop and institutionalize a new political order (Walker 2000). While it has not been possible within the limits of a chapter to develop the analysis that this approach demands, I hope enough has been said to show the promise of the SRA as one among several alternatives to be explored in future work on the European Union.

5

Multi-level Governance and Democracy: A Faustian Bargain?

B. GUY PETERS AND JON PIERRE

The restructuring of political authority in the Western European political and institutional context propelled by the growing powers of the European Union has given birth to a new school of thought in intergovernmental relations referred to as 'multi-level governance'. The search for alternative accounts of intergovernmental relations has also been fuelled by regional devolution in countries such as some of the Scandinavian and Southern European states (notably Spain) and the United Kingdom (Pierre and Stoker 2000). Relationships among institutions at different tiers of government in this perspective are believed to be fluid, negotiated, and contextually defined. Previously hierarchical models of institutional 'layering', for example, formal treatments of federalism, are being replaced by a more complex image of intergovernmental relations in which subnational authorities engage in direct exchange with supranational or global institutions and vice versa. In this context, multi-level governance has emerged as both an important real world phenomenon and a scholarly model.

There is little doubt that the continuing consolidation of the European Union and the devolution of political power within the state entail changes in institutional relationships that challenge our traditional understanding of those relationships. That said, most of the analytical models and interpretations of multi-level governance that we have seen so far have fallen in the same trap as some analyses of governance, that is, a previously state-centric and constitutional perspective has been almost completely replaced by an image of governing in which institutions are largely irrelevant (but see Bulmer 1993; Jordan 2001a). We believe that this account of recent changes in intergovernmental relations is exaggerated at best and misleading at worst. The institutional 'grip' on political processes within the state and between domestic and supranational actors, although recently relaxed, remains strong and can be further strengthened by the state if and when considered necessary. We are also frustrated by the idea that multi-level governance is all about context, processes, and bargaining. More specifically, we believe that the 'shift' towards multi-level governance should rather be conceived of as a gradual, incremental development in which institutions still play a defining role in governing. Institutions, not processes, are the vehicles of democratic and accountable government, hence we should only expect institutions not to surrender their leverage to contextually defined and *ad hoc* models of governing. While it is true that the challenge of governing has taken on a new magnitude along with the multi-'layering' of political institutions and authority, political control and accountability remain just as critical as ever to democratic government.

This chapter seeks to develop and sharpen existing theoretical models or conceptualizations of multi-level governance. Although the concept of multi-level governance is frequently employed in a wide range of analytical contexts, we still lack both a clear conceptual analysis of such governance as well as a critical discussion of multi-level governance as a democratic process. The basic argument in the chapter is that multi-level governance is frequently misconceived or misunderstood, either with regard to process or to outcomes, or both. Multi-level governance has become a popular model of intergovernmental relationships, partly because it draws on informal and inclusive ideals of decision making and partly because it appears to be a cozy, consensual, and accommodative process. We are less sanguine. In particular, we argue that the absence of distinct legal frameworks and the reliance on sometimes quite informal negotiations between different institutional levels could well be a 'Faustian bargain' where actors only see the attractions of the deal and choose to ignore the darker consequences of the arrangement.[1] To some extent, the 'Faustian bargain' stems from a tendency in multi-level governance thinking that it represents something radically different from traditional models of intergovernmental relations. Thus, we argue that the 'Faustian bargain' can be to some extent escaped if multi-level governance is not seen as an alternative but rather as a complement to intergovernmental relations defined in a regulatory framework.

As discussed elsewhere in this volume (Chapters 1 and 7) much of the work on multi-level governance appeared first among EU scholars who sought to develop a framework for the analysis of the relationships between EU institutions, the state, and subnational governments. While domestic multi-tier systems of governance were hierarchical in so far as communication, resources, steering and control normally moved up or down through all levels in the hierarchy, in the EU context transnational institutions frequently targeted subnational institutions thus circumnavigating the level of the state.

---

[1] This analogy draws on the play *Doctor Faustus*, which was written by Christopher Marlowe in 1592. In the play a well-respected German scholar, Dr Faustus, grows dis-satisfied with the limits of traditional forms of knowledge and decides that he wants to practice magic. His friends Valdes and Cornelius instruct him in the black arts, and he begins a new career as a magician by summoning up Mephastophilis, a devil. Despite warnings, Dr Faustus offers Lucifer his soul in exchange for twenty-four years of service from Mephastophilis. The phrase 'Faustian bargain' has entered the English lexicon, referring to a deal made for a short-term gain with great costs in the long run.

In addition to adding another institutional tier to the traditional equation of intergovernmental relationships, there was also a strong notion that the nature of the relationships between these tiers was distinctly different from domestic relationships between different institutional tiers. Thus, multi-level governance is assumed to differ from traditional intergovernmental relationships in four respects: it is focused on systems of governance involving transnational, national, and subnational institutions and actors; it highlights negotiations and networks, not constitutions and other legal frameworks, as the defining feature of institutional relationships; it emphasizes the role of satellite organizations, such as NGOs and agencies, which are not formally part of the governmental framework; and, it makes no normative pre-judgements about a logical order between different institutional tiers.

The chapter first conducts a conceptual analysis of multi-level governance; there is a need to sort out in some detail what multi-level governance is and is not. Following that discussion, we critically assess multi-level governance in terms of its alleged contribution as both a real world phenomenon and a scholarly model. Moreover, and something that has been largely absent in the debate so far, we highlight the perils and dangers associated with such governance in terms of participation, accountability, transparency, and inclusion.

Multi-level Governance: What is it?

The first task of this chapter is to define exactly what is meant by multi-level governance, at least for us in this discussion of the concept. There are four aspects of this concept that require some elaboration: the concept of govern- ance, the notion of governance that can include several levels of government, the negotiated order, which characterizes the relationship among these multiple and often at least partially autonomous levels; and the notion of multi-level governance as a particular form of political game.

The first and most obvious defining feature of multi-level governance is that it is *governance*; we share Smith's frustration by the fact that most approaches to multi-level governance have a 'paradoxical focus on government rather than governance' (Smith 1997: 725). That is to say, this concept should refer to a broader, more inclusive and encompassing process of coordination than the conventional view of government. The literature offers a host of definitions of governance (see Pierre 2000; Richards and Smith 2002). Rhodes (1996: 652–3, ital- ics in original) defines governance as 'a *change* in the meaning of government, referring to a *new* process of governing; or a *changed* condition of ordered rule; or the *new* method by which society is governed'. The novelty of governance is the emphasis of process over institution; it reflects a 'concern with governing, achieving collective action in the realm of public affairs, in conditions where it is not possible to rest on recourse to the authority of the state' (cf. Stoker 1998,

2000: 93). In a similar vein, Kooiman (1993: 2) defines governance as 'the patterns that emerge from governing activities of social, political and administrative actors'. And Jessop, in a regulation theory perspective, suggests that 'theories of governance are primarily concerned with a wide range of "social" modes of social co-ordination rather than with narrowly political (sovereign, juridico-political, bureaucratic or at least hierarchically organized) modes of social organization' (Jessop 1995: 317).

Thus, the common denominator in these different definitions of governance is that it refers to the process through which public and private actions and resources are coordinated and given a common direction and meaning. That having been said, we are less convinced about the alleged novelty in the style of governing that some of these definitions of governance imply. To some extent, the emergence of new forms of governance may appear more overwhelming in the historically speaking state-centric British political milieu than in many other European national contexts where institutionalized consensual cooperation between the state and societal actors have a long history. Indeed, if we think of governance as the process through which collective interests are defined and pursued (see Pierre and Peters 2000), then some degree of exchange between state and society should be expected.

Furthermore, these images of governance are focused on the process of coordination, in the strictest sense, and tend to ignore the question of how governance challenges the traditional institutions of the state. Pierre and Peters (2000) take a more state-centric view on governance. Their notion of govern-ance is similar to that of Rhodes, Stoker, and Kooiman in so far as they argue that contemporary governance serves to bridge the public–private border in the pursuit of the collective interests. However, they take issue with the notion that governance should be an alternative to government in the definition and pursuit of collective goals; for them, the state remains the most powerful actor in soci-ety, hence the key question is what is the role of government in these emerging forms of governance.

The significance of these defining features of governance in the present context is that unlike traditional models of intergovernmental relationships, multi-level governance refers to connected processes of governance incorp-orating both public and private actors in contextually defined forms of exchange and collaboration. Governance is to some extent more about process than institution; hence managing multi-level governance becomes a matter of integrating processes at different institutional levels with each other in ways which promote the interests of the system overall. However, the institutional dimension of multi-level governance remains critical, partly because it is institutions that define the linkages between different levels of government, partly because institutions as actors on more than one level help coordinate multi-level governance, and partly because multi-level governance—as all types of governance—is embedded in institutional webs which 'shape and constrain' political action (March and Olsen 1989). Thus, for instance, institutions of the state define their relationship with subnational authorities at the same time as they are actors in international governance processes.

Second, the concept of multi-level governance refers to a particular kind of relationship, both vertically and horizontally, between several institutional levels. The basic idea here is that in multi-level governance, actors, arenas, and institutions are not ordered hierarchically but have a more complex and contextually defined relationship. As Marks and his associates put it,

> political arenas are interconnected rather than nested . . . Subnational actors . . . operate in both national and supranational arenas, creating transnational associations in the process. States do not monopolize links between domestic and European actors, but are one among a variety of actors contesting decisions that are made at a variety of levels . . . The separation between domestic and international politics, which lies at the heart of the state-centric model [of EU governance], is rejected by the multi-level governance model. (Marks et al. 1996: 346-7)

Thus, multi-level governance theory argues that although local authorities are embedded in regional and national webs of rules, resources and patterns of coordination, these webs do not prevent them from pursuing their interests within global arenas. The notion of 'embeddedness' should not be seen as the complete opposite to the hierarchical model of intergovernmental relationships but it does signify that lower-level institutions are not invariably constrained by higher-level institutions' decisions and actions. Hierarchy has to a significant extent been replaced by a division of labor, competence, and jurisdiction among largely self-regulatory governance processes at different tiers of government.

Similarly, competencies and jurisdictions are increasingly defined at one institutional level only and not—as was previously often the case—as sectoral 'silos' where central, regional, and local government had clearly defined roles and relationships to each other. Indeed, it could be argued that hierarchy has been replaced by stratarchy, an organizational model where each level of the organization operates to a large extent independently of other organizational levels. For example, as a result of the decentralization in Western Europe, many local and regional authorities are less monitored by central government compared to a decade or so ago. Instead, central government agencies tend to concentrate on exchanges within central government while local and regional authorities receive 'lump grants' from the state to be spent largely on their discretion. There is some similarity to this pattern in the United States where the 'New Federalism' launched in the 1980s served to give the states some of their historical autonomy in relationship to the federal government. In both cases, it makes more sense to talk about a division of labor among institutions at different levels than a hierarchy.

Governance including several institutional levels raises the question of what constitutes the linkages between these levels. While individual actors can occasionally serve as such linkages, the most important continuous linkage between different levels of governance is institutions. These institutions can play either a direct or an indirect linking role; they can either themselves, as political authorities, operate at multiple levels; or, they can, in the shape of arenas for political actors, indirectly facilitate this type of linkage. Either way, however, it seems clear that it is only institutions that can provide continuous linkages between governance at different levels of the system. This institutional linkage often evolves in situations where the jurisdiction of institutions at different levels overlap to a smaller or larger extent.

Needless to say, the institutional arrangements and relationships that are said to be typical of multi-level governance differ from traditional intergovernmental relationships in several important respects. True, central government in most Western countries have relaxed some of their previous political and/or financial control over subnational authorities, but this decentralization has not been critical to the emergence of multi-level governance. Since most of these states have also sought to 'hive off' financial responsibilities to local governments (Sharpe 1988) it has become clear to subnational authorities that future strategies of resource mobilization should not be targeted at the state but should look elsewhere for financial resources (Harding and Le Galés 1998). This is part of the explanation to why international initiatives have become a popular strategy among local and regional authorities in several countries (see, e.g. Hobbs 1994; Fry 1998; Beauregard and Pierre 2000).

Moreover, multi-level governance could be said to be a way of capitalizing on the growing professionalism of regional and local authorities. Their increasing assertiveness vis-à-vis central government in many jurisdictions is proof of a self-reliance that stems in part from having the administrative and organizational capabilities to make autonomous decisions regarding their resource mobilization strategies without having to submit to the central state. Indeed, in many countries, Germany and Belgium, for example, subnational governments have modernized more rapidly and effectively than have central governments and are more capable of managing policies than are central governments. This reversal of the usual balance of capabilities alters the conduct of politics and presses towards the type of networked and largely inchoate pattern associated with multi-level governance.

All of this having been said, however, it should also be noted that the constitutional definitions of institutional competencies have remained remarkably intact; apart from the decentralization mentioned earlier, we have seen very few cases of constitutional reform accompanying the emergence of multi-level governance. Subnational authorities launching ambitious international initiatives, even up to the point of signing agreements with overseas authorities, do so in violation with the constitutional definition of their competencies (Beauregard and Pierre 2000). It is difficult to see how long any major discrepancy between the formal and de facto definitions of institutional discretion can be sustained.

A third feature of multi-level governance is that it denotes a negotiated order rather than an order defined by a formalized legal framework (Kohler-Koch 1996; Scharpf 1997). To some extent, the negotiated nature of multi-level governance is a reflection of the 'nested' nature of the institutional arrangements; the break-up of traditional hierarchies has disrupted the previous more distinct patterns of command and control (Pierre and Stoker 2000: 31). More importantly, however, multi-level exchanges in cases where supranational institutions such as the European Union are still in the process of developing their jurisdiction and their agenda tend to relate to actors and institutions in their external environment through negotiations. Put slightly differently, institutionalization entails negotiation; the evolving nature of the European Union necessitates a reliance on negotiations rather than resorting to some formal, constitutional power bases which are yet to be given their final design.

Therefore, to some extent multi-level governance represents a transnational version of the familiar network ideas employed to understand the domestic level of governance. The similarity can be seen in several features. One is that there are multiple linkages of actors, with little or no hierarchical structure among the actors. In addition, these are negotiated arrangements in which there is little or no capability to predict outcomes in advance. Further, as in some treatments of networks, these structures may be self-referential and resist attempts to impose order, whether from without or from within.

Finally, multi-level governance is frequently conceived of as a political game. This notion refers less to a rational-choice inspired approach to multi-level governance but more to the idea that the relaxation of regulatory frameworks opens up for more strategic and autonomous behaviour among the actors. Another important aspect of the game-like nature of governance, as opposed to the conventional view of intergovernmental relationships, is that the definition of who is a player becomes an empirical question, as does the definition of the stakes. Further, as in networks of all sorts, playing the game may be as important as winning in each iteration of the game. Therefore, multi-level governance can be associated with some moderation of demands by actors in order to maintain their favoured position as players.

Any game must have players, and one of the characteristics of multi-level governance is that it is a game that many players can play simultaneously. The game extends well beyond Putnam's (1982) concept of a two-level game in which bargainers on the international level are to some extent constrained by domestic politics. In the multi-level governance game institutions from several levels of government may be engaged in bargaining over policy, each institution bringing with it a set of goals that may or not be congruent with those of the other players. Further, the goals may be institutional as well as substantive. That is, subnational governments may be using this governance process, and the arenas created by it, as a means of evading control from central government, and EU institutions may also conceive of this process as a means of enhancing their own powers vis-à-vis national governments.

This is primarily a governmental and institutional game, so that the major players and the major goals are those of the political entities involved rather than private sector actors that may have a concern about the substantive policies. This means that it is more difficult to restrict access to the game than if there were only interest groups or individuals who wanted to participate. Once in, however, the alignments of the players may not be readily predictable so that there is a real game. That is, on some issues the alignments may be by institutional level within the political system while on others players may align according to partisan control of the government, or perhaps functional or regional interests. In the European Union, the European Commission has some advantages as a player given that it has fewer political constraints and therefore may be freer to play without concern for the two or three level game concerns of national or subnational governments.

What Multi-level Governance is not

We now have developed a general idea about what multi-level governance is and the range of phenomena to which it refers. In order to take the definitional discussion further, and to sort out some of the apparent confusion over various manifestations of multi-level governance, we will now focus more closely on intergovernmental patterns more broadly. This will enable us to see where the multi-level governance model clearly differs from competing conceptualizations of such institutional relations.

First, it is clear, as has already been suggested, that multi-level governance does not refer to intergovernmental relations as they are usually conceived. Multi-level governance has a wider cast of actors than traditional models of intergovernmental relations; here, we should expect to see public as well as non-public actors to be involved in governance. 'Non-public' actors is shorthand for a wide variety of actors that have an interest in participating in any given governance process, such as private businesses, voluntary associations, organized interests, or single-issue pressure groups. Since one of the defining features of governance is the pooling of public and private resources towards collective goals and interests, we should expect a significant diversity of actors to be involved in governance. This diversity of actors adds an intriguing complexity to multi-level governance, as some non-public actors tend to be almost as hierarchically structured and vertically integrated as systems of political institutions. For instance, organized interests in the environmental policy sector are frequently involved in governance at the local, regional, national, and supranational levels. Thus, the diversity of actors tends to create multiple linkages between governance processes at different levels (see Fairbrass and Jordan, Chapter 9, this volume).

Second, multi-level governance should not be conceived of as a hierarchical order of governance processes. Instead, multi-level governance sees transnational institutions engaging in direct communication with subnational actors, or vice versa. Multi-level governance is thus not controlled from above as tends to be the rule in hierarchical systems. This absence of authority, coupled with the search for the definition of competencies, or the management of overlapping competencies and jurisdictional boundaries, creates institutional exchanges that are typically *ad hoc* and designed differently for each specific matter.

Not very surprisingly, actors at different institutional levels have very different interpretations of this type of governance. At the local level, the idea of being able to negotiate directly with powerful and resourceful transnational institutions is extremely appealing. For instance, regions within the European Union that have experienced increasing difficulties in mobilizing financial resources from the state attach great hopes to their exchange with the EU structural funds. Similarly, transnational institutions enjoy the possibility to choose whether to approach national or subnational institutions, owing to the nature of the specific problem at hand. Instead, it is actors at the national level that tend to be the main critics of this arrangement; concerned over loss of control over subnational institutions whilst simultaneously being expected to be able to ensure compliance with the policies, rules, and programs of international institutions.

While central governments may see power draining away as a result of this process it may also have positive aspects. In particular, the bargaining may make more explicit the transnational political processes that are in train and make the public more aware of the complexities of modern governance. Therefore, some more explicit recognition of multi-level governance may benefit a government that stands to lose hierarchical control. Moreover, given that the coalitions in these bargaining relationships are fluid and subject to a number of influences, national governments may be able to create coalitions to oppose either Brussels or their own subnational governments, depending upon the issues at hand and the bargaining capabilities of national elites.

Furthermore, multi-level governance could been seen as proof of the increasing mutual dependency that characterizes institutional exchanges in the contemporary state (Rhodes 1997). Several decades ago, central governments could exercise close political and economic control of subnational authorities within their nominal domain. Lately, some of that control has been relaxed; institutions have entered a relationship that recognizes that central government, while still the unrivalled locus of political power, has much to gain from acquiring advice from institutions at lower tiers of government. The nature of resource dependency has, however, shifted markedly towards the subnational level.

All of this having been said, it is also important to note that multi-level governance theory sometimes tends to exaggerate the hierarchical and legal nature of intergovernmental relationships before the emergence of this model of governing. There are several accounts of intergovernmental relationships in different national contexts that highlight the negotiated nature of the relationship between the state and local government (Rhodes 1986; Gustafsson 1987; Ashford 1990). Some degree of negotiation and informal advice has always characterized institutional exchanges and it is fair to assume that this institutional exchange has played a critical role in enhancing the efficiency and coordination of the institutional system. Even so, however, multi-level governance differs from such contextually defined institutional relationships in two important respects; new (horizontal) models of governance have emerged at each of these institutional levels and the previously rather strict hierarchical ordering of institutions has been down played.

Third, multi-level governance is sometimes believed to be 'post-constitutional' or 'extra-constitutional'. The processes that have emerged (often without formal planning or formal sanction) are not constrained by formal agreements or rules, although inevitably they can run up against formal barriers and limits on jurisdictions. Thus, these processes are more than federalism and more like the processes of 'intergovernmental politics' described by Wright (1989), Walker (1999), and other students of the changing nature of American 'federalism'. The arguments made by these scholars are that the informal bargaining has become at least as important as the formal allocations of powers among levels, and that politics rather than laws and formal structural arrangements is the determining factor for outcomes. This once again describes a political process that is less determinate than a system of hierarchical subordination, but also a system that may have the flexibility to adapt to changing requirements.

Finally, a defining feature of multi-level governance is that it is a model of governing which largely defies, or ignores, structure. As in most other accounts of governance, the focus is clearly on process and outcomes. The process of governing does not have a uniform pattern but is defined differently owing to the nature of the policy problem and sector and the institutional location of key actors. Indeed, the informality and absence of structural constraints that characterizes multi-level governance is often seen as some of its most attractive features since this is believed to produce a more accommodative and efficient governance. Thus, in multi-level governance, structures are not determinate of outcomes as can be the case in domestic politics (Weaver and Rockman 1993); the empirical institutional explanation has little to offer to an understanding of multi-level governance.

Summary: Political Complexity and Indeterminate Policy Outcomes

The joint outcome of globalization, decentralization, deregulation, and agencification has been erosion of traditional bases of political authority. Furthermore, although democratic government still resorts to its traditional institutional set-up, contemporary governance seems to by-pass or ignores traditional definitions of authority:

the realities of governance seem to escape the boundaries of the nation-state. Modern nation-states are neither all-powerful nor autonomous externally; the domains of administration, politics and international relations are intertwined in ways that considerably complicate their description and effective governance within them. (March and Olsen 1995: 123)

Multi-level governance theory shares March and Olsen's views on the discrepancy between governance and the constitutional map of political life.

The analysis so far raises two questions. The first question relates to the challenge, which emerging forms of governance, not least multi-level governance, pose to the traditional institutions of the state. What is at stake here is our understanding of governance (see Peters 2000); we can either conceive of emerging patterns as 'new governance' and ask questions about coordination is attained, or, in the 'old governance' perspective, ask questions about how the traditional institutional system of the state is geared to participate in governance. Multi-level governance, like all forms of governance, clearly offers some degree of political congruence in a complex web of institutions, actors, and interests. But is multi-level governance the outcome of political deliberation, and how do we hold multi-level governance to political account? Has problem-solving capacity (Scharpf 1997) and outcomes taken precedence over democratic input and accountability?

The other, related question addresses the consequences of governance that 'escapes' traditional boundaries and regulatory frameworks. The present authors question the cozy, accommodative nature of multi-level governance as it emerges in much of the literature. In particular, we believe that multi-level governance, while tempting and attractive in its informality and orientation towards objectives and outcomes rather than focused on rules and formal arrangements, could be a 'Faustian bargain' in which core values of democratic government are traded for accommodation, consensus and the purported increased efficiency in governance. Many regulatory frameworks were implemented in order to define the rights and entitlements of constituencies vis-à-vis the state and each other. Additionally, much of the regulation and legislation that states have enacted has been aimed at changing social behaviour; environmental policies and gender equality policies are two cases in point. An assessment of the benefits of relaxing the existing rules must depart from a recognition of the political nature of regulation (Horwitz 1986). Thus, informal patterns of political coordination could in fact be a strategy for political interests to escape or by-pass regulations put in place explicitly to prevent that from happening.

Multi-level Governance: The Faustian Bargain?

On its face the content of multi-level governance appears very benign, and as a recognition of many continuing processes of democratization in the European countries and within the European Union. Unlike some approaches to policy making in Europe (and in individual nation states), multi-level governance is inclusive and tends to assume that including more actors does not diminish the capacity to reach decisions. Therefore, for democratic reasons the system can be opened to a range of actors.

In addition, the assumption of many of the scholars working in this approach is that decision making will be non-conflictual and accommodative. Again, this is a benign assumption but may not capture the reality of the processes involved. After all, bargaining must be about something and it is likely that there will be divergent interests among the participants. In some societies, one might expect these differences to be worked out in a relatively consensual manner, but that political style does not appear to hold for European politics. Most of the evidence is that actors in Brussels are working very hard to defend their interests (national or sectoral) in very tough bargaining arenas (Kassim et al. 2000). Therefore, it appears excessively optimistic to assume that the bargaining can be accomplished without real conflict of interests, and therefore the use of means other than sweet reason to reach decisions.

Following from the above, the assumption in the discussion of multi-level governance has been that the outcomes of the processes are bargained and not imposed. Again, that is a benign assumption and perhaps largely true. Although true at one level, the bargaining processes may well hide a good deal of power. First, there is the power to set the agenda for the discussions, something that remains largely in the hands of central governments. Further, within the context of the European Union the choice of institutional locale for the crucial aspects of debate may shift powers in one direction or another—but usually away from the subnational governments. Whether at the EU level that advantages the European Council or the Commission, the regional and / or local governments are likely to find their interests less well represented.

Even if the assumptions about multi-level governance were completely correct, there might well still be difficulties in the bargain that has been struck. These problems concern more the governance aspects of the equation than the multi-level aspects. That is, can this arrangement really provide governance, meaning as we indicated above the steering of a society or a set of societies towards some common goals? In the first instance, it appears that goal setting through means other than imposition is difficult. This is, in fact, always the case and determining goals is often a centralizing aspect of any political process.

In addition, having removed or simply not adopted formal means of making decisions there are few means of resolving conflicts among the participants. The rather happy assumption, similar to that contained in most network theory, is that there is some commonality of purposes and means of achieving those purposes among the participants in a multi-level governance process. That may happen, but it is not necessarily the most likely event. Indeed, there might be little need for these processes if there were so much agreement among the actors about means and ends. Therefore, the outcomes of multi-level governance processes are likely to be either conflicts that have to be resolved in other venues, or 'pork-barrel' agreements that give everybody something and do not necessarily resolve the fundamental policy problems that produced the need for the bargaining in the first place.

Another, and arguably more serious problem associated with multi-level governance is that the alleged cozy and consensual nature of this arrangement in fact is a consensus dictated by the stronger players. Formal and legal arrangements are often seen as excessively complicating and rigid frameworks for political decision-making, but one of their virtues is that they the do delineate power relationships and often provide the less powerful with formal means of combating the more powerful. With those constraints removed, or at least de-emphasized the more powerful players—usually still national governments—may be able to dominate the processes. These national governments may themselves have difficulties in agreeing on goals and desired outcomes, and these differences may create opportunities for subnational governments to achieve some of their goals, but the process remains one that will be dominated by the more powerful. It could well be that the outcome of multi-level governance is a benign model of governing for all concerned; the point is that we have no guarantees that it will be benign. Just as constitutions in many countries, notably the United States, rest on a distrust of the benevolence of resourceful political actors, so does the absence of any clear and comprehensive rules for institutional exchange in multi-level governance raise questions about its ability to cater to the interests of weak actors to ensure that multi-level *governance* means something more than multi-level *participation* (Bache 1999: 42).

Another way of describing this problem is to what extent informality entails inequality. Formal rules serve, *inter alia*, an important role in safeguarding equality in terms of the capabilities of the actors. For example, constitutional principles tend to ensure some equality of power for all states or provinces in a federal structure. True, such equality can be safeguarded by less coercive instruments, but informality basically means that it is incumbent upon the actors themselves to permit different actors to participate and to de facto define their relative leverage. For instance, (informal) multi-level governance in the context of the European Union may generate significant differences among different local and regional authorities with regard to their access to EU funds owing to differences in their political access or their ability to launch campaigns to lobby within the European Union.

We should also ask to what extent informality entails outcomes reflecting the status quo and/or the interests of dominant players. It could be argued that the legitimacy of multi-level governance is contingent on broad political and institutional support, which in turn, depends on the extent to which multi-level governance caters to the interests of all actors. In the European Union therefore, multi-level governance may in practice favour the interests of the nation states as the dominant players, even though it is conceptualized as providing greater power to the structurally less powerful subnational actors. Again, however, we find that informality will respond to the interests of weaker constituencies if and when dominant players find a reason to do so.

Although multi-level governance has some severe problems for governments in the real world, political analysts are perhaps in even greater peril of losing their souls by accepting this doctrine. While multi-level governance has the virtue of being capable of being invoked in almost any situation, that is also its great problem. Any complex and multi-faced political process can be referred to as multi-level governance. Second, and perhaps more importantly, multi-level governance appears incapable of providing clear predictions or even explanations (other than the most general) of outcomes in the governance process. As already noted, this approach has some similarities with network analysis, and one of those similarities is its indeterminate nature. It is very nice to say that a range of actors were involved and negotiated a solution but we would argue that a more definitive set of predictions are needed.

Why is this a Faustian bargain? The argument is that the capacity to govern has been sold, or at least has been downgraded, in an attempt to achieve more open and inclusive bargaining, and in order to circumvent formal structures that have been central to governing and to intergovernmental allocations in many systems. On the one hand, that may not be possible, especially when the players involved may be relatively new and rather jealous of their prerogatives. On the other hand, if it is possible then the system of governing that is implied may not really be a system of governing.

Conclusions: How Do We Save Our Souls?

The account of multi-level governance in this chapter may appear excessively bleak and pessimistic. We believe, however, that multi-level governance, both as a real-world phenomenon and as a scholarly model, needs to be critically assessed in order to facilitate a debate regarding its outcomes. Clearly, there is much in multi-level governance suggesting that it has a high problem-solving capacity and that it is likely to generate efficient outcomes. That said, multi-level governance also has features, which call its democratic nature into question. This refers primarily to the fuzzy instruments of accountability and political control.

If multi-level governance is a Faustian bargain, how do we save our souls, that is, how do we achieve the positive sides of the bargain without experiencing the downsides of the agreement? Unfortunately, the debate on multi-level governance—as the debate on governance more generally—has to some degree been framed in dichotomies; the novelty that has been said to be typical of governance exaggerates the extent to which it differs from the conventional system of government. On closer inspection, it becomes clear that for the most part intergovernmental relations in most advanced states have always been characterized by two concurrent types of exchanges; a formal, constitutionally defined exchange and an informal, contextually defined exchange. Most intergovernmental relations probably require both of these exchanges to operate efficiently. Informal exchange helps explain the more formal communications and help lower-tier institutions implement decisions by institutions higher up in the hierarchy. Similarly, high-level institutions need information about how their policies work 'on the ground' in order to design future policies. Thus, alongside the formal exchange there is a mutual need between institutions at different tiers of government for some kind of informal exchange. More importantly, however, all actors have the option to resort to the constitutional definition of their institutional capability if and when it is believed to be necessary to safeguard important institutional interests. Thus, what makes the informal exchanges efficient is that it is embedded in a regulatory framework.

Scholars of intergovernmental relations have long acknowledged the importance of the types of informal exchanges among levels of government that we have been identifying here (see, for instance, Wright 1989). The debate on multilevel governance probably has much to learn from the large existing literature on intergovernmental relations, as broadly defined, in the United States and other countries. Multi-level governance embedded in a regulatory setting that enables weaker actors to define a legal basis for their action might be the best strategy to escape the Faustian bargain and to cheat darker powers.

Part Two

Levels

6

Multi-level Governance and British Politics

IAN BACHE AND MATTHEW FLINDERS

At the beginning of the twenty-first century the British State is at a critical juncture. A range of exogenous and endogenous forces is producing a decision-making structure that a number of authors have referred to as an emerging structure of 'multi-level governance' (see Gamble 2000; Pierre and Stoker 2000; Hay 2002; Wilson 2003). Our purpose in this chapter is to explore the analytical notion of multi-level governance as a means for understanding the changing nature of British government and politics.

Recent constitutional reforms have accelerated, both formally and informally, the transition from 'government' to 'governance' by increasing the inter-organizational complexity and institutional hybridity of the British State. The process of devolution, in particular, has in the terms of multi-level governance, transferred competencies, created cracks, and provoked conflicts within the constitutional configuration. Moreover, as devolution is a dynamic process rather than an event, the British State is unlikely to reach a stable equilibrium. Within this context we need to adjust our conceptual frameworks to understand how the role of the British State has been altered. However, we suggest that while multi-level governance provides potential insights into the changing nature of British politics and government, this does not imply that state power has been eviscerated. Instead, we suggest that there is evidence that new strategies and mechanisms are being developed in response to maximize state power in this changing context. Through the creation of new structures, processes, institutions, and even cultures, state actors are seeking to 'fill in' the 'hollowing out' of strategic state capacity. Moreover, the transferral of certain functions and responsibilities, either upwards or downwards, could be interpreted as an exercise in 'overload reduction' that empowers the British State by allowing it to prioritize strategic issues.

Following on from these themes it is clear that studying the changing relationships in British policy-making demands the construction of a new research agenda, the refinement of conceptual and methodological tools and a break with the largely atheoretical and narrow focus of traditional approaches to the study of British politics (Marsh et al. 1999): most prominent among these

approaches is the Westminster Model (WM). Moreover, it necessitates tran-
scending the compartmentalism that often exists between sub-disciplines of
political studies. In Britain the sub-disciplines of public administration, constitutional studies, and public law have tended to eschew explicit theoretical
frameworks and questions of epistemology (Marsh and Furlong 2002).
Moreover, there has been a long-standing divide between academics studying
domestic and international politics.

The increasing complexity and uncertain trajectory of the British State
demands a more coherent and rigorous structure of inquiry than those analyses
drawing on domestic politics approaches alone. Multi-level governance directs
attention to a complexity, cross-sectoral engagement, and contestation of legitimate authority between actors organized at different territorial levels, which
increasingly speaks of the nature of British governance. This, in turn, stimulates
a reappraisal of the traditional dichotomy between 'domestic' and 'international' policy, and the growth of the 'intermestic'—national governments
increasingly operate in a context shaped by the intersection of internal and
external jurisdictions. Multi-level governance emphasizes that new methods of
cooperation and conflict resolution are required (Benz and Eberlein 1999a).
However, we argue that in its application to the study of Britain, multi-level
governance is strengthened by the insights of a 'domestic politics' approach: the
'differentiated polity' (Rhodes 1997).

In summary, our argument is that multi-level governance provides an increasingly suitable organizing perspective for the study of British governance. We
define an organizing perspective as a framework for analysis that provides a map
of how things (inter)-relate and leads to a set of research questions (Greenleaf
1983; Rhodes 1997). The value of an organizing perspective is that it provides a
framework to explore complex issues and it identifies areas that are important
and worthy of study. However, an organizing perspective is explicitly not a theory. The latter would present distinct hypotheses that may in principle be falsi-
fied (Gamble 1990: 405). It follows therefore that an organizing perspective is
always partial, it is not falsifiable, and it never provides a comprehensive or even
definitive account of the topic of analysis. In other words, we cannot expect
multi-level governance to explain everything in relation to British government
and politics but it can aid our understanding of dynamic processes and help us
to isolate key variables. Incorporation of the insights of the differentiated polity
can deepen this understanding.

Theoretical Issues

The WM has been the traditional organizing perspective for the study of British
politics and government (e.g. Jennings 1966; Mackintosh 1977). The influence of
this model cannot be overstated in terms of providing a structure for academic

research, for shaping the behaviour of politicians, and in influencing the public's expectations and criticisms of government (Judge 1993; Smith 1999). Moreover, the WM contained a strong normative dimension, describing not just how government was thought to work but how it *should* work.

Throughout the twentieth century problems with the WM emerged. These included: its over emphasis on the political elite, its narrow conception of politics, its simplistic assumptions about the location, and focus of power leading to false dualities (e.g. cabinet versus prime ministerial power, politicians versus judiciary, etc.) and its essentially insular (domestic) focus. The development of the behavioural school in the 1950s and 1960s posited new questions and advocated new methodological techniques (Benney et al. 1956). And yet the behaviouralists had no alternative organizing perspective to propose. In the 1970s and 1980s, the WM continued to provide the key conceptual lens for analysing British politics and government.

During the late 1980s and 1990s a range of factors combined to undermine the continuing efficacy of the WM. The increasing influence of the American and European political studies communities presented new and transferable approaches and methodological techniques, while also encouraging an appraisal of epistemological and ontological issues. Political and economic events also weakened the validity of the WM. These events included: the economic crises of the 1970s; concerns about 'ungovernability' and political 'overload'; the advent of neoliberalism, privatization, and the introduction of market mechanisms in the public sector; a belated acceptance of Britain's relative economic decline in the international economy; and, Britain's changing relationship with Europe (King 1975; Rose and Peters 1978; Birch 1984).

Similar issues were creating debates on 'governability' in a range of advanced liberal democracies (Crozier et al. 1975). However, in Britain the perception that the WM was failing to deliver 'effective' government, the evolution of an increasingly fragmented and marketized bureaucratic structure, and the obvious impact of international economic events and trends on domestic British politics, encouraged academics to develop more sophisticated approaches to the study of the state. These over-lapping and interrelated approaches included core-executive studies, policy networks, rational choice, and governance. To date, however, the juxtaposition of a 'multi-level' analysis with these approaches has been absent.

Multi-level Governance

Multi-level governance describes the dispersion of authoritative decision making across multiple territorial levels (Hooghe and Marks 2001b: xi). It emerged in the context of EU Studies, and seeks to develop and unify a number of related strands of writing that share the viewpoint that European integration has challenged the role of the state. It is therefore an alternative approach to the state-centric model of intergovernmentalists (Hoffman 1966; Moravcsik 1993, 1994).

Hooghe and Marks (2001b: 3–4) outline three central tenets of the multi-level governance model as applied to the European Union. First, that while nation states remain central actors in policy making, decision-making competencies are shared and contested by actors organized at different territorial levels rather than monopolized by national governments. Second, collective decision making among states in the European Union involves a significant loss of control for individual national governments. Third, political arenas are interconnected, both formally and informally, rather than nested. Subnational actors operate in both national and supranational arenas, creating transnational networks in the process. The 'gatekeeper' role of national executives is therefore increasingly challenged: the effectiveness of the response varies considerably, in large part according to domestic territorial structures of governance. (Hooghe 1996; Bache 1999; Bache and Bristow 2003).

In an early article on the subject, Gary Marks defined multi-level governance as 'a system of continuous negotiation among nested governments at several territorial tiers—supranational, national, regional, and local—as the result of a broad process of institutional creation and decisional reallocation' (1993: 392). In developing this definition, he drew on analysis of domestic politics, specifically the policy networks approach, in describing how within multi-level governance 'supranational, national, regional, and local governments are enmeshed in territorially overarching policy networks' (Marks 1993: 402–3). The multi-level governance concept thus contained both vertical and horizontal dimensions. For Marks, 'multi-level' referred to the increased vertical interdependence of actors operating at different territorial levels, while 'governance' signalled the growing horizontal interdependence between governments and non-governmental actors. To draw out the distinct features of the 'multi-level' and 'governance' aspects of this approach, we discuss these dimensions separately and draw on a broader literature than multi-level governance in doing so.

Governance

Perhaps more than any other concept, governance has been smoothly assimilated into the discourse of academics and practitioners alike. Yet often the term is used loosely and perhaps inappropriately. An easy starting point for understanding what governance means in the political studies literature is to make clear what it does not mean. That is, governance is not simply a new phrase for describing what governments do. However, what governance does mean is more controversial. Smouts (1998: 81) notes how the concept has 'a high mythification potential . . . the more seriously the notion is taken, the less content it has'. Its ubiquitous usage in contemporary literature is rarely accompanied by definitional clarity (for a discussion see Jessop 1995).

In broad terms, 'governance' (in most usages at least) describes the increased role of non-governmental actors in public policy making and delivery. The term is used to imply an appreciation of an increasingly complex state-society relationship in which network actors are prominent in policy making and the state's primary role is policy coordination rather than direct policy control. This raises important questions about the challenge of governance to state power and related questions of democratic accountability (Flinders 2001: Peters and Pierre, Chapter 5, this volume).

Pierre (2000: 1) suggests that the 'institutional strength' of states has been challenged from a number of sources. 'External' factors include the deregulation of financial markets and the subsequently increased volatility of international capital that has deprived the state of much of its traditional capacity to govern the economy. Subnational governments have become more assertive vis-à-vis the state; cities and regions—frequently propelled by ethnic and cultural identification—are positioning themselves in the international arena, seeking to bypass central and state institutions and interests (Le Gales 2002). 'Internal' factors focus on the impact and unintended consequences of new public management (NPM)—deregulation, contracting-out, agencification, privatization, etc. (see Hood 1991). The introduction of quasi-autonomous relationships in order to mimic market style relationships has increased the level of fragmentation and created a complex bureaucratic topography (see Skelcher 1998; HC 209 1999).

In the context of these developments, there has been little long-term strategic thinking regarding the steering capacity of the centre. As the then Head of the British Civil Service, Sir Richard Wilson (1999: 5), stated, 'I would not claim that the manner in which we implemented all these reforms over the years was a model to emulate. There was not enough overall vision or strategic planning.' The combination of these external and internal factors brought a challenge to traditional state power that led Rhodes (1994) to describe the process as the 'hollowing out' of the state.

While there is a view that states are losing control in the context of governance, the alternative view focuses on new state strategies for coping with the challenge of governance. Whichever view of state control is taken, the emergence of governance as policy making through complex networks has now secured its place alongside state hierarchy and markets as means through which authoritative decisions are made.

Multi-levels

The concept of intergovernmental relations is not new to the study of British politics, but has traditionally focused on the relationship between central government and local authorities (e.g. see Rhodes 1981). However, other territorial levels of authority have become increasingly important. Above the nation state, the European Union has grown in competence in a wide range of policy

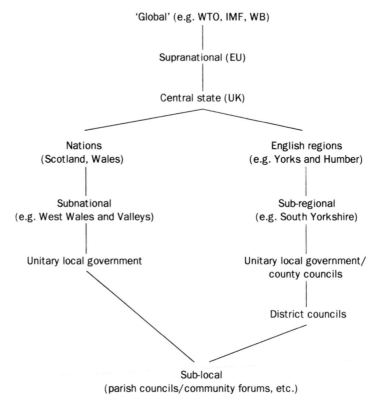

FIGURE 6.1 Territorial levels of decision making

domains. Other international institutions and agencies such as North Atlantic Treaty Organization (NATO), the World Trade Organization and the World Bank place constraints on the autonomy of domestic policy making (Held and McGrew 2002). Political devolution has occurred within the domestic arena and both the sub-regional and sub-local level have been activated or reactivated in recent years in some policy domains. We provide a basic map of authoritative decision-making levels as they presently apply to Britain. (see Fig 6.1.)

The lines connecting the various levels of decision making over-simplify the complex relationships between actors in a multi-level polity. Not all relationships are channelled hierarchically and a more sophisticated diagram would represent a complex network or web of relationships linking subnational to supranational, sub-local to regional, etc. Where multi-level relationships have been investigated, variation is found in their nature and importance across different policy areas (Marks 1998). However, this research agenda is relatively new and part of our purpose here is to highlight the need for further research exploring these relationships.

Multi-level Governance and the Differentiated Polity in Britain

In developing the multi-level governance framework for understanding British government and politics, we draw on Rhodes's (1997) attempt to capture the changing nature of British governance through the 'differentiated polity'. His point of departure is a critique of the WM.

Our grasp of this world is fragile. All too often we simplify to impose an order that is not there. Our theories fall about our ears as our methods collect data with no inherent meaning. All that is solid, including political institutions, can seem as if it is melting into air. The Westminster model has not, and will not, evaporate. But its institutions have been eroded and transformed since 1945. The narrative of governing without Government in the differentiated polity seeks to capture the transformation. (1997: 200)

The narrative of 'governing without government in the differentiated polity' perhaps implies a demise of state power that Rhodes does not intend. The important point, however, is that the WM, with its focus on the strong executive and tradition of 'leaders know best' 'founders on the complex, multiform maze of institutions that makes up the differentiated polity' (1997: 3). In its place, Rhodes puts forward the differentiated polity to describe 'the new institutional setting of British government' and to 'identify the constraints on executive power' (1997: 3). For Rhodes (1997: 7–9) this perspective fulfils a range of functions: it identifies important weaknesses in the WM, it poses distinct questions about British government; and, it explains key problems confronting policy making and implementation.

From a structural perspective, the differentiated polity offers a more realistic interpretation of the modern British State than does the WM, particularly post-NPM. However, acknowledging the emergence of governance as a challenge to state power is not the same as assuming that state power is ineffectual. Rhodes (1997: 15) states:

It would be foolish to argue that the British centre can never intervene effectively. Its relationships with other units of government and with policy networks are 'asymmetric'; for example, the centre has more legal resources than any other domestic actor does. However, it is equally foolish to ignore the clear limits to, and constraints on, central intervention; there is asymmetric interdependence.

So for Rhodes, fragmentation and centralization coexist, in a manner akin to the concept of 'fragmegration' offered by Rosenau (Chapter 3, this volume), within a polity characterized by 'persistent tension between the wish for authoritative action and dependence on the compliance of others' (Rhodes 1997: 15).

Despite its merits, a weakness of the differentiated polity is that it is a pre-devolution analysis and, as such, does not account for the transferred competencies and subsequent tensions within the new constitutional configuration. It is here that the increasingly multi-level dimension of British politics must now be

TABLE 6.1 Comparing the WM with the multi-level polity

Westminster Model	Multi-level polity
Centralized state	Differentiated state
General Principles	
Hierarchy	Heterarchy
Control	Steering
Clear lines of accountability	Multiple lines of accountability
'External' Dimensions	
National sovereignty	Shared/negotiated sovereignty
British foreign policy	Multiple foreign policy
'Internal' Dimensions	
Unitary state	Quasi-federal state
Parliamentary sovereignty	Inter-institutional bargaining
	Multi-level bargaining
Strong executive	Segmented executive
Unified civil service	Fragmented civil service
Political constitution	Quasi-judicial constitution
British foreign policy	Multiple foreign policies

highlighted. In Table 6.1, we bring together the tenets of what we now describe as a multi-level polity in Britain in contrast to those of the WM. In essence this table seeks to hypothesize the reorganization of authority in contemporary Britain.

Our argument is that the extent to which state power has been weakened in a multi-level polity remains an empirical question, the answer to which is likely to vary across policies and territories within the United Kingdom. However, as we illustrate in our study of devolution below, the British State is developing new mechanisms for maximizing central steering in the emerging multi-level polity.

Devolution

The *Scotland Act 1998, Government of Wales Act 1998*, and *Northern Ireland Act 1998* replaced a unitary system of government in Britain with a quasi-federal struc-ture. Moreover, the *Greater London Authority Act 1999* facilitated the direct elec-tion of a mayor and an elected body for London. In addition, an emerging structure of English regional governance can be identified. These devolution-ary reforms have transferred decision-making power from the centre.

As emphasized by Hooghe and Marks (Chapter 2, this volume) devolution and decentralization is not unique to the United Kingdom but is characteristic of a trend in many Western, and particularly European states. However, some issues arising from these processes are unique to the United Kingdom due to its distinct constitutional structure and the framework of parliamentary sovereignty within which changes have been accommodated. Other challenges are shared by other decentralizing states. These include: the distribution of policy competencies; fiscal autonomy; judicial review; issues of accountability; the tension between parliamentary sovereignty and quasi-federal structures; and, the need for coordination and cooperation between levels of government.

All complex multi-level constitutional systems (Canada, Australia, Spain, Germany, Belgium, Switzerland, etc.) have developed new formal methods of intergovernmental coordination to distribute competencies, ensure cooperation and resolve disputes between levels. In a multi-level polity, coordination has both horizontal and vertical dimensions and should therefore be viewed as the management of complex matrices. Consequently, the formal methods of coordinating intergovernmental relationships in a multi-level polity can be both horizontal (e.g. concordats and agreements between national or subnational units) and/or vertical (i.e. concordats and agreements between units organized at different territorial levels). Moreover, these agreements can be either multi-lateral or bilateral. Informal methods of coordination may develop as devolution progresses and are worthy of further investigation. Here we focus on the formal arrangements established in Britain to date.

The emerging structure of intergovernmental agreements and mechanisms of conflict resolution in Britain are complex. The main document for coordinating relations between the centre and devolved institutions is the *Memorandum of Understanding* (MOU) (CM 4806 2000). This is a multi-lateral agreement signed by the UK government, the Scottish Executive, the Cabinet of the National Assembly of Wales and the Northern Ireland Executive. The MOU established general principles of information sharing, cooperation and confidentiality. It established the Joint-Ministerial Council (JMC) and functional sub-committees of the JMC to act as the apex of the intergovernmental cooperation machinery. The MOU is supported by a burgeoning number of multi-lateral and bilateral concordats covering specific issues such as EU policy, financial assistance to industry and international relations. In addition to the MOU and the concordats are a large number of bilateral agreements between Whitehall departments, the Scottish Executive, and the Cabinet of the National Assembly of Wales. These bilateral agreements are supported by a number of 'best practice' guides.

The JMC represents the main arena for assuaging the tensions of devolution within the United Kingdom. Indeed the MOU highlights that the role of the JMC is primarily conflict resolution. The MOU (CM 4806 2000: 8) notes, 'Where a dispute cannot be resolved bilaterally or through the good offices of the relevant territorial Secretary of State the matter may formally be referred to the JMC secretariat'. However, the JMC is just one of a range of intergovernmental committees in existence to support and coordinate the multi-level framework that now exists. These include the British–Irish Council, the North/South Ministerial Council, the British–Irish Intergovernmental Conference, and the Council of the Isles. However, the British multi-level polity is in a state of flux. The fledgling units of national and regional governance are still developing their operating procedures, analysing the capacity of their respective powers and seeking to build relationships at both the local, national, and international levels. New forms of intergovernmental relations are developing that demand adjudicatory mechanisms to ensure composed conflict resolution (see HL 28, 2002). This issue will take on greater saliency should the 2003 elections in Scotland and Wales result in the creation of new governing arrangements that do not include representatives of the Labour party, which governs at the national level.

Much of the literature analysing devolution in the United Kingdom has understandably focused on the relationships between the UK centre and the national structures introduced in Scotland and Wales. However, multi-level governance highlights the insularity of such an approach. The Scottish Parliament and Welsh Assembly are now responsible for the operation of local government in their respective countries. Local government is wary of far-reaching reforms and fears the loss of functions to the regional and national tiers of government. Consequently, it is likely that the Welsh Local Government Association, for example, will seek to build dual networks. These would exert pressure on the National Assembly directly but also seek to apply indirect two-step leverage via Whitehall and Westminster. Both local and sub-central authorities are also likely to seek representation at the European level in order to apply two-step leverage on the British government (see Gargiulo 1993; Ansell et al. 1997). This has been clearly seen in response to the European Commission's White Paper of July 2001 on governance. The Scottish Executive and the Convention of Scottish Local Authorities (COSLA) produced a joint response document. It is arguable that the post devolution structure may provide a more rewarding environment for subnational actors to operate. Moreover, there has been a rapid increase in the number of horizontal subnational regional agreements that cross-national boundaries. For example, Scotland has been a key member of the regional association that published a Common Declaration on European Governance in May 2002. This association, which includes Aquitaire, Emilia-Romagna, Flanders, Hessen, Marche, Skane, Scotland, Tuscany, Wales, and Wallonie, aims to produce a 'networked response' to the debate about European governance that will support a greater role for the regions of Europe. The Welsh Assembly has been similarly active in building sub-regional linkages in other countries in order to develop and protect common interests. For example, in April 2001 Wales signed a MOU with the Spanish region of Catalunya in order to strengthen economic and cultural links. The circumnavigation of levels of government demonstrates the innate complexity of multi-level governance and suggests that intergovernmental relations may demand increased resources and new institutional frameworks (see HL 28 2002).

Although England was hardly mentioned in the devolution legislation, the Labour party's 1997 manifesto had committed the party to introducing legislation to allow the public to decide, on a regional basis, whether they wanted directly elected regional government. In power the Labour government has been cautious (Tomaney 2000*a*,*b*). The central thrust of new regional governance to date has been the creation of Regional Development Agencies (RDAs). However, regional governance in England is complex and fragmented. The RDAs operate in a bureaucratically 'thick' stratum that includes the Government Offices in the Regions (GORs), regional chambers, and a range of regionally organized quangos (Environment Agency, Housing Corporation, Highways Agency, etc.). This dense regional topography has been further complicated by the creation of a range of area based initiatives (ABIs) since 1997 (Health/Education/ Employment Action Zones, Sure Start Schemes, New Deal Schemes, etc.).

New tools of governance are being developed in order to ensure better coordination within English regions. For example, a number of concordats have been signed between the RDA, GOR, and the regional chamber (in Yorkshire and Humber, for example). In other regions, particularly the North East, the regional chamber and the RDA have worked together to secure greater funding from central government. Alongside these initiatives, more comprehensive and formalized mechanisms have been implemented at the national level. The Performance and Innovation Unit (PIU) report *Reaching Out* (Cabinet Office 2000) recommended that the GORs take on the primary role for ensuring coordination in terms of vertical governance along the local–regional–national axis and the horizontal axis between the various institutions of regional governance. As a result, from April 2000 a range of new functions (drawn from Ministry of Agriculture, Fisheries and Food (MAFF), Department for Culture, Media and Sport (DCMS), and the Home Office) were transferred to the GORs.

The PIU report also led to the creation of a 'Regional Co-ordination Unit' (RCU) within the Cabinet Office (transferred to the Office of the Deputy Prime Minister in May 2002). All departments are formally required to consult the RCU when introducing any new ABIs. The RCU is also designed to feed into the policy-making process within Whitehall and form a two-way conduit between the centre and the English regions. The RCU reflects a direct recognition and acceptance by central government of both the challenges of operationalizing devolution and the need for new steering mechanisms in the context of a multi-level polity. It acknowledges that governing via complex networks rather than traditional hierarchies demands not formal command and control processes but more conciliatory methods stressing coordination and cooperation. In other words, the creation of the RCU might therefore be interpreted as an attempt at 'filling in' the 'hollowing out' of the state (Holliday 2000; Taylor 2000; Flinders 2002). The government's preference for the GORs rather than the RDAs or the Regional Chambers as the lead actor reflects a degree of both bureaucratic and political realism. Neither the RDAs nor the Regional Chambers are yet sufficiently developed to take on such a role. Moreover, in terms of political and financial resources, the GORs provide an infrastructure through which national actors can effectively steer networks at the regional level (Bache 2000).

Regional devolution in England exemplifies the complexity of constitutional engineering and the dangers of proceeding without a coherent vision of how reforms in one area have implications and, often, unintended consequences for other parts of the constitutional infrastructure. In particular, it remains unclear how the government's plans for regional government fit with its agenda for local government. A comparative perspective demonstrates that serious jurisdictional and financial conflicts are likely to occur between the regional and local levels in the context of subnational reform. Such conflict has been pronounced in both Germany and Spain. Jeffery (1998: 12) notes that when formerly centralist states decentralize powers to the regional level, local government can suffer from the 'decentralism of centralism' as has, for example, been the case in Belgium and Spain: (the regional Catalonian government in Spain attempted to abolish local government completely in its territory).

In summary, the regional topography of the state in England is both dense and opaque. Moreover, the regional tier involves a range of sector specific organizations that would not traditionally have been incorporated under the 'governmental' framework. These include ABIs, regional arms of executive non-departmental public bodies and a range of projects utilizing public/private partnerships and the private finance initiative. Yet while the support for English regional government is growing, the position and capacity of the national government to control this process has not yet been seriously threatened. The creation of the RCU can be interpreted as a direct response to these pressures but the government remains in control of the process.

Yet it is also evident that the evolution of the regional tier of governance in England challenges the adequacy of the WM. Its top–down emphasis on hierarchy and clear lines of accountability appear inadequate in light of the complexity of the modern state and recent constitutional developments. This complexity is exacerbated by the fact that the topography of the British State consists of an increasingly diverse range of quasi-autonomous non-governmental organizations (Flinders 2003). Therefore understanding Britain as a *multi-level polity* highlights not just the interaction between different levels or different parts of government but the wider structure of what the Organization for Economic Cooperation and Development (OECD) (2001*a*) termed 'distributed public governance' consisting of agencies, authorities, and other autonomous bodies.

Conclusions

In terms of the way scholars from different academic backgrounds have utilized the concept of multi-level governance it is clear that, to date, observers of

British politics and public policy have focused attention primarily on the state and how it is attempting to manage contemporary governance challenges. This arguably stands in contrast to the society-centric approach of some international relations scholars, like Rosenau above, and sociological viewpoints, like that of Jessop above, who locate or at least attempt to appreciate the protean nature of the state in terms of broader processes.

While for some, the 'multi-level' component of multi-level governance is a limitation in that it connotes hierarchy, here it has the advantage of focusing attention on the backbone of the 'governmental framework' around which the broader context and structure of 'governance' in Britain exists. In this sense, we would not aver from Jessop's argument that multi-level governance exists in the 'shadow of hierarchy' (Chapter 4, this volume). The legitimacy of the state between elections is largely based around parliamentary mechanisms that seek to make transparent the operation of the state. It is in relation to the implications of emerging multi-level governance for democratic accountability, that research (and probably reform) are necessary. The British Parliament was designed to oversee a relatively stable state structure based around the departmental model headed by a minister. The transfer of functions upwards to the European Union and global actors and downwards to the Scottish Parliament and Welsh Assembly has reduced the breadth of policy areas that Parliament can oversee. At the same time, initiatives to foster greater horizontal or 'joined up' governance have led to the demise of the convention of ministerial responsibility as culpability is now commonly diluted amongst a team of ministers drawn from several departments. Only recently has Parliament begun the process of creating scrutiny mechanisms with the flexibility to mirror increasingly fluid state models, such as departmentally related parliamentary select committees launching joint inquiries into policy initiatives that transcend departmental boundaries.

The argument made at the beginning of this discussion was that multi-level governance provides a valuable organizing perspective for understanding the changing nature of policy making in Britain and that this concept is strengthened by the insights of the differentiated polity approach. Drawing on the theoretical chapters in Part One, we have argued that British politics is understood more effectively as a *multi-level polity*. In the context of devolution, there is greater evidence of a bargaining executive, rather than a strong executive; of interdependence between territorially distinct state organizations, rather than hierarchy; of multiple and confused accountability, rather than clear lines of accountability; of a quasi-federal state, rather than a unitary state. We also suggest that further investigations would be likely to cast doubt on other pillars of the WM in the context of devolution: in particular, those of a unified civil service and the notion of a single foreign policy. However, despite the emergence of a multi-level polity, the erosion of the power of central government should not be taken for granted, but should continue to be examined empirically. The new reality is likely to reveal variations in central government power across different parts of the United Kingdom and in relation to different issues and policies. Our discussion of devolution reveals that while the centre faces new challenges in this new context, it has begun to develop new means through which to achieve coordination, steering, and gatekeeping.

Yet, while the WM has lost much of its explanatory power, it has not become irrelevant to those who govern. Marsh et al. (2001) noted: 'whilst the Westminster model is not an accurate description of the British political system, it does reflect, to varying degrees, the conception that politicians and senior civil servants have on the process of government. In other words, it underpins their belief systems and so affects what they do.'

Indeed, it is a paradox of the Labour government's approach to reform of the constitution and the State that 'the mainframe has remained sacrosanct' (Nairn 2000: 70). The challenges facing the British State stem from its attempt to maintain elements of the traditional governmental framework (parliamentary sovereignty, ministerial responsibility, etc.) while introducing constitutional and bureaucratic reforms that directly undermine those concepts. For the political elite, the WM endures because it legitimizes a centralist (and elitist) framework. It describes a system in which ministers, via their party's effective control of parliament, enjoy stability and the capacity to govern. Ministers must always make the final decision as ministerial responsibility holds them ultimately accountable to the public. The WM therefore provides ministers with a legitimating foundation with which to base their desire to retain the power of finality.

In conclusion therefore, we suggest that the power of central government has not been eviscerated; it remains the primary governance level and as Jessop notes (Chapter 4, this volume) will remain so until supranational governance mechanisms enjoy democratic legitimacy. However, governments operating at the national level must increasingly exert their powers via different governance mechanisms and techniques. This illustrates the contribution of multi-level governance to our framework. To paraphrase Hooghe and Marks (2001: 3–4), while the British State remains a central actor in policy making, decision-making competencies in Britain are increasingly shared and contested by actors organized at different territorial levels rather than monopolized by national governments. In this context, the emergence of a multi-level polity in Britain 'challenges much of our traditional understanding of how the state operates, what determines its capacities, what its contingencies are, and ultimately of the organisation of democratic and accountable government' (Peters and Pierre 2000: 131).

7

Multi-level Governance and the European Union

STEPHEN GEORGE

As the editors discuss in Chapter 1 of this volume, the term multi-level governance emerged first in the study of the European Community (EC) and the European Union. Originally it was only a particularly neat descriptive phrase devised by Gary Marks (1993) to express a characterization of EC regional and structural policy that had already been described in similar terms by Anderson (1990), and indeed in an earlier article by Marks himself, where he used the rather more cumbersome phrase 'a complex, multilayered, decision-making process stretching beneath the state as well as above it' (Marks 1992: 221). At this stage Marks (1992: 223) thought that there was 'little reason to believe that the experience of structural policy will be replicated in other policy areas in the EC'. It was apparently only after he had coined the term 'multi-level governance' to describe this experience of structural policy that Marks decided that it had more general applicability.

Given its origins, it is not surprising that multi-level governance has been applied more extensively to the European Union than to any other area of study. It has also been extensively criticized in its application to the European Union (for a summary, see Jordan 2001*b* and Jordan and Fairbrass, Chapter 9, this volume). These established criticisms provide a useful way of structuring the discussion in this chapter of the application of multi-level governance to the European Union. They allow a focus on the debates specific to the European Union, while at the same time opening up several of the core themes of the book as identified by Bache and Flinders in Chapter 1.

Andrew Jordan (2001*b*: 201) identifies seven key criticisms of multi-level governance as applied to the European Union:

- multi-level governance is nothing new, but an amalgam of existing theories
- it provides a description of the European Union, but not a theory
- it overstates the autonomy of subnational actors (SNAs)
- it adopts a 'top–down' view of SNAs
- it focuses on SNAs to the exclusion of other subnational actors
- it mistakes evidence of SNA mobilization at European level as evidence of SNA influence
- it ignores the international level of interaction.

Multi-level Governance is an Amalgam of Existing Theories

The study of European integration, of the EC and subsequently the European Union, has been dominated for decades by a division between an 'intergovernmental'[1] perspective on the one hand, and what is sometimes, rather lamely, called a 'supranational' perspective on the other. A review of Hooghe and Marks (2001) accurately summarizes a general view that: 'Multi-level governance has come to be regarded as one of the more fruitful of the approaches to move beyond the moribund intergovernmental/supranational dichotomy' (Grewal 2002). However, this chapter will argue that general view is entirely wrong: multi-level governance does not escape the dichotomy, but is simply a more sophisticated restatement of one side of it; and the dichotomy, far from being moribund, has been extremely productive and is continuing to be so in its revised form. This represents broad agreement with the observation that multi-level governance is nothing new, but without seeing that as necessarily a criticism.

The Intergovernmental/Supranational Dichotomy

The original form of this theoretical divide was between conceptualizations of the process of European integration as, in one view, controlled by the governments of states or, in the other view, out of the control of governments. In the original version the protagonists on the intergovernmental side were Hoffmann (1964, 1966) and Milward (1984, 1992), while the 'supranational' side was represented by the 'neofunctionalists' (Haas 1958, 1970; Lindberg 1963; Schmitter 1970). Each of these theoretical positions subsequently developed. Intergovernmentalism was redesigned and presented in the form of Liberal Intergovernmentalism by Andrew Moravcsik (1993, 1998). Many, but not all, of the theoretical positions of the neofunctionalists were revived by Wayne Sandholtz and his collaborators (Sandholtz and Zysman 1989; Sandholtz and Stone Sweet 1998); and this chapter will argue that multi-level governance is also descended from that same set of theories.

Neofunctionalism was a multi-faceted theory of European integration, containing within it many elements. Central was the concept of functional spillover, hence the name given to the theory as a whole. Neofunctionalists used the concept of functional spillover to help them to explain how, once national governments took the initial steps towards integration, the process took on a life of its own, and swept the governments along further than they had anticipated

---

[1] The term is derived from the discipline of international relations, and refers to a perspective that emphasizes the relationship between the national governments of different sovereign states. It is potentially confusing, because the same term is used in the discipline of comparative politics to refer to relations within a sovereign state between different levels of government, for example, central government, regional government, local government.

going. This argument was based on the perception that modern industrial economies are made up of interconnected parts, so that it is not possible to isolate one sector from others. Following that understanding, neofunctionalists argued that if member states integrated one sector of their economies, the interconnectedness between that sector and others would lead to a 'spillover' into the other sectors: the integration of one sector would only work if other functionally related sectors were also integrated (for further explanation and specific examples, see George and Bache 2001: 9–12).

However, functional spillover was not the whole of the analysis offered by neofunctionalism. In addition, it also embraced a theory of the politics of European integration. This gave a privileged role to supranational institutions, particularly the European Commission. The Commission was seen as an institution with genuine autonomy from the governments of the member states; an actor that could manipulate the pressures on governments so as to push forward the process of European integration. The pressures that the Commission could manipulate included those from functional spillover, but the neofunctionalists also theorized a pluralist political process that the Commission could exploit.

In this pluralist analysis, interest groups were central to the dynamics of integration. Neofunctionalists assumed that interest groups in sectors that were integrated would benefit from the integration, and would therefore act as barriers against governments deciding to abandon the experiment and retreat to national policy making in the sectors that had previously been integrated. They also expected the Commission to cultivate the interest groups by involving them in European decision making, so winning allies in any confrontation with national governments over their proposals. At the same time interest groups in other economic sectors would see the benefits accruing to the interest groups in the sectors that were already integrated, and would press for integration in their sectors.

A third set of pressures on governments would come from functional departments of state, such as departments of trade or the environment, which would form alliances with the Commission and with their counterparts in other member states. The central state executive would therefore find itself faced with an alliance of its own civil servants in favour of European solutions to policy problems.

Hoffmann's original intergovernmentalist critique of neofunctionalism included an attack on the pluralist version of the political process. Hoffmann was a close and sympathetic observer of French politics. He therefore had a better feel for the nature of European democratic politics than some American political scientists, whose starting point was a pluralist analysis of the US polity (not necessarily itself accurate), which was then generalized to other systems.[2] While not denying that interest groups were influential in western Europe, Hoffmann

---

[2] This may be a slight caricature of the position of Haas and Lindberg, but such a view was dominant in US political science at the time. For a review and critique of pluralist theories see Smith (1995).

insisted that governments did not *only* respond to the prompting of these groups. They also responded to the demands of electoral politics, *and* they had an independent view of what constituted the 'national interest'.

In contrast to Hoffmann's dismissal of the pluralist foundations of the neofunctionalist analysis, Moravcsik's later reformulation of intergovernmentalism embraces those same foundations, but with one important difference. Where the neofunctionalists assumed that the interest groups would start to turn their attention to the European level, and would become allies of the Commission in pushing for further integration, Moravcsik (1993) assumes that the pluralist political process will be confined to the national level, and that the interest groups will not take a consistent position on whether European integration is a good thing. Instead, they will react to each issue on its merits in the light of how they perceive that it will affect their interests. Each will then apply pressure on its own national government accordingly. Governments will decide their position on particular proposals for integration on the basis of the balance of domestic pressures, and will then take this position into their negotiations with the governments of the other member states.

This 'Liberal Intergovernmental' position was first applied to explain the negotiation of the Single European Act (Moravcsik 1991), where it was opposed to an explanation that represented a partial revival of the ideas of the neofunctionalists. However, functional spillover, the central element of the neofunctionalist theory, and the one that had given it its name, was not taken up by the new theories that tried to explain the revival of European integration from a supranational perspective. Sandholtz and Zysman (1989) are quite clear that in their view functional spillover cannot explain the 1992 programme to create the single European market, because the functional pressures had been present since the late 1960s, so they could not explain the timing of the single-market programme. It is therefore inappropriate to refer to the revival of neofunctionalism. Instead, certain aspects of that multi-faceted theory were revived, particularly the idea of the ability of the Commission to form alliances with interest groups to lever governments into agreeing to more integration. According to supranational explanations, the key actors in the agreement to the single market programme were the Commission, under the leadership of Jacques Delors, and the European Round Table of Industrialists, a supranational interest group consisting of the major European multinational corporations (Sandholtz and Zysman 1989; Fielder 2000).

From this brief review, it should be obvious that the intergovernmental/supranational dichotomy is far from 'lacking vitality or vigour', to quote the definition of 'moribund' given in the *New Oxford Dictionary of English*. The debate has not stagnated, but has evolved. The Liberal Intergovernmentalism of Moravcsik is not just a rehash of Hoffmann's position: indeed, its theoretical starting point is that it 'takes seriously the self-criticisms of neofunctionalists' (Moravcsik 1993: 480). Equally, although Stone Sweet and Sandholtz (1998: 6) acknowledge that, '[t]he three constituent elements of our theory are prefigured in neofunctionalism', they are also quite clear that, '[w]e do not, however, embrace the whole of . . . neofunctionalism'. The vigour of the debate has produced the two classic studies of the Single European Act and the single market programme (Sandholtz and Zysman 1989; Moravcsik 1991), and two very significant books on the process of European integration (Moravcsik 1998; Sandholtz and Stone Sweet 1998).

The Relationship of Multi-level Governance to the Intergovernmental/Supranational Dichotomy

Despite attempts to distinguish it from neofunctionalism, multi-level governance actually marks a revival of one part of the theory that does not really feature in the reformulation by Stone Sweet and Sandholtz (1998). However, this is *not* the idea of functional spillover. That idea has been abandoned so comprehensively that there is no justification for referring to this side of the dichotomy as 'neofunctionalism' any longer. Neither is it the idea that supranational interest groups, such as the European Round Table, will form alliances with supranational institutions, such as the Commission, to lever more competencies away from the national to the supranational level. That idea is revived by Stone Sweet and Sandholtz, and their intense focus on this level justifies describing theirs as a theory of 'supranational governance', a name that, oddly, they do not accept.[3] They also revive the idea that the Commission will forge alliances with national interest groups that stand to benefit from further supranational governance. But the aspect of neofunctionalism that Stone Sweet and Sandholtz do not revive, and multi-level governance does, is the idea that the Commission will form coalitions with subnational public-sector actors.

This relationship to neofunctionalism does not appear always to have been entirely clear to the advocates of multi-level governance. In her edited comparative study of multi-level governance and cohesion policy, Liesbet Hooghe (1996) distinguishes between 'neofunctional', and 'multi-level' perspectives. In this exposition, the multi-level governance perspective differs from the 'neofunctional' only in positing the role of subnational as well as supranational actors: it argues that alliances can be forged between the supranational Commission and SNAs that will weaken the ability of national central governments to play the role of gatekeepers between the European Union and national levels. However, Hooghe seems to be on slightly shaky ground in arguing that neofunctionalism did not see a role for SNAs, because this is just a special case of the third type of pressure that the neofunctionalists thought that the

---

[3] It is strange because their book is called *European Integration and Supranational Governance*, yet when Branch and Øhrgaard (1999) so described the theory, Sandholtz and Stone Sweet (1999: 144) retorted, 'we did not name our theory "supranational governance" and we object to the label'.

Commission could bring to bear on national governments. In its original form the pressure was represented by alliances between the Commission and the functional ministries of the member states (Lindberg 1963: 286–7; Coombes 1970: 86–91). This early disaggregation of the concept of the state did not go so far as explicitly to identify SNAs as potential allies of the Commission, but the logic is the same. The national state is not a unified entity, and parts of the state can defect from central control and ally themselves with the supranational actor. Multi-level governance therefore simply presents a special case within one aspect of the neofunctionalist analysis.

Attempts to distance multi-level governance from neofunctionalism are ultimately unconvincing. The two theories share a common position on the role of supranational institutional actors. In order to establish that the autonomy of SNAs is increased by the Europeanization of a policy sector, it is necessary to contest the state-centric view that supranational institutions are simply agents of the central executives of the member states, because if the supranational institutions are simply the agents of national central governments, there is no prospect of them forming alliances with SNAs against the policy preferences of the central governments.

This logic is implicitly accepted in Marks et al. (1996), where instead of the three perspectives identified in Hooghe (1996)—intergovernmental, neofunctional, and multi-level—only two are set out. As the title of the article indicates, the debate is framed here as 'state-centric versus multi-level governance'. By the time that this article was revised for inclusion in a book on multi-level governance (Hooghe and Marks 2001b) it had become an essay on the ability of national executives to control the process of European integration. SNAs are still in there, but have become just one part of an argument that reads as a more modern and sophisticated version of neofunctionalism, although minus functional spillover, which of course is why it needs a new name.

The relationship of multi-level governance to the 'intergovernmental/ supranational dichotomy', then, is that multi-level governance has effectively taken the place of neofunctionalism as the alternative theory to intergovernmentalism. It incorporates all the main elements of the neofunctionalists' theory, except for their central emphasis on functional spillover. It is a more comprehensive successor to neofunctionalism than the theories of 'supranational governance', which only pick up on some aspects of the neofunctionalist framework, and which therefore essentially form a subset of hypotheses within the multi-level governance framework. Because nobody really defends functional spillover as an explanatory mechanism today, there is no justification for continuing to use the term 'neofunctionalism'. The theoretical debate about the nature of the European Union should therefore properly be called the intergovernmental–multi-level governance debate.

In that form the debate has continued to be remarkably productive. Much of the credit for it being so productive must go to Andrew Moravcsik, who has consistently taken a rigorous Liberal Intergovernmental position, and has thereby forced multi-level governance theorists like Gary Marks and Liesbet Hooghe to defend their position equally rigorously. The search for knowledge is a communal activity, and Moravcsik has fully played his part in preventing the intergovernmental/supranational dichotomy from becoming moribund, as have Marks, Hooghe, and other theorists of multi-level governance. So, it is true that multi-level governance is nothing particularly new, but then novelty can be overrated.

Multi-level Governance provides a Description of the European Union, but not a Theory

This seems a strange assertion. Jordan (2001*b*: 201) in further explication of the point, says that multi-level governance 'lacks a causal motor of integration or a testable set of hypotheses', and suggests that multi-level governance 'needs to be fleshed out with causal accounts drawn from other theoretical traditions (e.g. historical institutionalism)'.

The Lack of a 'Causal Motor of Integration'

There are two ways of dealing with this criticism. The first is to dismiss it immediately as unfair. Multi-level governance did not set out to provide an explanation of European integration. It was part of the 'turn to governance' in the study of the European Union that essentially said the attempt to discover the dynamics of the process of European integration should be set on one side and a start made on using concepts derived from comparative politics to try to understand the European Union as a political system that is already functioning. This is a perfectly legitimate intellectual exercise, and to criticize it for not solving the problem that it had started by setting to one side would be totally unreasonable.

However, as Jordan (2001*b*: 205) acknowledges in an end-note, this issue actually has been addressed by Marks (1996*a*). It has been further considered by Hooghe and Marks (2001: 69–80). The fundamental question considered is why government leaders have allowed decision-making authority to slip out of their hands. Three possibilities are identified: because government leaders want it to happen; because, although they do not intrinsically want to see their authority eroded, they see an advantage to themselves in allowing it to happen in particular instances; and finally, because they are powerless to stop it happening (Hooghe and Marks 2001*b*: 71).

Government leaders may want to diffuse power away from the central state for at least three different reasons. First, they might see the diffusion of power as a means of increasing their leverage in either international or domestic intergovernmental negotiations. A government that goes into a negotiation with the governments of other states with its hands tied by a domestic diffusion of power has a much smaller possible 'win-set' in the negotiations than it would have if domestic constraints were tighter. This gives it a negotiating advantage: other governments accept that it can make few concessions if it is to be able to sell the deal in the domestic arena. On the other hand, a central government that can claim in negotiations with SNAs that its hands are tied by agreements previously reached at the supranational level has a powerful resource for resisting demands for a shift in policy (Hooghe and Marks 2001b: 72).

Second, as well as tying their own hands, government leaders might wish to tie the hands of their successors. Agreements reached in the European Union are legally binding on the member states, and remain binding even if there is a change of the political party or coalition of parties in government. The rules for amending EU legislation are such that it is difficult for a new government to reverse what its predecessor accepted (Hooghe and Marks 2001b: 72). So, the Thatcher governments in the United Kingdom had to live with social legislation that had been accepted by the previous Labour government; and the subsequent Labour governments had to accept the single-market rules to which Thatcher agreed.

Third, government leaders might want to avoid the political consequences of making unpopular decisions that they believe to be necessary, but which might lose them the next election (Hooghe and Marks 2001b: 72–3). The enthusiasm of Italian governments for European Monetary Union was presented as a commitment to the ideal of European integration, and as a matter of national pride, that Italy must be involved in any major development in the European Union. However, it might also have owed something to the difficulty of getting the Italian electorate otherwise to accept the economic consequences of monetary discipline, which if not accepted might have undermined the continuing prosperity of Italy.

The unwilling transfer of competencies away from national central government can happen when a government pursues a policy objective that cannot be achieved without making concessions, if the concession of authority to supranational institutions is the cheapest option. Hooghe and Marks (2001b: 74) use the example of Margaret Thatcher's acceptance of qualified majority voting in the Council of Ministers on issues related to the creation of the single European market. The single market was a high policy priority for the British government. Although it was accepted in principle by the governments of all the other member states, it was obvious that in the negotiation of detail there would almost invariably be one or more governments who stood to lose from any shift away from the status quo, and if each had a veto they would either block progress or use the threat of the veto to extract increasingly costly concessions from the states that were most committed to the single market. Margaret Thatcher certainly did not want to surrender her own veto, but it must have seemed like the lowest-cost option to achieve the overriding policy option of the single market.

Governments may prove unable to prevent the transfer of authority away from the central state. Using principal–agent theory, Hooghe and Marks

(2001*b*: 76) demonstrate how multiple principals, such as the member states of the European Union, find it difficult to achieve the degree of unanimity that is necessary effectively to exercise control over the supranational agents that they have brought into existence (the Commission, the European Parliament, the European Court of Justice). Once agencies have been created, and competences transferred to them, a new status quo is in existence. Incomplete contracting is endemic in agreements between the member states: if every ambiguity had to be removed from treaties or legislation, agreement would never be reached. It is a consequence of using diplomatic means to draw up legislative texts. The gaps in the contracts leave spaces for the supranational agents to escape the control of the principals. Reining them in is difficult because the multiple principals may not be able to agree on doing so, because voting rules make changing the status quo difficult to effect, and because the principals might be able to ally themselves with powerful actors who can damage the principals.

Multi-Level governance emerges once national governments surrender authority to supranational agents. This shifts the balance of resources between levels of government. It has an impact on SNAs, who may find that the resources they have traditionally been able to deploy to achieve some autonomy from central government control have been eroded. For example, central government leaders can claim to have their hands tied by EU-level agreements; or they can manipulate their superior informational resources about what is happening at the EU level to give them an advantage in internal negotiations. To redress this imbalance, Hooghe and Marks (2001*b*: 78) argue that SNAs will adopt a number of strategies. They will:

- establish their own offices in Brussels
- intensify their contacts with each other
- demand more information from central governments about developments in Brussels
- demand formal channels to influence ministerial representation in the European Union
- form direct links with Commission officials
- campaign for direct representation in the Council of Ministers
- participate in the Committee of the Regions
- erect additional barriers to treaty amendment
- demand recognition of subsidiarity in EU treaties and legislation.

These responses will set up a national/subnational dynamic that will further pull authority away from the national centre.

All of this analysis, and especially perhaps the last point, the creation of a dynamic that will pull the governments of states further along the road of diffusion of authority than they ever originally intended, is either taken directly from neofunctionalism, or is fully compatible with it. Given the comments made already about the intellectual origins of multi-level governance, it is not surprising that this is the case.

The Lack of a 'Testable Set of Hypotheses'

This criticism is simply unsustainable. Even without being supplemented by other theories, multi-level governance does generate hypotheses. The initial hypotheses relate to the question of whether the European Union does represent a system of multi-level governance rather than one dominated by national governments. Out of this investigation other hypotheses are generated in a logical sequence of enquiry that represents genuine scientific progress.

Hooghe (1996: 19–20) sets up three models that structure her study of cohesion policy in the European Union: the state-centric, the neofunctionalist, and the multi-level governance. The state-centric approach 'claims that European policies have generally empowered state executives to concentrate control in their hands in the European and national arena. The state has effectively strengthened its autonomy vis-à-vis subnational actors, and the supranational institutions are its agents'. The neofunctionalist model argues that 'subnational or transnational private actors, especially business and multinational corporations, are often able to manipulate the EU agenda, and can shape considerably the options put forward to the state executives'. The multi-level governance model argues that 'power . . . is dispersed through at least three governmental levels' and it seeks to understand 'how the interlocking happens between them'.

Each of these models generates testable hypotheses. The state-centric model suggests that subnational mobilization should remain weak. The neofunctionalist model suggests that 'subnational mobilization could grow as a result of supranational entrepreneurship or institutional learning; it should probably happen rather evenly across the Union, and should be accompanied by a shift of state sovereignty to the supranational and subnational level' (Hooghe 1996: 20). Then, in an apparent confirmation of the criticism that multi-level governance does not generate testable hypotheses, Hooghe (1996) goes on to say that multi-level governance does not generate a similar hypothesis; however, this simply represents a failure of Hooghe to acknowledge that multi-level governance is identical to neofunctionalism in the hypotheses that it generates, because it is nothing more than a partial restatement of neofunctionalism without the functionalism.

The conclusion of the book is that the empirical evidence demonstrates 'that subnational involvement has increased, but it has happened highly unevenly across territory' (Hooghe 1996). This does not sustain either the first or the second set of hypotheses, but it is more damaging to the first (intergovernmental) set. Yet this qualification of the generalization generated by neofunctionalism is simply indicative of the greater sophistication of multi-level governance. Theoretically multi-level governance turns its back on broad generalizations about the nature of the European Union and asks empirically testable questions about specific policy sectors. In asking such questions about cohesion policy, Hooghe (1996) finds that the empirical evidence demands a further differentiation be made between the position in different member states. The logic of enquiry then leads on to the next question: Why has there been such variation?

The obvious answer, and that offered by Hooghe (1996) and Marks (1996*b*), is that the interaction of SNAs with the European level is mediated through different national institutional arrangements. However, both Smyrl (1997), looking at France and Italy, and Garmise (1997), looking at the United Kingdom, conclude that there is also differential empowerment within a single state. Smyrl (1997: 297–304) attributes this to differences in leadership and in whether a 'regional policy community' existed in the region prior to the arrival of the European funds. In similar vein, Jeffery (2000*a*: 11–18) identifies the factors that affect whether a particular SNA will be effective in influencing national European policy as:

- constitutional position
- the quality of intergovernmental relations within the state
- the level of entrepreneurship displayed by the SNA (which in turn will be affected by the level of internal institutional adaptation, leadership, and the strategies of coalition-building adopted)
- the legitimacy of the SNA: the extent to which it has the backing of a local/regional population with a strong sense of common identity and purpose.

This is an ongoing academic debate, but it indicates that multi-level governance can generate testable hypotheses to guide empirical research, the findings from which can lead to further research questions, and to answer which further testable hypotheses can be formulated.

Does this establish that multi-level governance is a theory? Or does it mean that it is a 'paradigm' (Jordan 2000: 204), a '(dis)ordering framework' (Rosamond 2000: 111), or a 'compelling metaphor' (Rosamond 2000: 110)? Or, as this author suspects, does it not really matter so long as a disciplined research agenda emerges that uncovers new knowledge about and understanding of, the nature of the European Union?

Multi-level Governance and New Institutionalism

Jordan (2001*b*: 201) says that multi-level governance needs to be combined with other theories, and suggests historical institutionalism, but does not expand on the suggestion. Keating (2001), on the other hand, argues that both Liberal Intergovernmentalism and multi-level governance are what he describes as 'American theories' based on rational choice institutionalism.[4] Certainly Moravcsik's approach is entirely in line with rational choice, while the insistence of Marks (1996*a*) and Hooghe and Marks (2001*b*) that multi-level governance is

---

[4] This is a slightly puzzling description as neither Marks nor Hooghe is American, and the fact that they are both attached to North American universities renders them no less European than did Keating's attachment to the same university as Hooghe at the time. However, there is a widespread assumption that rational choice is somehow a quintessentially American scientific approach, while social constructivist approaches are somehow quintessentially European. Since when, one is left to ponder, did scientific theories hold passports?

an actor-centred approach, and their use of principal–agent theory, drawn from the public choice branch of rational choice literature, suggest that Keating's is a defensible characterization. If multi-level governance is to develop as a branch of rational choice analysis, though, it needs a stronger theory of the resources available to actors, such as that outlined by Moravcsik (1994) or by Rhodes (1997). So Jordan's argument that multi-level governance needs to fill out its own framework by borrowing from other theories is sustained.

In this context, it is interesting to note the position of Thielemann (1999). He analyses the dispute between the Commission and the German *Land* of Saxony over the granting of state aid to Volkswagen, and argues that it cannot be fully understood in terms of an actor-centred approach, but that it is necessary to invoke concepts drawn from sociological institutionalism. A complete understanding of both the specific dispute and the general run of such disputes between the Commission and Germany has to take into account that actors choose their preferences according to a particular institutional logic, and if the actors operate with divergent institutional logics, mutual distrust will prevail. It also has to take account of the structural bias whereby different sets of institutional arrangements legitimize and empower different sets of actors. The Commission is blind to the role of the *Länder* in the German system of state aids. This blindness results in bitterness, because what the German actors consider to be proper behaviour is not followed by the Commission. It also leads to problems such as the German federal government being taken to Court by the Commission over an action by a *Land* which the federal government had neither been involved in nor approved.

It is of course quite feasible that multi-level governance can be combined with more than one form of new institutionalism. The danger is that it will become caught up in a dichotomy quite different from the intergovernmental / supranational dichotomy, and far less productive, which is threatening to take EU studies down a total blind alley: the dichotomy between rational choice and social constructivist approaches. Both sides in this dichotomy are equally adamant that the other is wrong. In so far as historical institutionalism tries to drive a middle way between the two doctrinal positions, it might yet be that Jordan is right to see it as the most productive partner for multi-level governance.

Multi-level Governance Overstates the Autonomy of Subnational Authorities

Marks frequently says that multi-level governance makes no assumptions about the autonomy of SNAs. The extent of such autonomy is precisely one of the questions that the multi-level governance research agenda addresses through empirical research. As the discussion above of Hooghe (1996) makes clear, the answer is that sometimes SNAs appear to be influential, and sometimes they appear to be less influential, leading on to the question of under what conditions they can exercise influence. That question has already been addressed above. However, since Jordan (2001*b*: 201) quotes Bache (1999) in support of his contention that multi-level governance overstates the autonomy of SNAs, it is perhaps worth reviewing the particular debate to which that work is a contribution.

Because variations in pre-existing institutional patterns are seen as the one key variable determining the impact of Europeanization on the different national systems, the United Kingdom and the Federal Republic of Germany have tended to be seen as polar opposites. The United Kingdom has a highly centralized system of government, and especially under the Conservative governments from 1979 to 1997, had a culture of top–down decision making. Germany has a federal constitution that gives considerable resources to the *Länder*, together with a cooperative political culture based on compromise. If it can be shown that the ability of the British central government to play the role of gatekeeper has been weakened as a result of the Europeanization of structural and regional policy, and that SNAs in the United Kingdom have been empowered by the process, strong support will be given to the multi-level governance view of the nature of the European Union. On the other hand, if it can be shown that there has been no weakening of the ability of the German federal government to play the role of gatekeeper, and no further empowerment of SNAs in Germany, that would lend strong support to the intergovernmental view of the nature of the European Union.

It is perhaps because of the perception of the United Kingdom as a polar case that so much debate has centred around one particular dispute involving the British government. The dispute concerned the Community Initiative (CI) programme for the economic regeneration of coal-mining areas, RECHAR. CIs were introduced as part of the 1988 reform of the structural funds. They 'were programmes devised by the Commission to meet outstanding regional needs' which 'would primarily address the needs of specific types of regions, such as those suffering from the decline of a dominant industry' (Bache 1998: 71). The Commission had considerably more institutionalized autonomy in the selection of these initiatives, which accounted for 9 per cent of the total allocated to the European Regional Development Fund (ERDF), than it had for the selection of projects under the five main objectives that governed the ERDF as a whole.

The RECHAR programme for the conversion of coal mining areas was one CI. It aimed to promote the economic conversion and social renewal of coal-mining areas that had been seriously affected by decline in the sector. Across the EC, twenty-eight areas were identified by the Commission as eligible for funding, and no less than twelve of these were in the United Kingdom. The announcement of eligibility was made in 1990, after the British central government had set out its spending priorities for the coming financial year. As all EC structural fund expenditure is required to be additional to planned national expenditure, the eligible local authorities expected that the money would be passed directly to them once it had been received by the UK Treasury. It soon became evident, though, that the Treasury had no intention of passing on these funds. It intended to absorb them into the general revenues accruing to central government, and not pay out to local authorities any more than had already been allocated.

This was the normal manner of proceeding for the Treasury. Its argument was always that in the annual spending review it anticipated the revenues that would be coming in from Brussels and allocated funds accordingly. This excuse did not work for RECHAR because when the expenditure allocation had been made the CI did not exist, so there was no way that the revenues could have been anticipated and allocated in advance. Under the circumstances, the Commissioner, the former British Labour politician Bruce Millan, refused to release the funds. After a protracted stand-off, the British central government appeared to back down and to allocate additional funds to the local authorities.

Marks (1993: 399–403) argues that the RECHAR dispute provides evidence in the case of the United Kingdom that the ability of British central government to ensure that its own preferences on regional spending prevailed was undermined by the ability of SNAs to form a coalition with the Commission at the implementation stage. This is the multi-level governance case. Against it, Moravcsik (1994: 54) argues the intergovernmental case: 'Whitehall continues to employ EC monies primarily as an alternative source of funding for existing priorities. Even the conflict between Britain and the Commission over . . . additionality, widely cited a year ago as the victory of a supranational–subnational alliance over London, now appears to be resolving in favour of the latter.'

Bache (1999) puts empirical flesh on this point. The British Treasury was able subsequently to claw back the extra expenditure through new arrangements that came into effect after the April 1992 general election. This demonstrated the ability of central governments to play the role of gatekeeper even at the implementation stage, the stage where Marks et al. (1996: 365) argue that multi-level governance will be most prominent. Central governments are not only gatekeepers at the policy-making stage, they possess resources that allow them to play the role of 'extended gatekeeper', reasserting at the implementation stage control over any aspect of policy that, as a result of the need to reach agreements with the other member states, has slipped past them at the earlier stage.

This conclusion does not lend support to the argument that SNAs have gained autonomy from the Europeanization of a policy sector, but it is not such a surprising finding. The surprising finding was the original one: that in the case of RECHAR there had been an apparent breach of the ability of the central government to control the application of EU policy within the United Kingdom. The British case is at the 'centralized' end of the centralized–decentralized spectrum, and the findings of the cross-national studies in Hooghe (1996) would actually lead us to expect a variation in outcomes in which the United Kingdom would be one of the states least likely to exhibit evidence of a significant weakening of the gatekeeper role of central government.[5] That the Treasury had to concede ground, even only temporarily, indicates that the dominance of the core executive could not simply be taken for granted, even if the deviation from the preferred policy option was slight.

This is not the whole of the story, though. While the Treasury successfully reasserted its ability to control overall levels of public expenditure, there was some consequent 'Europeanization' of the sector due to this dispute. One concession given to the Commission by the Treasury was the introduction of transparency in the domestic procedures for accounting for ERDF spending. This meant that while there would be no significant additional spending as a result of the RECHAR dispute, it would be possible for the first time to identify the extent of 'EU' spending by local authorities. In other words, the Commission would be able to monitor whether EU spending went on domestically determined priorities or on projects that were closer to EU priorities. The Commission's task was aided by the gradual move away from national quotas to a system of indicative allocations to member states, which allowed the Commission some discretion in the selection process. The result was a gradual move away from spending both EU grants and the domestic match-fund components on domestically determined projects towards increased spending on EU-approved projects (Bache and George 2001).

Moving to the other end of the centralized–decentralized spectrum, there seems to be support for the view that the German *Länder* have been empowered by the Europeanization of policy, and that the eastern *Länder* in particular have formed 'a new territorial constituency in Germany, one that has had the opportunity, the desire, and the means to avail itself of Commission resources' (Anderson 1996: 164). However, Thielemann (1999) provides a timely warning not to assume that the result of the Europeanization of a policy sector will necessarily be beneficial to SNAs. It might have the opposite effect, placing new limits on their autonomy, even in a decentralized system such as that of Germany.

Thielemann looks at the relationship between the German *Länder* and the Commission in the context of EU policy on state aids. He notes that most work on multi-level governance in the European Union focuses on EU structural policy, and that it comes to the conclusion that the Europeanization of a policy sector opens up new resources that can be jointly utilized by the Commission and SNAs to strengthen their positions relative to national central governments. Their ability to do this varies between member states according to the constitutional arrangements prevailing in each state, but because of its federal structure, Germany is a case where there might be expected to be a particularly strong effect. However, if the focus shifts from structural policy to policy on state aids, the picture looks very different. Relations between the *Länder* and the Commission

---

[5] It should be noted that Bache was also one of the authors of the chapter on the United Kingdom in Hooghe (1996).

in this field are strained, and were seriously strained in the case that he particularly examines of state aid given to Volkswagen by the *Land* of Saxony. Far from forming an alliance with the Commission, Saxony found itself in bitter conflict with it, and found that the federal government was unable to defend it. This research of Thielemann, taken together with that of Bache, does suggest that there might be some validity in the criticism that the empowerment of SNAs that multi-level governance leads us to expect, could be overstated.

Multi-level Governance Adopts a 'Top–Down' View of Subnational Authorities

The original for this criticism is Jeffery (2000). Although Charlie Jeffery (2000: 20) accepts that 'the existing architecture [of authoritative decision making] is being chipped away into a new, diverse and dynamic pattern of multi-level governance by a profusion of larger or smaller waves of subnational mobilization and policy influence', he denies that multi-level governance is an accurate theorization of what is occurring because it is too 'top–down' in its perspective (Jeffery 2000: 8). It is primarily concerned with the relationship between national central governments and supranational EU institutions, one of the spin-offs of which is to empower SNAs. The SNAs are therefore more or less passive beneficiaries of a struggle over competences between other actors. In contrast, the record suggests that SNAs are actively claiming a role in EU policy making by exploiting factors such as the problems posed for central governments by economic globalization and the adoption of new strategies of public management, including decentralization.

This is a useful corrective to a narrow view of the underpinning of multi-level governance in the European Union. Neofunctionalism suffered from the weakness of analyzing European integration as though it was a self-contained and self-sufficient process (George and Bache 2001: 12). There are other influences on the relative power of different levels of government. Devolution in the United Kingdom is changing the balance of constitutional resources, allowing some SNAs to assert more autonomy in both domestic and EU policy making and implementation. The chapters in this volume, though, indicate that multi-level governance has outgrown its origins in the study of the European Union, and is now being understood in its wider context.

Multi-level Governance Focuses on Subnational Authorities to the Exclusion of Other Subnational Actors

This has been largely true of the studies of multi-level governance in the European Union that have appeared (as is obvious from what has been said above). If the argument of this chapter in the section titled 'Multi-level Governance is an Amalgam of Existing Theories', is accepted, that multi-level governance is a direct descendant of neofunctionalism and that the relationship between the European Commission and SNAs is just a special case of the relationship that neofunctionalists expected to see develop between the Commission and other types of actors, there should be no problem in extending the focus. In fact, Jordan (2001b: 201) is careful to qualify this criticism by referring to it as a criticism of multi-level governance 'as originally proposed', and providing a reference to Marks and McAdam (1996), which is a discussion of the changing structure of political opportunity in the European Union for social movements.

Another way in which multi-level governance can and should be extended is to move the focus from simply SNAs to look at the changing patterns of relations between different sections of national central government. As noted above in the section titled,'Multi-level Governance is an Amalgam of Existing Theories', neofunctionalism incorporated a general theory that disaggregated the concept of the state and argued that bureaucrats in the functional ministries of national governments might form alliances both with their counterparts in other member states and with the relevant Directorate-General(s) of the Commission. This insight is easily incorporated into multi-level governance, and the dynamics of such a process have been explored by researchers such as Lewis (2000).[6]

Multi-level Governance Mistakes Evidence of Subnational Authority Mobilization at European Level as Evidence of Influence

This is another criticism that Jordan takes from Jeffery (2000). Marks, et al. (1996) provide evidence of considerable mobilization of SNAs in setting up offices in Brussels, and provide a number of competing hypotheses for explaining this. These incorporate the type of differences between SNAs in the same state that Smyrl (1997) identifies. Although Jeffery (2000: 7–8) accepts that considerable SNA mobilization has occurred in recent years, he argues that extrastate channels of access to EU decision making, such as the Committee of the Regions, have only limited influence. It is therefore important not to exaggerate the extent to which SNAs have been liberated from national central governments in trying to have an impact on EU policy. 'SNAs have not moved in anything other than limited and symbolic senses beyond the nation state' (Jeffery 2000: 7). On this view, presumably the main advantage of their mobilization at the EU level is primarily to overcome the informational advantages that central

---

[6] Interestingly, Lewis studied under Leon Lindberg at Stanford.

government executives derive from their role as gatekeepers between the national and European levels (Moravcsik 1994: 12–14).

According to Jeffery (2000: 7), the main game that is still being played is the domestic political game between SNAs and the central state. However, he is keen to assert that his position is not meant to support the intergovernmentalist argument that central executives can effectively maintain a gatekeeper role between the national political arena and the European Union. The exclusion of SNAs from European policy making is becoming increasingly impossible, and SNAs across the European Union are succeeding in claiming from their own central governments a share in the management of European policy. The alternative perspective that Jeffery offers on this process adopts the phrase coined by the German *Länder*: 'European domestic policy'. It describes a situation where SNAs pro-actively claim a role in determining national European policy, which will occur where EU policy impinges on the domestic policy competences of SNAs, and will vary across the member states.

Although Jeffery is clearly anxious not to associate himself with the intergovernmentalist position, it is actually quite difficult to see how his position differs from that of Moravcsik (1993), except that where Moravcsik adopts an intergovernmentalist position that privileges the role of economic interests in the process of national preference formation, Jeffery adopts an intergovernmentalist position that privileges the interaction between different levels of national government in national preference formation. In both cases, though, the process that is envisaged is compatible with the idea of EU policy making as a 'two-level game'. Preferences are formulated first at the national level as the result of a domestic political game, and the preferences so formed are then carried into the Council of Ministers where the second game of intergovernmental bargaining around those preferences is conducted.

Multi-level Governance Ignores the International Level of Interaction

Like several of Jordan's criticisms, there is truth in this as a factual statement of what has been done to date, but there is nothing inevitable about multi-level governance ignoring the international level. The same ideas and analyses that have been applied to understanding the relationship between levels of governance within the European Union can be extended to the position of the European Union in the global system. Indeed, the whole theory is one that tries to grapple with the governance of a capitalist system that is globalized more than it is regionalized.

Some attempts have been made to theorize the wider economic role of the European Union, for example as a three-level game (Collinson 1999). The opportunities for the Commission to achieve autonomy under circumstances where it, rather than national central government, is the potential gatekeeper between levels are intriguingly similar to those analysed for the national executives in Moravcsik (1994). There is much more potential for research here, as Collinson (1999) recognizes in her title.

Conclusion

Jordan's seven criticisms of multi-level governance as applied to the European Union prove to be of variable validity. The first, that multi-level governance is nothing new but an amalgam of existing theories, is central to the whole understanding of multi-level governance as it has been applied to the European Union. It is a true comment, although scarcely a criticism. Placing multi-level governance in the context of the intergovernmental/supranational debate in EU studies allows an informed understanding of it as an alternative to state-centred perspectives, and therefore the substantial section of this chapter devoted to doing just that is a contribution to addressing the first of the core themes of this book, that is, the theme of the definition of multi-level governance.

As a distinct perspective on the European Union, multi-level governance offers not a description, but a theory of what sort of organization the European Union is. It is hypothesized to be an organization in which the central executives of states do not do all the governing but share and contest responsibility and authority with other actors, both supranational and subnational. This is still disputed, and much of the debate about the European Union has involved trying to establish through a process of empirical testing whether the central hypothesis is valid. In the course of this exercise, this book's core themes four and five are directly addressed.

In response to theme four, multi-level governance as applied to the European Union does not imply hierarchy. On the contrary, it sets up an alternative hypothesis that the hierarchy of levels of governance is being eroded. The role of the central governments of states is important, but multi-level governance looks for evidence that it is diminished in the system of governance that is the European Union. On the other hand, Moravcsik (1994) suggests that the nation state can and does use multi-level governance as a means of enhancing its independence from societal actors, and therefore as means of increasing its steering capacity. Again, multi-level governance needs to be seen as one voice in a debate with state-centred intergovernmental perspectives.

The limitations of multi-level governance as applied to the European Union (this book's theme seven) include those identified in Jordan's criticisms five, six, and seven. Work adopting the multi-level governance perspective has tended to focus on SNAs to the exclusion of other actors, although there is no necessity for this to be so. It has not sufficiently addressed the question of whether the mobilization of SNAs has made a real difference to outcomes in the policy process.

It has also not been applied sufficiently to the international level where the European Union itself stands in the role of potential gatekeeper between different arenas. All of these point the way forward to the future agenda of EU studies within the multi-level governance framework, and will throw further light on this book's theme three of the differences between policy sectors, some of which are already apparent in research reported above.

8

Multi-level Governance and International Relations

STEPHEN WELCH AND CAROLINE KENNEDY-PIPE

Variations on the theme of governance reflect disciplinary and sub-disciplinary research agendas, leading to much conceptual confusion. As such, our discussion of multi-level governance here sits alongside the related notions of governance and good governance that have been more common in the field of international relations (IR). Our purpose here is to assess the usefulness of the rapidly developing concept and theory of multi-level governance to the study of IR.

Hopes for a large analytical pay-off from the multi-level governance concept have been high, as it has been applied to a succession of fields of study within the European Union (see George, Chapter 7, this volume) and domestic politics (see Bache and Flinders, Chapter 6, this volume). In the realm of IR, hopes for the concept's intellectual yield combine with a generally optimistic reading of the empirical progress of governance. It is perhaps rather early to evaluate the potential of this conceptual innovation. Nevertheless, the chapter will argue that much of the sense of intellectual anticipation surrounding the term is premature. There can be no doubt that really existing trends in international politics have been grasped by the concept of governance; but this does not mean that the concept of multi-level governance has provided, or will provide, the surest grasp of these trends that is available within our conceptual toolkit. The concept indeed contains some crucial ambiguities even in its general usage; these are considerably compounded, we will argue, in its putative application to the field of IR.

This chapter is organized into three sections. In the first, we offer an outline of the conceptual issues generated by the governance research agenda, considering specifically the linked concepts of good governance and multi-level governance, and the relationship of governance to government. We also indicate and justify our argumentative strategy. The second section offers a synoptic review of issue areas in IR where the question of governance might be said to arise. In the final section we draw together the implications of the first and second sections and assess the utility of the governance concept within IR.

Concepts and Strategy

The terminological field surrounding 'governance', including 'good governance' and 'multi-level governance', demands some preliminary exposition. As
noted above, these differences in terminology are largely the product of different disciplinary and sub-disciplinary research agendas. Good governance has
been closely associated with development studies, and multi-level governance
with the study of European countries and the European Union.

The emergence of a concern with good governance can be fairly precisely
dated to the publication of a 1989 report by the World Bank (WB), *Sub-Saharan
Africa: From Crisis to Sustainable Growth* (Leftwich 1993: 610; Abrahamsen 2000:
47–8). The WB is precluded from expressly mandating political forms by its
founding Articles of Agreement. Nevertheless, it has been argued and it seems
plain that the Bank's pronouncements have triggered a discourse in which
'democracy emerges as the necessary political framework for successful economic development', and in which 'bad governance equals state intervention,
good governance equals democracy and economic liberalism' (Abrahamsen
2000: 51). The UN Development Programme expresses these concerns as follows: 'Good governance is participatory, transparent and accountable—its
social, political and economic priorities are reached by consensus and the poorest and most vulnerable have their say in matters affecting their well being and
in the allocation of development resources. Bad governance, rife with bribery,
corruption and maladministration, has the opposite effect' (quoted in
Marquette 2001: 396).

Good governance evidently has a significant normative and prescriptive
dimension. Multi-level governance, on the other hand, is at least a less nakedly
normative concept. It draws attention to various challenges to the ability
of political leaders 'to proactively "steer" society in the traditional sense'. It
'emerges as a coordinating instrument in institutional systems where hierarchical command and control mechanisms have been relaxed or abolished. It draws
on bargaining rather than submission and public–private mobilization rather
than public sector specificity' (Pierre and Stoker 2000: 30). While in the case of
a so-called 'unitary state' like Britain (where, however, different levels of government have always existed), multi-level governance reflects such a 'relaxation', the application of the concept to the European Union is a way of
referring to the enhanced capacities of EU institutions while avoiding the problematic categories of federalism and intergovernmentalism. This enhance-
ment, it is said, is a process in which 'the notions of sovereignty and democracy
are being prised away from their traditional rootedness in the national community and the territorially bounded nation state' (Held and McGrew, cited in
Hueglin 1999*b*: 251).

These usages considerably complicate the conceptual field. 'Good
governance' is largely a specification, arguably quite a narrow one, of good

government, or indeed of the scope of government (limited) and its economic policy (neoliberal). Contrast with government is not the point of the concept. Users of the concept of multi-level governance, on the other hand, usually seek to differentiate governance from government, where government may refer specifically to the nation state, or more generally to hierarchical, centralized and public-sector administrative arrangements, as opposed to negotiated, fragmented and public–private ones.

These contrasts are plausible but somewhat underspecified. Even in respect of the last and apparently most straightforward of them, a lack of specification is evident. Is 'privatization' definable *per se* as an increment of governance, on the grounds that it marks a reduction in the size of the state? Is it the increment in control by private enterprises that marks enhanced governance, as the state now has to deal with them as independent entities? Or, as Majone has suggested, does the regulation of privatized enterprises and the 'contractorization' of state–provider relationships (involving also an increased role for the courts) mark a new kind of control, the replacement of the 'positive' (redistributive) state by the regulatory state (Majone 1997)? More generally, as regards 'negotiation' and horizontal and vertical fragmentation, the articulation between governance and established concepts such as pluralism and corporatism, as well as federalism, needs clarification.

The same contrastive purpose is served, for some writers, by the unqualified term 'governance' (a usage we will largely follow in this chapter). For them, effectively, the qualification 'multi-level' is redundant. One such writer asserts that

the notion that government can be differentiated from governance as two ideal-typical poles of a scale which distinguishes centralised from fragmented political authority appears to be more fruitful. In this tradition, government refers to the political control of a centralized state, whereas governance denotes the coordination of social relations in the absence of a unifying authority. (Krahmann 2001: 7)

Furthermore, alongside this contrastive usage, the unadorned term 'governance' has a generic usage rather similar to that of authority or coordination, of which government good or bad, unitary or fragmented, and multi-level governance or governance in the contrastive sense, would simply be variants (Kahler and Lake 2003).

In this chapter we adopt a dual strategy. We are interested in exploring the analytical advantages arising out of the contrastive concept of governance that differentiates it from government—what is often but not invariably called multi-level governance. However, in order to undertake this exploration we exploit for heuristic purposes the scope of the generic concept of governance. This is a strategic choice that requires some words of justification.

Studies of governance, or multi-level governance, often take the form of case studies. This research strategy works well for the domestic and indeed the European research context, where distinct policy areas such as welfare and the environment allow for case-by-case testing. However, the international realm is different. Indeed the very idea of 'policy areas' begs a question that it would be better to leave open, namely: whose policy? We therefore opt to take a synoptic view, rather than expanding on the implications of a specific case study.

What, then, should be the scope of this synoptic view? Our proposal is to investigate issue areas in IR in which the question of the distribution of authority arises—the question, as it might be put, of governance in the generic sense. We allow that generic concept to guide our expansive choice of issue areas, but use these issue areas to interrogate the utility of the contrastive concept. The interrogation can be summarized in the following way. When we move from the domestic to the international arena, should we continue to think of governance as defined in opposition to the institutions of national government? Or should we alternatively think in more abstract terms of government as pertaining to some 'central' authority, of which the nation state is the expression only at the domestic level of analysis, so that governance is defined in conceptual opposition to this authority, and not to the state *per se*? To put the question more pointedly, if we find evidence of the emergence of some such authority in the international realm, and of the consequent depletion of national governmental power or capacity, does this count as more *government*, or more *governance*?

We are reminded of the terminological difficulty noted in *Fowler's Modern English Usage* about the term 'Cold War': when the Cold War intensifies, do we say it is getting hotter, or colder? However, the difficulty here is more than just a linguistic trap for unwary journalists. It is an ambiguity that is fundamental to the extension of the governance research programme to IR. Our survey of a number of areas of application of the governance concept in IR will show why.

Articulating Governance and International Relations: Five Issue Areas

We have identified an ambiguity in the application of the concept of governance to IR. In order to assess the problems generated by this ambiguity, we will consider a range of issue areas relating to the distribution of international authority. We want to ask which, if any, of these distributions is appropriately analysed using the concept and theory of governance, and how appropriate is the combination of some or all of them under that rubric.

We identify five issue areas: the *international system*, meaning the coexistence of a plurality of states as well as the distribution of power among them; the role of *supranational organizations* such as the United Nations (UN), North Atlantic Treaty Organization (NATO), and the European Union; *international civil society*, consisting of social movements and non-governmental organizations (NGOs); *international civic norms*, the emergence of global norms such as democracy and humanitarianism; and *transnational threats and risks* such as trafficking and terrorism. This list is not far short of a prospectus of IR itself.

But that is just a preliminary indication of either the potential or perhaps the over-ambitiousness of the governance concept.

The International System

Much of the governance literature holds that the traditional or realist perspective on global politics has little resonance for the development of international affairs after the 1970s. The structural / neorealist model of international politics is usually characterized as a world of states endlessly entangled in violent con-frontation within an anarchic environment. Such a view is rejected by those engaged in the discussion and promotion of multi-level governance. Indeed, the central position of both the state and war in IR is challenged by those seeking to depict new patterns of global politics far removed from the traditional tales of balance-of-power politics. In this version of IR the emergence and growth of governance renders state sovereignty, territorial boundaries, and government as a source of authority increasingly obsolete. As James Rosenau puts it, 'world affairs can now be conceptualized as governed through a bifurcated system of two worlds. One a system of states and the other a dynamic multi-centric source of authority that sometimes cooperates but often competes with the state-centric system' (Rosenau and Singh 2002: 36).

However, if we begin by positing that one measure of the applicability of the governance concept is the limitation of the power and capacity of the nation state, we cannot help but notice that the first limitation presented by the inter-national environment is simply the multiplicity of states. The situation con-trasts with that of domestic politics, where the state is a first principle. Now this is not to say that the state is historically primordial: arguably, states emerged out of an international environment that demanded them as a basis for military organization (Tilly 1975; Downing 1992). In this sense, states may constitute the reification or crystallization of a prior set of social conflicts and are thus far from a first principle. Nevertheless, the state in the domestic environment is by definition (the definition of the word 'domestic') the starting point for the discussion of governance.

But the state has a dual face: its internal and external face. It is the sole pos-sessor of the legitimate means of violence within its sovereign borders, but potential victim of other possessors of these means in the external environment (Giddens 1985). Any discussion of the diminution of government and its replacement by governance in the international realm must therefore reckon with the absence of the monopolistic state as the existential and historical first principle of the discussion: externally, states are necessarily limited and weak (though the extent of this will vary over time and space) in a way that they are not domestically.

From this point of view, 'balance of power' is itself a form of governance, defined in terms of the inhibition of the power and capacity of government.

So are other kinds of international 'regimes', as they have been called (Krasner 1983). It is of course far from a novel form. If, in the domestic political environment, the state is increasingly having to contend with rival claimants on its power, then this means that the domestic environment may be becoming more like the international. But then the trade in concepts should be from the outside in, not, as with governance, from the inside out.

If other states constitute a limitation on nation-state power and capacity in the international realm, the same is true *a fortiori* of other states that are exceptionally powerful. Of course, the point can be made in reverse: that some states escape to varying degrees from the limitations of the anarchic system by virtue of their exceptional military (and other) capacity. However, historically these powerful states are in a minority; in global terms, indeed, a tiny minority. From this consideration have arisen the theories of hegemony and polarity: theories of the constraints imposed by unequal state power.

The theory of polarity, that is, the classification of the international distribution or power in terms of unipolarity, bipolarity, multipolarity, and so on, is perhaps the simpler of these two theories. It constitutes an extension of balance-of-power reasoning in the context of global blocs, allowing in particular the application of game-theoretic modelling in the study of diplomacy and international conflict. Hegemony constitutes in the first place a special case of polarity—unipolarity—but it deepens the theorization by drawing on Gramscian arguments about the cultural dynamics of domination and authority. Hegemony, for Gramsci, is a condition of the 'naturalized' and hence accepted inequality of power, in which overt displays of force have ceased to be necessary. Cox writes of 'a concept of hegemony that is based on a coherent conjunction or fit between a configuration of material power, the prevalent collective image of world order (including certain norms) and a set of institutions which administer the order with a certain semblance of universality (that is, not just as the overt instruments of a particular state's dominance)' (Cox 1986: 222–3).

For all states other than the pole(s) or the hegemon, the world describable by these concepts is one in which state power is severely limited. In the theory of hegemony, moreover, the limitation is multidimensional. If less nation-state government equals more international governance, then hegemony and polarity constitute conditions favourable to governance. Yet this is an issue area where the ambiguity of the governance concept in the international realm seems very obvious: the pole or hegemon (to take the singular case) is itself a nation state whose capacity for controlling its external environment (i.e. for extending the reach of *government*) would seem to be at a maximum under these conditions. In the domestic realm, the contrastive concept of governance suggests plurality in place of the singularity of government. By analogy, a tendency towards unipolarity or hegemony in the international realm would seem to imply a move away from governance, towards government.

It is scarcely necessary to add that, whatever the merit of the hegemony analysis, the order of polarity has changed since 1989, with arguably considerable consolidation since September 2001. Expectations of the emergence of multipolarity after the end of the Cold War have largely been disappointed, especially those expectations which focused on Europe as an emerging counterpoint to American power (Kagan 2002). The world is unipolar, in the terms of this analysis, and the United States is the pole. Again, we pose the pointed question: for the rest of the world, does this constitute more government, or more governance?

Supranational Organizations

Supranational organizations are clearly not all of a piece. Indeed their very variety and numerousness offers initial support to the application of the governance concept. Here it would emphasize the complexity of the array of constraints which supranational organizations present for nation states. However, that is only a very preliminary observation: closer scrutiny, while it does not lessen and might reinforce the impression of multiplicity and complexity, nevertheless reveals order and pattern in the world of supranational organizations. This order and pattern has two dimensions: of hierarchy and of function.

Some supranational organizations are more powerful, and represent more of a challenge to or a substitution of nation-state power, than others. The World Trade Organization (WTO), for instance, presents more of a constraint on national governments than the International Labour Organization. In the area of overlap of their terms of reference, it is the WTO which prevails: it 'is unique both in the extent of its contractual obligations . . . and in the enforcement mechanism built into its system for resolving disputes (Blackhurst 1998: 32). So while their co-presence in this area of overlap suggests multiple and complex constraints, hierarchy simplifies the matter somewhat. State power remains constrained, but by an entity that in its singular power more closely resembles the pole or hegemon we discussed in the preceding section.

Function also gives order and pattern to the world of supranational organizations. While, as in the example just mentioned, there are cases of overlapping terms of reference, such overlap is far from universal. Different organizations have competence and power in different fields. This at least reduces complexity for the nation state. There may, moreover, also be a kind of hierarchy across functions, so that we can speak of more or less important areas of constraint on state power. The trend in IR has been to deny such a functional hierarchy, which has traditionally placed military and security concerns at the apex. Arguments from International Political Economy (IPE), from proponents of a normative international order, and from feminism, among many others, have sought to deconstruct this notion of 'high' and 'low' politics. Attempts to broaden the concept of security to encompass economic, environmental, and humanitarian concerns are an important token of this (Buzan et al. 1998). Nevertheless, salutary though some of these efforts have been in bringing neglected issues to wider attention (this is especially true of feminist scholarship), it is not clear that a hierarchy of functions has been abolished. Among the effects of 11 September 2001 has been to reassert the primacy of security (traditionally defined). As we will shortly see, some observers doubted the retreat of this traditional concern even during the so-called 'humanitarian interventions' of the 1990s.

Despite these qualifications to an initial impression of the complex multiplicity of supranational organizations, there can be no doubt that they exist and present growing constraints on national governmental power and capacity. There is still a need to pose our main question, however: does this trend mean more governance, or more government? One example will suffice to highlight the issues.

Paul Cammack has analysed the WB's 'Comprehensive Development Framework' of January 1999 in terms that go right to the heart of our question. The Framework's centrepiece is a 'matrix' of policy objectives and actors, about which Cammack concludes: '[It] is unequivocally a management tool through which the Bank and other agencies can monitor government policy across the board and in detail, against objectives and programmes agreed with the Bank . . . . IMF surveillance of macroeconomic policy is to be matched by Bank surveillance of social and structural policy'. The Bank seeks to establish a 'Global Architecture of Governance', but in Cammack's view what this amounts to is an aspiration to be 'the mother of all governments' (Cammack 2002: 44, 49, 50). Rather than 'more governance, less government', what we seem to have here is more of each, specifically more government *through* more governance. To say this is to call to our attention precisely the problem of articulating these two concepts in the international realm.

Aside from the order we may discern in the world of supranational organizations, a further important question for governance is how supranational they in fact are. Are they not, in fact, rather intergovernmental? Answers will have to be given case by case, but taking the example we have already considered, it is interesting to note the WTO's insistence on its own intergovernmental character in its attempt to delimit its dealings with NGOs. Its *Guidelines for Arrangements on Relations with NGOs* state as guideline VI:

Members have pointed to the special character of the WTO, which is both a legally binding intergovernmental treaty of rights and obligations among its Members and a forum for negotiations. As a result of extensive discussions, there is a broadly held view that it would not be possible for NGOs to be directly involved in the work of the WTO or its meetings. Closer consultation and cooperation with NGOs can also be met constructively through appropriate processes at the national level where lies primary responsibility for taking into account the different elements of public interest which are brought to bear on trade policy-making (quoted in Wilkinson 2002: 202).

In such a 'forum for negotiations', the question naturally arises of the relative influence of the negotiating parties, defined by this guideline as nation states.

To the extent that predominant influences from powerful states can be discerned, we will have additional grounds for asking whether tokens of governance are not in fact signs of the increased reach of government.

International Civil Society

In speaking of civil society, whether national or international, we seem to be on safer ground regarding the relationship of governance and government. Civil society has indeed been defined largely in terms of a disjuncture, allegedly characteristic of liberal–democratic nations, between itself and the formal institutions of the state. Specifically, it is characteristically defined not just as 'society', but rather as society in an organized form; moreover not organized as a mass (which is compatible with, indeed characteristic of, totalitarian regimes), but rather as a network of spontaneously formed and intermittently coordinated groups. Several research programmes compete within the paradigm of civil society. A Tocquevillian perspective, which emphasizes the interconnectedness of spontaneously formed groups, has been prevalent, under the modern rubric of 'social capital' (Putnam 2000). But earlier research traditions such as pluralism within the empirical theory of democracy, and the study of pressure or interest groups, as well as the study of social movements, fall under this heading too.

With this background in the study of liberal–democratic polities, we can see that international civil society must consist of a range of activities and organizations arrayed along a spectrum of formality—informality, at one extreme distinguished from the state, and at the other from society in a purely aggregate sense. We might consider Amnesty International as an example at the more formal end of the spectrum, along with other NGOs, and the anti-globalization movement at the informal end (without succumbing to the error of seeing more unruly and violent protest as necessarily a sign of lack of organization or rationality).

From time to time, students of civil society have seen in it a potential not only to stand against the state, but also to replace the state. For instance, Andrew Arato claimed to discern this possibility in the activities of the Solidarity movement in Poland in 1980 (Arato 1981). Similarly novel forms of organization were glimpsed by Stephen Gill in the anti-globalization protests in Seattle in 1999 (on the occasion of a Ministerial Meeting of the WTO): 'Global collective action cannot, in my view, be understood as a singular form of collective agency . . . . It is more plural and differentiated, as well as being democratic and inclusive' (Gill 2000). Some authors have seen in these occurrences and alleged potentials scope for applying a broad concept of governance, as a way of describing non-state social coordination (Rosenau and Singh 2002). In this view, governance is defined at its greatest distance from government, tantamount to informal social organization and indeed empirically antipathetic to state power.

More common, though, is to apply the concept of governance not in these imaginary scenarios of state substitution by civil society but in the area of overlap and interpenetration between civil society and the state. At the domestic level, this occurs when, for instance, the state intervenes in civil society to create and sponsor organizations to serve as constituencies for its activities (Walker 1991). The well-known typology of 'insider' and 'outsider' pressure groups, whereby the former receive acknowledgement and recognition by the state in return for contributing expertise, allowing close relationships to develop over time, is a more general illustration that the analytical distinction between state and civil society need not translate into an empirical one. The same is true of the phenomenon of corporatism.

In IR, the 1990s provide several examples of international civil society's role alongside governments. It was actively engaged, for example, in transforming the way in which wars could be fought. The treaty banning landmines was negotiated amongst individuals, a number of NGOs and liberal states in a bid to stop this particular and grotesque form of warfare (Kennedy-Pipe and Jones 2000). Increasingly, groups such as Amnesty International have been actively engaged in the drafting and implementation of human rights legislation. NGO involvement in this specific area goes back to the 1948 Universal Declaration of Human Rights (Korey 1998). The 1984 Convention against Torture came about through intensive lobbying by Amnesty, which also contributed to the drafting the treaty. NGOs such as Amnesty International or Human Rights Watch provide crucial information about human rights violations to national governments as well as international organizations such as the UN Human Rights Commission.

Analytically, this conception of governance in terms of the influence of international civil society on states, its participation in the development of policy, and the delegation to it of monitoring functions, seems unproblematic. Empirically, though, the case is not so clear. How far are states constrained by international civil society, and by what mechanisms? The answer obviously varies across states. The United States, for instance, is not a signatory to the landmines convention. For all the NGO emphasis on this problem, unexploded US cluster bombs remain scattered over large areas in south-east Asia. Where states *are* constrained, is this directly, or by democratic political pressure stimulated by NGO activity with the help of the media? The latter may well be an important if unpredictable mechanism, but to say that it represents the growth of governance is again to equate governance with everything but the state.

International Civic Norms

We adopt the somewhat unfamiliar label 'international civic norms' in order to suggest broadly liberal, democratic, and humanitarian values while being minimally prescriptive about what these amount to. A variety of arguments in IR can be grouped under this heading, including arguments about the liberal or democratic peace, about the normative status of human rights, about 'humanitarian intervention', and about democratization. 'Good governance', too, falls under the heading of 'international civic norms'.

A 'constructivist' perspective has predominated in the discussion of international norms within IR (e.g. see Katzenstein 1996). While useful in charting the changes in meaning and application of norms, this approach has less to say about their precise nature, viewing normativity as a species of discourse. Less clear in such an analysis is the manner in which norms constrain governments—but just this is what we need to be interested in if we are to assess the extent to which international civic normativity invites description in terms of governance. For this purpose, it is useful to distinguish three kinds of process that can be involved in the development of international civic norms: their *diffusion*, *imposition*, and *invocation*.

We may speak of the diffusion of civic norms when these spread in a largely spontaneous fashion; where external pressure, while it need not be absent (we are talking here of analytical categories, not neat empirical divisions), is not the paramount influence on their adoption. Within this category there are likely to be two main mechanisms. One is the emulation of behavioural norms (for instance, but far from exclusively, in the form of legal codes) by policy makers or elites on the grounds of some direct appeal that these norms have, through increased exposure to them in international forums, or perhaps through exposure of cohorts of policy makers to non-indigenous educational experiences. The other is through popular but still internal pressure on governments by social elements responding for instance to greater media penetration or to a 'wave' of elite collapses appearing to suggest a revolutionary conjuncture (the party-state collapses or 'revolutions' of 1989 in Eastern Europe are the classic example).

External imposition may in practice be difficult to distinguish from the 'demonstration effects' that might lead to the diffusion of civic norms, but analytically the distinction is clear. Numerous kinds of external pressure tend towards the universalization of civic norms. These range from international agreements like the Universal Declaration of Human Rights and the Helsinki Accords, and 'political conditionality' as demanded of candidates for accession to the European Union or for WB credits, to more *ad hoc* diplomatic pressure that might be associated with aid packages or arms sales, and beyond this activity of other states to the demands of foreign investors or non-governmental aid donors.

A final process that can be said to have promoted international civic norms is the invocation of them in justification of military interventions by powerful states. NATO's intervention in Kosovo has been widely regarded as a key token of 'humanitarian intervention', promoting (for the rest of the world by a demonstration effect; for Yugoslavia by rather more direct means) two norms at once: the norm prohibiting large-scale ethnic harassment or cleansing, and the norm allowing state sovereignty to be breached in the service of this prohibition (Prins 2002: 139–53). As an example of the latter argument, the 'Independent International Commission on Kosovo' has described the NATO intervention in Kosovo as just but not legal, and called for a change in 'the "default setting" of the UN Charter, revising the so-called inviolability of sovereign states so that sovereignty becomes conditional on observance of certain minimal but universal and clear standards of behaviour' (Independent International Commission on Kosovo 2000: 289, 291).

But despite widespread and powerful support for this extension of international civic norms, and approval of the Kosovo example, questions can still be put as to alternative motivations, as well as the success of that particular instance in averting ethnic catastrophe (critics argue that the intervention did not prevent but precipitated just this catastrophe: Chomsky 1999; Carpenter 2000). If, as critics such as Chomsky maintain, the establishment of a new post-Cold War mission and a reassertion of the 'credibility' of NATO was the real motive (see Petras and Vieux 1996 for a similar argument regarding Bosnia), while we could agree that a norm of intervention might be in the making, its civic credentials would be questionable. Its governance credentials are at least put into serious question by the methods used: the classic governmental instrument of military force. They are further put in doubt by the administrative residue of such interventions, illustrated by the case of Bosnia where there has been minimal inter-ethnic rehabilitation and the consequent need for indefinitely extended quasi-military occupations (Chandler 1999).

The three processes of diffusion, imposition, and invocation have different implications for the application of the governance concept. At one extreme, the diffusion of norms through shared educational experiences or by the seepage of media broadcasts seems to fall outside the scope not only of government but also of governance. At the other, the use of military force, and its 'peacekeeping' or 'state-building' sequel, in order to impose norms (whatever the possible benefits), does little to encourage the idea of a diminution of governmental hierarchy. We are left with a middle zone of the imposition of norms. Here our attention must be on the nature of the agencies doing the imposing—and the key question will be whether we can be clear that the effect is the not the work of government. As suggested above, the prevailing constructivist or discourse-analytical approach to norms in IR is likely to ignore the distinctions between the diffusion, imposition, and invocation of norms: any of these would mark the extension of the normative discourse. This extension alone, we suggest, in the absence of a more discriminating analysis, provides only a facile justification for suggesting the growth of international governance.

Transnational Threats and Risks

Much of the international environment we have already described is of course replete with threats and risks. Other states are a threat to small states; poles and hegemons are a more general threat to those who, advertently and otherwise, oppose them. Threat and risk is inherent in the international realm. Nevertheless, sensitivity to threats and risks that can be labelled 'transnational' has grown, and new kinds of threat and risk have come onto the agenda of a wider range of policy makers and commentators (Coker 2002).

If, as several analysts have asserted, globalization is characterized fundamentally by the greater ease and cheapness of communication and transportation, a properly dialectical view of world history will lead us to expect an increase in the trade of 'bads', as well as goods. Such trade is what we call 'trafficking'. It is, of course, like trade and communication, not a new phenomenon. Moreover, standards vary over time and place as to what can be legally traded and what perforce must be trafficked. Nevertheless, the incentives and the channels for trafficking opened up by the ongoing process of globalization of trade have given the phenomenon unprecedented political salience.

At bottom, as trafficking is defined in terms of criminality, control of it is a matter of policing. However, this response takes a variety of forms with equally various implications for the concept of governance. An initial problem here is to define the relationship of police and policing to governance in general (i.e. in the domestic realm), which is far from a straightforward preliminary. Putting aside the far broader concept of police, meaning the promotion of order, security, and welfare, which scholars influenced by Foucault have excavated (though this literature could add considerable historical depth to explorations of governance—see for example Neocleous 2000), even the narrower concept of police as an institution has a complex relationship to the concept of governance. While the police institution, pioneered in Britain in 1829 with the formation of London's Metropolitan Police, clearly marks an increase in the state's surveillance and intervention capacity, at the same time it marked a taming and regularization of the use of force by the state, and also a localization of this force (Welch 2001: 111). Such localization exists to varying degrees in different countries, reaching an extreme in the United States where local election of law enforcement officials is wide spread.

Such developments allow a role for both the concept of (multi-level) governance and that of government in the analysis of domestic policing. In the international realm, however, the local and the non-military character of policing are each diminished. In fact, not only the local, but also the national, distinctiveness of police institutions is disappearing, partly under the pressure of common threats such as international crime (Reiner 2000: 202). Moreover, the scale and nature of international threats has led to the mobilization of substantial military force in an effort to police them.

An example is America's 'War on Drugs'. The domestic scope of this effort far outweighs its international impact; nevertheless its implications for international relations are considerable. The 'Andean Initiative', launched in 1989, involves a programme of police and military assistance to countries with cocaine-producing regions. The militarization of the war against drugs produces significant 'collateral damage' in terms of human rights abuses and threats to democracy in these countries. Two commentators conclude: 'Enhancing drug control performance often requires changes in the military, police, customs services, courts, agriculture and rural development policy, regulation of financial systems, laws governing drug production and use, and legal or constitutional restrictions on the extradition of citizens and control of sovereign territory' (Bertram and Spencer 2000: 13). In other words, a veritable programme of government for the target countries, whose content flows from the determinations of the US administration and US electoral politics.

International terrorism is another dialectical inversion of the process of globalization. Like trafficking, it relies on the exploitation of channels of communication that globalization continually enhances, operating in the interstices, or the lapses, of governmental regulation and surveillance. With a novel combination of the long-established techniques of hijacking and suicide bombing, the attackers of 11 September 2001 were able to inflict enormous real and symbolic damage on their enemy, the United States. Some commentators and policy makers inferred a heightened threat from evidence of a new indifference to loss of life on the part of the attackers, though this reasoning projects onto earlier terrorists humanitarian impulses whose existence is highly debatable. More persuasive was the indication provided by the coordinated nature of the attacks that a highly developed 'network' of terror existed.

Whatever the actual increment in threat marked by 9/11, perception of threat drastically increased, internationally, but particularly in the United States. Anxieties about threats from weapons of mass destruction (WMD) and biological weapons, typified by the anthrax scare in the United States in 2001, became common currency. Almost immediately, a 'War on Terrorism' was announced, and it soon became clear that, like the War on Drugs, in the international realm this was no empty metaphor. An actual war, the invasion of Afghanistan, was its first major expression.

This environment gave the opportunity for the promulgation of a strategic and military doctrine that seems an epoch away from the optimistic prognoses for international humanitarian intervention of the late 1990s. The *National Security Strategy of the United States*, published by the White House in September 2002, asserts a doctrine of pre-emption:

Traditional concepts of deterrence will not work against a terrorist enemy whose avowed tactics are wanton destruction and the targeting of innocents; whose so-called soldiers seek martyrdom in death and whose most potent protection is statelessness. The overlap between states that sponsor terror and those that pursue WMD compels us to action (*National Security Strategy of the United States* 2002).

The last sentence establishes a broad remit for pre-emptive intervention against 'rogue states' as well as terrorist networks; indeed, it assimilates these phenomena. The doctrine is, at the time of writing, in the process of being tested in the case of Iraq, though it is noteworthy that British Prime Minister Tony Blair has also tried to emphasize a 'humanitarian' basis for the proposed invasion and forced regime change (Blair 2003), an attempt to place the invasion under the heading of international civic norms.

The rights and wrongs of these various responses to international threats and risks are not our present topic. We are interested in their implications for the related concepts of governance in general and multi-level governance in particular. While responses to international threats and risks have sometimes taken the form of policing, the implications which domestic policing carries in relation to localization and civilianization have been muted in the international version. Recent developments have drastically increased the role and visibility of military power, of which the United States is the preponderant possessor. Its interventions in Afghanistan and in Iraq, whatever their merits and justifications, seem clearly designed to restore to acceptable performance the governments of these countries, as well as to send a message to other governments. The American doctrine of pre-emption, as now established, undoubtedly constitutes a limitation on the policy choices of other states, but it is a limit that seems a poor fit for the concept of multi-level governance.

The Use and Usefulness of the Governance Concepts in International Relations

The preceding survey has been undertaken in order to investigate, across a broad spectrum of issue areas in which the question of the international distribution of authority arises, whether a contrastive concept of governance, often termed multi-level governance, has utility. We have framed this question in terms of a more pointed one: do the trends in the distribution of authority in the international realm constitute more governance, or more government?

What is immediately apparent, and what a case-study approach might have concealed, is the contradictory nature of the evidence. A multitude of contexts and trends can be perceived, which are far from uniformly suggesting a single answer to our question. In fact we argued above that the same can be said of the evidence for the growth of governance at the domestic level too. Governance is drastically conceptually underspecified. As we noted above, it refers in its contrastive sense to a negotiated as opposed to compulsory mode of authority; to a fragmented as opposed to centralized, and a multi-level and stratified, as opposed to hierarchical, distribution of authority; and to private or public–private provision in place of the public sector, but even the last of these, seemingly the most empirically precise, may be interpreted in several ways, as Majone's account of the regulatory state illustrates.

Such problems of conceptual specification are compounded in the field of IR. One obvious problem is a lack of reference for the term 'public sector'. Whatever may be in the process of replacing the public sector in domestic politics, it is reasonably clear what it was to begin with. Not so in the international realm. This problem for the IR application of governance is however just an aspect of a more general one that we highlighted at the outset: how far is the question of governance to be tied to the question of the powers and capacities of the nation state?

Confusion abounds here. To return to a definition cited earlier, Krahmann sees as 'more fruitful' a definition of governance which highlights its 'fragmented political authority', and immediately continues: 'In this tradition, government refers to the political control of a centralized state'. But how do we apply such a definition in a context in which states always have to deal with other states, and in which the relative power of states varies widely? If one state has a hegemonic relationship with another, how should we describe this in terms of governance and government?

Such considerations, which arise in the first of our five issue areas, might lead us to offer a contrastive definition with a more abstract basis, seeking out an international analogue of the centralized, hierarchical state, and posing the question of increase or decrease in *its* power as a test of government versus governance. The bewildering choice of candidates for such a role might itself offer support to the diagnosis in terms of governance. If states have to deal with the UN, NATO, the EU, the WTO and (to continue the example of Europe) a host of other organizations such as the Council of the Baltic Sea States or the Visegrad Nine, is this not a sign of the fragmentation of authority that the idea of governance draws upon?

The problem does not, however, go away that easily. As we pointed out above, it is arguable that a hierarchy exists among this array of supranational organizations. In formal terms, the UN (specifically its Security Council) stands at the apex of this hierarchy. In practical terms, th order may differ. Arguably, NATO significantly displaced the UN in the case of the Kosovo intervention, where even the UN's retrospective authorization has been interpreted in a fashion highly favourable to NATO's authority, as opposed to its role as agent. The hierarchy is therefore not fixed, and it cannot be specified with the precision of a military order of ranks. Nevertheless it does somewhat simplify the dizzying multiplicity presented by a first look at the world of supranational organizations, and therefore reduces the need for immediate recourse to the governance concept's implication of complexity as opposed to hierarchy.

Moreover, the relationship of these organizations to the more and less powerful states is clearly variable. At the time of writing, the UN Security Council is in the process of being superseded in the role of interpreting and effecting its own resolutions by an American administration bound on pre-emption of the threat supposedly presented by Iraq. Needless to say, similar questions about the role of powerful states can be raised about the operations of the WTO, the International Monetary Fund (IMF), and the WB.

It is therefore arguable that supranational organizations feature some of the hierarchy defined as characteristic of government, so that the question will then be, is this intensifying, or diminishing? It is furthermore arguable that in any case powerful national governments exercise predominant influence within this hierarchy, and in a unipolar world it will follow that the distribution of authority is far from fragmented.

Emphasis on the anti-hierarchical and negotiated character of governance, as well as on 'privatization' or 'partnerization' of state activities, allows the concept some utility in the analysis of what we have termed international civil society. Conceptual difficulties nevertheless arise. Again, the key problem is whether state power, or the power of international state-analogues, is the contrastive term for governance. If we agree that elements of international civil society, such as charities or protest organizations, constrain states as well as supranational organizations, it remains unclear how to code this in terms of governance and government. If the WTO were to be constrained by international civil society, would this be a reduction, or an increase, in governance?

We may, moreover, not agree on the extent of the constraint in the first place. While states have outsourced expertise to NGOs in various cases, and responded to the political pressure brought by NGOs on subjects such as human rights violations, we cannot speak of a permanent or consistent delegation of power. In many cases, states retain a capacity to ignore pressures from international civil society. In democracies, for example, it is uncommon for international affairs to be electorally significant, while in general the resources of direct pressure available to NGOs or organized protestors pale in comparison to those of states. States, moreover, are able to adapt to and in part neutralize pressure from protestors: innovation is not all on one side. Preventing the disruption of international meetings has become costly; but the cost of erecting high fences and creating safe zones for international leaders in meeting sites remains minute compared to the resources of many states.

We sought in our review to condense the wide topic of international civic norms into three aspects: diffusion, imposition, and invocation. These three dynamics of international normativity carry different implications for the concept of governance. If 'not the state' is a definitional parameter for governance, processes of the diffusion of norms, such as shared educational experiences, seem to fall most readily under its scope. It would, however, be extremely difficult to distinguish empirically between such factors in the generation of normative consensus and factors of imposition such as the WB's good governance agenda. These raise the kind of difficulties we have already addressed, concerning the identity and nature of the agency doing the imposing. When the spread of normativity may in this way be traced back to institutions, it is the nature of these institutions (and the governments which may predominate in them), not merely the presence of state-constraining norms, which will determine the applicability of the concepts of governance and government.

Finally, responses to transnational threats and risks show the contradictory nature of the redistribution of international authority. Efforts at 'policing' evoke, and may involve, domestic police institutions. They bring into play international norms of criminality and legitimacy which may initially be highly contested, as indeed they were when policing institutions were first introduced in nation states, as well as being possibly conflictual (as in the case of drug prohibition and human rights norms in Latin America).

It is, however, in this issue area that developments offer to clarify with some force the question of the priority of government and governance. The threat of international terrorism, and of the 'rogue states' which either support it or have been categorically assimilated to it, has met a response from the United States that leaves little room for governance. Indeed, the contrastive term 'government' is here manifest in its most hierarchical and centralized form, utilizing its classic instruments of surveillance and intelligence as well of course as military power. Post-intervention 'state-building' efforts will doubtless leave some room for non-state actors, in the form of Western corporations; but even so, the occasion and the authorship of these efforts leave the governance debate looking marginal at best.

Too much should not be inferred from the immediately topical. That would be to replicate the errors that can flow from over-extending the lessons of governance case studies. Our main aim in this chapter has been to show what difficulties arise for the concept of multi-level governance in IR from the ambiguity of its contrastive definition. However, it is equally an error to ignore the immediately topical. Our conclusion is that in international relations this is an exceptionally unpropitious time to be suggesting, as the concept of multi-level governance does, a general trend of the eclipse of the government of the nation state.

Part Three

Sectors

9

Multi-level Governance and Environmental Policy

JENNY FAIRBRASS AND ANDREW JORDAN

Introduction

At its founding in 1957, the European Economic Community (EEC) did not have any laws, policy, or bureaucracy dedicated solely to environmental issues. The environmental policies that could be said to have existed at that time were chiefly concerned with safeguarding human health rather than protecting the environment for its own sake and were largely formulated and implemented *within* and *by* states. More than 45 years later, the EEC has evolved into the European Union and has created some of the strongest and most progressive environmental policies of any polity in the world. This remarkable achievement has been accomplished with the involvement of a variety of state and non-state actors at different levels of governance, ranging from the local to the global. Clearly, the EU's own supranational institutions, such as the Commission, Parliament, and Court have played a decisive role in this policy development. So too, have a range of national and subnational actors encompassing central government departments, regional and local government authorities, national regulatory agencies, and many private and voluntary sector, non-state actors such as firms and environmental interest groups. Of course, environmental policy in the European Union is also partly the product of global (or at least international) negotiations, such as the 1992 United Nations (UN) Conference on Environment and Development, held in Rio de Janeiro. The EU's supranational institutions and individual member states were parties to the agreements reached.

Crucially, whilst the EU's own supranational bodies enjoy powers in the realm of environmental policy that are normally the sole preserve of states, the European Union itself is not a sovereign state. Although the Commission, Parliament, and Court wield considerable influence over the EU's environmental policies, they ultimately share responsibility for environmental policy decision-making and implementation with the range of actors identified above. For example, although the European Commission initiates new policies and oversees the implementation of common policies at the national and subnational level, disputes about compliance regularly flare up between it and individual member states. These are often adjudicated by another of the EU's supranational institutions, the European Court of Justice (ECJ). In a number of cases, the commission relies on its allies among non-governmental organizations (NGOs) to provide the information to pursue such legal action. In sum, the EU's environmental policies are typically the product of the competition and collaboration between state and non-state actors situated at the local, national, regional (i.e. European), and international levels. This complicated, contested, and evolving distribution of authority and competences is one of the most intriguing features of EU environmental governance.

Scholars have sought to capture this unique and contested vertical allocation of powers by employing the concept of multi-level environmental governance (Sbragia 1998; Weale et al. 2000; Jordan 2002a). Since the EU's environmental policy is characterized by such dispersed decision-making competences and the involvement of state and non-state actors it would seem to provide an excellent vehicle for analysing multi-level governance in general, and the utility of Gary Marks' model in particular. In fact, we would argue that environmental policy is a case *par excellence* of 'the dispersion of authoritative decision-making across multiple territorial levels' (Hooghe and Marks 2001: xi). Therefore, in this chapter we use recent developments in EU environmental policy as a prism through which to examine four of the seven themes that form the framework of are said to this book.

First, in order to explore theme 1 (How should multi-level governance be defined?) we highlight certain aspects of the multi-level governance model developed by Gary Marks and his associates, and relate them to EU environmental policy. We focus on four noteworthy features of this literature on multi-level governance. They are: the mobilization of subnational interests; the complex, uncertain and contested nature of decision making; the entrepreneurial action of EU level policy-makers (especially the Commission and Parliament); and the unintended and often unwelcome policy outcomes that are said to emerge from multi-level governance.

Second, although most scholars of the European Union agree that European integration is a multi-level phenomenon, they diverge on the question of precisely which level is the most important. We reflect upon the role played by member states, and in doing so consider theme five concerning the role and power of the nation states, by comparing multi-level governance to its most obvious rival, Moravcsik's liberal intergovernmental (LI) theory of European integration. Put very simply, LI characterizes the European Union as an exercise in conventional statecraft, in which states fight to advance their national economic interests. According to this view, the nation state is the single most important source of EU policy and the most influential level of governance. Indeed, Moravcsik argues, *contra* multi-level governance that European integration has succeeded in making states *more* not less powerful (Moravcsik 1994).

Third, we explore the explanatory value of these two perspectives (i.e. multi-level governance and Liberal Intergovernmentalism) by relating them to two sub-areas of EU environmental policy, namely biodiversity protection (i.e. measures that seek to conserve flora and fauna and their habitats) and land use planning (i.e. the decision-making process in which areas of land are allocated to different functions). We concentrate on the UK's implementation of directives in these two policy areas. We have selected these because they represent 'critical' cases of European integration (see subsequently for an explanation). The two biodiversity measures are Directives 79/409/EEC (the Birds Directive) and 92/43/EEC (the Habitats Directive). The ones relating to land use planning are Directives 85/337/EEC (the Environmental Impact Assessment (EIA) Directive) and 2001/42/EC (on Strategic Environmental Assessment (SEA)). By relating multi-level governance to a new empirical area (most of the testing to date has involved EU structural policy) we should be in a better position to judge how far multi-level governance differs across policy sectors. This relates to theme three— to what extent does multi-level governance differ across policy sectors?

Finally, our analysis explores the involvement of UK actors in the development and implementation of these four items of legislation. The main actors include the UK national executive (primarily the national environment ministry, which was (until 1997) the Department of the Environment (DoE)) and a number of environmental pressure groups, namely the Royal Society for the Protection of Birds (RSPB) and the Council for the Protection of Rural England (CPRE). By adopting a 30-year perspective (c.1970 to c. 2000) we are able to scrutinize the aims and actions of the UK central administration and the UK-based environmental groups over the full policy cycle (from agenda setting to implementation) and are able to compare policy *objectives* to actual *outcomes*. Significantly, this not only exposes the underlying preferences of the actors involved, but also allows us to measure the extent to which they were satisfied by the process of European integration. This allows us to reflect upon the strengths and the limitations of multi-level governance and LI as general frameworks for understanding European integration.

The remainder of this chapter unfolds as follows. Section 2 briefly highlights several key features of Gary Marks' model of multi-level governance. Section 3 compares multi-level governance to its main theoretical rival, LI. Having identified the main points of dispute between these two perspectives, in Section 4 we justify our exclusive focus on the United Kingdom. In Section 5, we explore the development and implementation of the four directives. The final section uses these empirical findings to identify the most important strengths and weaknesses of multi-level governance (and LI), and looks forward to the next phase of research on European integration in general and multi-level governance in particular.

Multi-level Governance

According to Gary Marks (1993: 392) multi-level governance in the European Union amounts to: 'a system of continuous negotiation among *nested* governments at several territorial tiers—supranational, national, regional, and local—as the result of a broad process of institutional creation and *decisional re-allocation*' (emphasis added).

His ideas arose out of empirical work conducted on the reform of the EU's structural policies. Generalizing from this case, he went on to claim that states remain pre-eminent but are incapable of fully controlling the integration process, which escapes their collective command in many important respects. A contributory factor is the tendency for domestic interest groups to 'outflank' national executives (Marks 1992: 215) by establishing direct relations with EU institutions. Another is the fact that EU institutions are not wholly dependent on states; they have their own role interests and are partially autonomous. Marks (1992: 221–3) eventually concluded that the EU exhibits emerging political disorder with complex, multi-layered decision-making above and below the state. In the following sections we examine a number of the most prominent features of Marks' conception of multi-level governance.

Subnational Mobilization and Potential Rewards

Marks notes (1992) that there has been a mobilization of regional, national, and subnational actors (e.g. local authorities), who have sought direct contact with EU level policy-makers. This has been achieved in a number of ways including, *inter alia*, establishing direct representation (e.g. an office or a pan-European grouping base) in Brussels. He appears to link this development (Marks 1992: 214–15) with the availability of new 'rewards' at the EU level (e.g. obtaining EU funding, being able to exert some influence over the content of EU/national policy, and/or having access to information).

Although the bulk of the literature on multi-level governance concerns regional or local government, some of Marks' later work does refer to interest groups (see Marks and McAdam 1996). In a way that is reminiscent of early neo-functionalist ideas, Marks et al. (1995: 19) argue that interest groups will mobilize at the EU level once they think that the institutions have acquired (sufficient) decision-making authority and competence. This mobilization, in turn, is said to enhance the legitimacy of EU decisions. Crucially, for Marks (1992: 217), one of the potential repercussions of the direct interaction between domestic interest groups and EU policy-makers is that national executives may not be able to dictate the future evolution of these relationships.

Complexity, Uncertainty and Contested Decision-making

According to Marks (1992: 215), the reform of EU structural funding produced a fluid and ill-defined situation, which states struggled to control even though they had initiated it, distinguished by rival understandings of the extent and the location of decision making. One implication for our study is that if there is a significant increase in the intricacy of the decision-making process and a rising lack of predictability about which level of governance wields the greatest influence over policy development, subnational actors may want to create and maintain close relationship with *both* national and supranational levels of governance.

Supranational Entrepreneurial Action and Alliance Building

In contrast to LI (see below), advocates of multi-level governance believe that supranational actors play a decisive and proactive (i.e. entrepreneurial), rather than a subordinate, role in EU policy-making. Marks et al. (1996: 359), however, recognize that like other policy actors, the Commission is not a wholly independent or autonomous actor. It is still an unresolved question (Pierson 1998: 37) as to the extent to which member states, the Commission, and other EU level actors take the initiative in the European Union. It is conceivable that the supranational institutions merely 'anticipate' the wishes of the national executives of the member states (Garrett 1992). Nevertheless, for Marks and his associates, part of the Commission's potency derives from its ability to foster and exploit a variety of contacts (presumably both state and non-state actors), its ability to anticipate demands from a variety of sources, its capacity for handling difficult negotiations, and its decisional efficacy.

Marks et al. (1996) argue that the Commission is uniquely well placed to influence EU policy-making because it a focal point for demands and information. However, the Commission is not the only EU institution credited with some independence of action. Hooghe and Marks (1996: 37) contend that the ECJ can also be a decisive player in policy development because its decisions are an accepted part of the legal order in the European Union (i.e. via the doctrines of direct effect and supremacy). Consequently, decision making has become even more multi-level. Moreover, the ECJ creates opportunities for a variety of policy actors, namely the Commission, interest groups, and national courts to influence policy.

Unintended Outcomes and Learning

Given the features identified above, states find it very difficult to control policy making in the European Union. So, far from strengthening the state, European integration is, 'part of a new political (dis)order that is multilayered, constitutionally open ended, and programmatically diverse' (Marks 1992: 221). No one, not even the most powerful state executive, is capable of predicting fully what will eventually emerge when a new policy is pitched into this swirling pattern of alliances. States cannot therefore know exactly what they are agreeing to when they sign on to particular policies (Marks 1993: 403). States 'share, rather than monopolize, control over many activities that take place *in their respective territories*' (Hooghe and Marks 1996: 24) (emphasis added). However, states do not watch passively as unintended consequences accumulate. On the contrary, they actively intervene to tighten or regain their grip on subnational actors. By way of an example, in the sphere of regional policy and structural funding, the UK central administration can maintain control over the impact on public expenditure because it holds the purse strings of subnational government. In other words, it can act as an 'extended gatekeeper' at the policy implementation stage (Bache 1999).

Criticisms of Multi-level Governance

Multi-level governance has attracted a fair deal of criticism. First, it has been claimed that it is not especially novel, being an amalgam of existing theoretical statements. For example, Puchala (1972: 278–9) portrayed the EU as a 'concordance system' emphasizing many themes and issues, which are central to contemporary debates surrounding multi-level governance. Second, although it provides a compelling *description* of contemporary changes in European governance, it lacks an explicit causal motor of integration. It only hints at what might prove to be the reasons (i.e. rewards) for the mobilization of subnational actors (but see Fairbrass 2002, for the application of the strategic decision-making model to interest group behaviour, and Fairbrass and Jordan 2002). Third, it overstates the autonomy of subnational and supranational actors (see Pollack 1995; Bache 1999): the state is still an important shaper of post-decisional politics and a powerful, post-decisional gatekeeper (Jordan 1997). Fourth, it implicitly adopts a top-down view of subnational actors, who are assumed to accept passively power handed down to them from Brussels/national capitals rather than fighting to achieve it for themselves (Jeffrey 2000: 8; but see Marks et al. 1996). Fifth, as originally proposed, multi-level governance focused exclusively on subnational authorities rather than other subnational actors such as pressure groups (but see Marks and McAdam 1996). Sixth, just because subnational actors bypass states and operate independently in Europe does not necessarily imply that they have the power to shape outcomes. In other words, *mobilization* and *influence* are not synonymous (see Jeffery 2000: 3). Finally, advocates of more state-centred theories have claimed that multi-level governance is symptomatic of redistributive policy areas such as structural funding that were expressly designed to empower non-state actors (Moravcsik 1994: 53). Critics of multi-level governance, therefore, claim that analysts should look at 'essential structures [i.e. the state] and major policy decisions [i.e. the periodic revision of the Treaties]' (Moravcsik 1994: 52).

State Dominated Theories: Liberal Inter-governmentalism

In contrast to multi-level governance, more state-centred theories, such as LI argue that the nation state is *the* most important source of EU policy. It is the most influential tier of multi-level governance and acts as a gatekeeper at all stages of the policy-cycle. Five of its guiding assumptions are especially noteworthy. First, states direct the process of integration: the bargaining between them more or less determines the course of integration. Policy outcomes reflect the relative strength of the most powerful member states. Second, states are rational, self-interested actors. Domestic, societal forces determine the state's preferences. However, domestic political systems are biased against diffuse interests. A state's core task is first to aggregate national societal preferences (the 'L' in LI) then to take them to the international level, where the necessary policies are supplied through interstate negotiation (the 'I' in LI).

Third, states keep the gate between national and international politics: despite the explosion of lobbying in Brussels, national channels of representation are pre-eminent. Four, states enjoy little flexibility in making concessions beyond their own domestically determined preferences: this drives EU agreements towards the lowest common denominator of state preferences. Finally, integration strengthens the state: states use the European Union as part of a two level game to overcome domestic opposition by pushing through important but unpopular policies that might otherwise have been blocked (i.e. slack cutting).

Several criticisms have been levelled at LI (see Wincott 1995; Peterson 1997; Jordan 2001, 2002b). First, LI assumes that states function as a single agent in Europe (Moravcsik 1994: 5), rather than an amalgam of different and very often competing organizations and ministries. The former is a credible enough assumption to make if one is (like Moravcsik) looking solely at Intergovernmental Conferences (IGCs) and traditionally unitary states such as the United Kingdom, but it becomes more questionable when the focus is shifted to the day-to-day process of policy making involving more decentralized states. Second, a number of key terms and concepts underpinning LI are unclear (e.g. state, state executive, and national leader). It would seem that Moravcsik (1994: 4) is mainly concerned with the head of state (i.e. chief executive) or minister in a particular issue area. Rather confusingly, societal groups are said to comprise interest groups and political parties, but also civil servants and other cabinet ministers. In other words, having assumed the state is unified he promptly disaggregates it!

Third, the conditions under which slack cutting arises are, at best, very poorly theorized and, at worst, internally contradictory. So, on the one hand state preferences are said to be determined domestically, yet when these constraints are 'loose' the executive can 'shirk' tasks and pursue 'her preferred policies' in Europe (Moravcsik 1994: 5). According to the definitions supplied above, this could conceivably include one Minister going beyond their brief, although only by undercutting one of the central tenets of LI: state coherence. There is, of course, another important aspect to this: if societal groups do not determine state preferences where do they come from? Finally, in spite of the slack cutting argument, LI still struggles to explain why states/state executives, which (under an earlier elaboration of the model) are preoccupied primarily with 'safeguarding their countries against the future erosion of sovereignty' (Moravcsik 1991: 27), are progressively undermining their own existence by relinquishing state authority to other actors.

In spite of these criticisms, Moravcsik's faith in the power of state-level actors to shape major decisions is essentially undiminished. Yet, he remains fundamentally unwilling to apply LI in the very areas of secondary (or day-to-day) policy making where advocates of multi-level governance claim to find greater evidence of pluralism and unintended consequences. Moravcsik (1999: 179) has, however, conceded that 'it remains an open question to what extent the pattern of national preferences . . . remains a, perhaps the, decisive factor in daily decision making'. If LI were correct, we would expect to find that long-term outcomes in our four cases of secondary policy making would be closely aligned with the objectives and actions of national level state actors (i.e. central government departments such the UK's DoE).

Environmental Policy in the Untied Kingdom: A Critical Case of Multi-level Governance?

Having summarized the two approaches, we now set out a number of reasons for treating biodiversity and land use planning policy in the United Kingdom as 'critical tests' for multi-level governance. First, the United Kingdom has been characterized as an 'extreme case' of a unitary state, because of the subservient position of local government (John 1996: 132), with a relatively strong, centralized bureaucracy and internal coordinating mechanisms (Metcalfe 1994). Second, the UK Government has traditionally approached European negotiations with great scepticism (Wallace 1995). Across a whole range of different issue areas, the United Kingdom has regularly found itself isolated from and at odds with continental Europe (Wallace 1997). For example, Golub (1995) claims that the British judiciary, encouraged by an ambivalent public, has retarded legal integration by refusing to make references to the ECJ. Consequently, Jordan (2002b: 48) suggests that the United Kingdom is closer than most other member states to the rational, hierarchical model of action that is commonly found in state-based theories of the European Union. Third, it seems reasonable to expect a state such as the United Kingdom, which had in the past demonstrated enthusiastic support for the single market and its attendant measures (Moravcsik 1998: 324–5), would readily accept or promote those EU polices that would advance market liberalization but resist those policies that do not directly assist in achieving these objectives or are themselves, potentially, a constraint on economic development, such as environmental regulation (Moravcsik 1998: 319; Jordan 2002b). Among the EU's policy competences, biodiversity and land use planning stand out as being only very tenuously connected to the logic of the single market. Finally, unlike structural policy, environmental policy is primarily *regulatory* in nature. Recall Lowi's celebrated typology: redistributive policies typically involve a relatively open competition for (newly distributed) resources (Lowi 1964), whereas regulatory policies tend to be more narrowly drawn and conflictual in nature. Crucially, since the costs of regulatory policies, such as environmental policy, fall most heavily on national actors (i.e. not the European Union), member states can be expected to defend vigorously their national economic interests as LI predicts (Pollack 1994: 110–11).

Given the characteristics identified above, we would not therefore readily expect domestic non-state actors in the United Kingdom successfully to outflank national government policy-makers, by seeking common cause with European actors, thereby, limiting the extent of multi-level governance. If LI claims are correct, we would not expect environmental policy making and implementation in the United Kingdom and the EU to be either 'multi-level' or dominated by 'governance'. On the contrary, it is more likely to be predominantly 'single level' and 'government' led (i.e. the product of bargaining between states).

Biodiversity Policy

EU biodiversity policy comprises an array of different statutes, encompassing subjects as diverse as forestry protection and seals. However, the two main planks of EU policy are Directive 79/409/EEC on the conservation of wild birds, and Directive 92/43/EEC on the conservation of natural habitats and wild fauna/flora.

The Birds Directive

It was not until the Single European Act came into force in the mid-1980s, that the European Union acquired a solid legal foundation for biodiversity policy. Nevertheless, from the early 1970s, the European Union began to establish environmental principles and programmes. Haigh (1997) argues that here was a recognition that species and habitats were under considerable threat. This concern had resulted in the signing and adoption of some important international intergovernmental conventions, which eventually provided the impetus for EU level action. The first EU level proposal to include an undertaking to protect birds and certain other species was the First Action Programme in 1973, which exploited Article 2 of the Treaty of Rome (that refers to improvements in the quality of life). The signing of this programme signalled the endorsement, by the member states, of the need for species protection.

Other sources of pressure for nature conservation measures were the public, sections of which were outraged at the annual slaughter of migratory birds, and interest groups such as Save our Migratory Birds. The latter petitioned the European Parliament, which later issued a Resolution (February 1975).

This Resolution led in turn to proposals from the Commission. However, these were not the Commission's first involvement in the policy area. From the 1970s onwards, it had undertaken a number of desk studies and consulted national experts (Haigh 1997: 9.2–5) about the need for the EU's involvement. In December 1974, the Commission reminded member states of their obligations to comply with the international agreements on bird protection such as the 1971 Ramsar Convention (Wils 1994: 219), which they had voluntarily entered into earlier. As a result of the broad public and political support for protection measures for birds, the Birds Directive was proposed in December 1976 (COM (76) 676). It was not actually adopted until April 1979 (OJ L103 25.4.79), largely due to the opposition from the French and Italian governments. Under the terms of the Directive, member states were required to designate their own Special Protection Areas (SPAs) and to notify the Commission of these sites by April 1981 (i.e. 2 years after formal adoption). Despite this deadline, unlike the Habitats Directive, the Birds Directive lacked a strict timetable for compliance. Consequently, there were widespread implementation problems in most EU member states. The European Parliament (1988) reported on these in the late 1980s.

Previously, as early as 1983, the Commission had begun to respond to growing concerns about the implementation deficit articulated particularly by nature conservation groups. As a result, the Commission initiated infringement proceedings against every single member state. EU level legal action concerned three main issues: non-designation of candidate SPAs; derogations; and the legal transposition of the Directive. Two of the most important cases upon which the ECJ ruled were C-57/89 (CEC v. Federal Republic of Germany with the United Kingdom intervening, a.k.a. *Leybucht Dykes*) in 1991 and C-355/90 (CEC v. Spain, a.k.a. *Marismas de Santona*) in 1993. Crucially, the ECJ's decisions in these two cases appeared to elevate *ecological* considerations over *economic* ones during the designation and development of protected sites (Ball 1997: 217). Employing the principles upheld in the above cases, the ECJ ruled against the UK Government in the *Lappel Bank* case in July 1996. In this case, which was brought against the UK Government by the RSPB, the ECJ ruled that the government had been wrong to exclude an area of land from a SPA to allow development of a nearby port. Again, the Court supported a much more maximal interpretation of EU law than the United Kingdom had anticipated or been prepared to accept. This decision carried significant political costs for the UK Government (i.e. its inability to pursue certain economic development plans). Significantly, several of the cases above drew upon information submitted by national environmental groups, such as the RSPB, which had consciously adopted a 'watchdog' role (RSPB 2000).

The Habitats Directive

In common with the Birds Directive, the Habitats Directive was the product of the efforts of more than one type of political actor operating at different levels of governance. Governments formally recognized the link between protecting species and the habitats they depended upon (Haigh 1997: 9.9–6) by adopting the Third Action Programme, which covered the period 1982–1986. This programme called for the integration of environmental considerations into other policy areas such as transport and agriculture (the so-called Environmental Policy Integration (EPI) principle), reinforced the preventative dimension of EU environmental policy, and highlighted a number of areas for action, such as fresh water and marine pollution, and the protection of sensitive areas (McCormick 2001: 53).

However, other, non-state actors were also actively involved in driving EU action. Thus, from the early 1980s onwards, national and transnational conservation organizations continued to campaign for increased protection (Dixon 1998: 224; WWF-UK 2000; RSPB/WWF Joint Campaigner 2000) and exhorted the European Union to implement fully the provisions of the Bern Convention—another international agreement—through EU legislation. The Bern Convention on the conservation of European wildlife and natural habitats had been adopted in 1979, and had come into force in 1982. However, nature conservation groups (WWF-UK 2000) felt that its objectives had never really been fully realized by the European Union. These included the conservation of natural habitats, flora and fauna, the promotion of cooperation between states, and particularly, the protection of endangered and vulnerable species, including vulnerable migratory species. Once again, the Commission and European Parliament responded to the various demands by developing proposals for an EU directive, based in large part on this international agreement.

The Habitats Directive was proposed in September 1988 (COM (88) 381) but was not finally adopted until 1992 (OJ L206 22.7.92) (Haigh 1997: 9.9–8). Progress was once again obstructed by member states. On this occasion, the UK Government was one of the chief agents of delay, primarily because it wanted to reverse the unintended effects of the *Leybucht* ruling (see above). This had been in progress while the Habitats Directive was being negotiated, and when the ECJ decision was announced in February 1991, it alarmed and surprized the UK Government (Jordan 2002b). Amendments were duly made to the draft habitats directive, which strongly resembled a UK central government circular that had been issued to local planning bodies in 1987 (Freestone 1996: 248), suggesting that the UK Government had successfully shaped the wording of the Directive. In addition to the UK's objections, negotiations over the Habitats Directive also foundered over the issue of providing financial assistance to 'ecologically rich' but 'economically poor' countries (e.g. member states such as Spain). Negotiations stalled until such states were satisfied that they would receive 'adequate' financial support in the form of cohesion funding.

The UK Government's successful campaign to restore member state discretion over protected sites resulted in the inclusion of a number of crucial articles in the final Habitats Directive. Thus, Articles 6(4) and 7 of the Habitats Directive replaced Article 4(4) of the Birds Directive, thus appearing to render the former a rather weaker piece of species protection legislation. The Habitats Directive and the amended Birds Directive appeared to give member states greater autonomy with regard to protected sites (e.g. to use economic reasons to allow damage to sites). Nevertheless, the final text places obligations on member states to protect plant and animal species, and their habitats. Crucially, member states are required to avoid deterioration of such sites and to carry out appropriate assessments of any plans or projects that might potentially damage them.

As with its predecessor, the implementation of the Habitats Directive has been problematic (Ledoux et al. 2000). Despite the inclusion of a strict but still quite generous, 10-year implementation timetable that was demanded by the UK Government (WWF-European Policy Office (EPO), the Commission soon began to issue warnings and to initiate infringement proceedings against a majority of the member states. For example, in 1998 the Commission initiated legal action against nine member states (not including the United Kingdom) for their failure to comply with various aspects of the two directives, but especially the identification of protected sites. As a result of this pressure, the UK's executive has been forced to identify many more SACs than it ever intended to (Department of the Environment, Transport, and the Regions (DETR) 2000). Environmental protection has also had to be extended to areas that were previously exempt from national nature conservation measures, such as marine areas within the 200-mile territorial limit, thereby imposing potentially significant constraints on future economic activities such as oil extraction in the North Sea.

Land use Planning Policy

Environmental Impact Assessment (EIA) Directive

In 1969, the United States Government introduced EIA. This is a tool for evaluating the impacts of proposed developments such as a road or power station. Ideally, the systematic collection of information should enable the most environmentally damaging impacts to be alleviated or mitigated entirely. This eventually inspired similar systems in many European states and, eventually, the European Union. By the time the European Union adopted an EIA Directive in 1985 (85/337/EEC), some of the most environmentally advanced member states were already experienced at undertaking their own, domestic assessments (West Germany, France, and the Netherlands, since 1975, 1976, and 1981 respectively). However, for the rest, EIA was a novelty (Haigh 1983: 592; Wood 1995).

In common with the biodiversity directives outlined above, a number of policy actors operating at different levels of governance contributed to the development of the EIA Directive. These included the Commission, which had begun preparing the ground in the mid-1970s by commissioning a series of expert reports. In fact, the first of these two reports was produced by two British academics (Lee and Wood 1978). The European Environmental Bureau, the main pan-European environmental pressure group that represents the interests of national environmental pressure groups in Brussels, tried to crystallize public and expert opinion by holding an information-sharing seminar for national experts and Commission officials in 1975 (Sheate 1997: 270).

On the basis of these discussions, the Commission began drafting a formal proposal in 1977. However, almost immediately negotiations foundered because the proposal represented the EU's first intrusion into national land use planning practices. It is reported that the proposal went through as many as twenty different drafts before finally being published in 1980 (COM 80 313) (Wood 1995: 32). Once again the UK Government presented a significant obstacle to agreement. During the drafting stages, important changes were made to accommodate its demands for a less intrusive and environmentally less ambitious form of EIA that would not be too disruptive in terms of national economic development priorities. Nevertheless, the final draft still contained a number of elements that the UK Government opposed, such as a long list of the so-called Annex I projects where EIA was mandatory (Wood 1995: 32).

The 1985 Directive requires developers to undertake an environmental assessment for those projects that are considered, potentially, to have *significant* impacts upon the environment. This assessment must be completed prior to planning consent being granted. Article I of the Directive lists nine types of project that must receive an environmental assessment, although exemptions can be made in exceptional circumstances. Annex II includes thirteen categories of development project covering eighty separate types of project that require an EIA where states 'consider that their characteristics so require'. Article 4(2) requires member states either to specify a priori certain types of projects that will fall under Article II, or establish the criteria and thresholds to determine which apply. In the United Kingdom, the simple test used is 'significant' environmental impacts (although such a test can clearly provoke controversy as it is fundamentally subjective).

As with nature conservation, the UK Government believed that it was a pacesetter in land use planning policy and thought that the EU law would only formalize existing national best practices, dating back to the 1947 Town and Country Planning Act. Initially, formal compliance with the EIA Directive in the United Kingdom was attempted using secondary regulation adopted under the European Communities Act 1972, which in practice required more than forty separate pieces of legislation. When this failed to produce adequate compliance with the strict terms of the Directive (since it did not cover developments like agriculture and forestry), the UK Government was obliged to introduce the 1991 Planning and Compensation Act.

As with EU biodiversity policy, Commission-initiated rulings by the ECJ have played an important part in giving the EIA Directive greater legal and political bite. The ECJ's judgements, which stemmed from continuing disagreements about the interpretation of the Directive at the national level, have confirmed that states have far less leeway than they expected in determining the precise scope of EIA and have imposed restrictions on national economic development. Most significant among the ECJ cases were C431/92 (Germany supported by the UK *v.* Commission) in 1995 and C133/94 (Belgium and Germany *v.* Commission) in 1996. In both cases the ECJ ruled in favour of the Commission and against the member states.

In terms of its general impact on the United Kingdom, the EIA Directive has resulted in far more EIAs being undertaken than anyone expected, particularly with respect to activities under Article II, which the UK Government hoped would be spared almost entirely from the process (Wood and Jones 1991). Between 1988 and 1993, over one thousand environmental impact statements (EISs) were produced under EU law (of which only 10 per cent were related to Article I) and over 300 outside it, indicating the tremendous interest in EIA generated by the Directive (Wood 1995: 53). In fact, the growing popularity of EIA among developers, environmentalists, and local planners has meant that it is now formally applied to projects falling outside EU rules. Interestingly, the UK Government's lukewarm enthusiasm for EIA has also grown considerably in the period since 1988, as the dire warnings of delay and excessive litigation failed to materialize.

Strategic Environmental Assessment

Strategic Environmental Assessment (SEA) has been one of the Commission's strategic policy goals for almost as long as the European Union has had an environmental policy. The Commission understandably regarded strategic environmental assessment as being of greater long-term importance than EIA. This is because SEA shifts the focus of attention from individual projects (e.g. a road) to the overarching policies (e.g. to improve accessibility) and programmes (e.g. a road building programme) that guide them. In the late 1970s, the two British academics, Lee and Wood (see above) first recommended the idea of SEA to the Commission. There were also plans to introduce it in the Commission's 1980 draft EIA proposal (Jordan 2002*b*). However, it was only with the 1987 Fourth Action Programme that the member states and the Commission formally committed themselves to introducing it. Environmental groups and the European Parliament have long been enthusiastic advocates of SEA, but the Commission has had to tread carefully in order to win all of the member states around to its way of thinking. It failed conspicuously to read the rules correctly in the early 1980s, and SEA was deleted from the early drafts of the EIA Directive.

However, by the 1990s the political context had become much more supportive of SEA. By then, environmental policy, or to be accurate sustainable development policy, was a Treaty-based objective of European integration. EU environmental policy had moved even further from being just an adjunct to the single market, and pressure group lobbying in Brussels had reached unprecedented levels. At the same time, many states, including the United Kingdom, were experimenting with informal, national-level systems of SEA to achieve sustainable development—the emerging *leitmotif* of EU environmental policy. The Commission was then able to use the prospect that national systems might develop in rather different ways as a justification for proposing SEA at the European level, though, not without much delay and patient negotiation. Work commenced on a formal proposal in 1990, which was released to national experts in March 1991. Early drafts implied that SEA would be applied to virtually all policies, programmes, and projects that gave rise to development.

In December 1992, the UK Government used the subsidiarity debate to kill off the SEA proposal, which in any case had never achieved formal status and was strongly disliked by many other states. This setback did not deter the Commission from making efforts to extend SEA by other means, for example, via the structural funding process, in certain directives such as those addressing habitats, and also in the construction of roads (Therivel et al. 1992: 53; Sheate 1997: 279–81). Subsequently, following further extensive discussions with member states, the Commission finally issued a formal SEA proposal in 1996 (see COM (96) 0304 and COM(96)511 as amended by COM (99)73). This required an environmental assessment of all plans and programmes adopted under national town and country planning legislation but not (as originally suggested) over-arching policies and programmes (see above). The scope of SEA was also narrowed to specific land use planning documents such as local development and waste plans. Other changes made to appease member states provided greater discretion and flexibility to tailor the directive to suit national circumstances.

Thereafter, the proposal remained in limbo as a succession of Council Presidencies ignored it. Interestingly, during its Presidency in 1998, the UK Government shunned SEA and opted instead to try and 'green' strategic, long-term policies via the so-called 'Cardiff process' of review and reporting instead of SEA (Jordan and Lenschow 2000). However, the 'history making' decision at Amsterdam in 1997 to strengthen the legal commitment to achieve EPI in the European Union gave the SEA proposal a much needed shot in the arm. In 1999, first the Finnish and then the German Presidencies, picked up the initiative in response to the EU-wide challenge of implementing the newly strengthened commitment to achieving EPI. By 1999, even the UK Government was said to be broadly in favour of the proposal, which by now was a weaker proposition. Following some delays associated with the process of conciliation (ENDS 2001), Directive 2001/42/EC was given formal approval by the European Parliament and the Council on the 27 June 2001 (OJL 197, 21-07-2001, 30–37). Member states will have until 21 July 2004 to introduce suitable national legislation in order to comply with the Directive.

Together the EIA and SEA Directives have combined to produce policy implications for the UK Government that were unforeseen and unwelcome. For example, they resulted in intense conflicts within Whitehall and environmental protection has been extended into areas of national policy making that were previously closed off to the DoE (Jordan 2002b: 186–7).

Discussion and Conclusions

In this chapter we have examined two specific areas of EU environmental policy; biodiversity and land use planning. We now use this evidence to address four of the seven themes outlined in the introductory chapter. These focused on the following questions: how should multi-level governance be defined; what role does the state play in multi-level governance?; to what extent does multi-level governance differ across policy sectors; and, what are the limitations of multi-level governance as a general theory of European integration?

The implementation of EU biodiversity and land use planning measures in the UK share several common features with structural funding policy (see Chapter 11, this volume). They are both characterized by subnational mobilization, complex, uncertain, and contested decision-making, entrepreneurial action on the part of the Commission and Parliament, unintended policy outcomes and learning on the part of member states. If multi-level governance refers to 'the dispersion of authoritative decision-making across multiple tiers' (Hooghe and Marks 2001: xi), then our two cases could easily be classified as examples of multi-level governance. This is because UK-based environmental groups have mobilized at the EU level, have made direct contact with staff and the Commissioner in DG Environment (RSPB/WWF Joint Campaigner 2000; WWF-EPO 2000) and have established close links with leading MEPs on the Environment Committee of the European Parliament (such as Caroline Jackson and Hemmo Muntingh) and rendered the process even more multi-tiered. In addition, they have worked with the Brussels based group, Birdlife International, in providing information to the Commission (Birdlife International 2000) with a view to influencing biodiversity policy via legal channels, notably the ECJ. Actions on the part of both the Commission and the European Parliament were specifically intended to build political support and provide them with the means to influence policy development. Both EU institutions actively encouraged links with the environmental groups and the resulting alliances have helped to shape environmental policy (Birdlife International 2000; WWF-EPO 2000).

That such a picture should emerge in our two specially selected (or 'critical') cases is especially important to the debate about the role of the state in the context of multi-level governance. The development of biodiversity and land use planning policy in the United Kingdom arose out of a conflict between a sizeable number of actors, not just states. Complexity arises partly from the sheer number of vested interests that colonized the two policy domains: the public, environmental groups, land owning and economic development interests, different and competing UK government departments (for a brief account of the opposition encountered by the DoE from other UK central government departments see Fairbrass and Jordan 2001: 10), other member state national executives, the European Parliament, and, the Commission. Conflicting objectives were very much in evidence. The DoE's objectives had been to install policies, paradigms, and practices (i.e. a flexible, case-by-case, voluntary approach) at the EU level that simply replicated those already in place in the United Kingdom, to amend the Habitats Directive, and to dilute the Birds Directive. However, in contrast to the UK Government's aims, EU institutions successfully promoted and adopted a more formalized system that gave the Commission and the ECJ sufficient leverage, with help from the environmental groups, with which to discipline member states such as the United Kingdom (e.g. the *Lappel Bank* and Twyford Downs cases).

The degree of uncertainty faced by the various stakeholders and the potential for unintended outcomes in the development of biodiversity and land use planning policy is reflected in the way in which the four directives mutated from their original drafts, through negotiations, to adoption, and especially during implementation. On several occasions the UK Government found that policy assumed a form that was wholly unexpected and undesirable. In other words, there were unintended consequences. The *Leybucht Dykes* ruling clearly shocked DoE officials; the *Lappel Bank* ruling was equally unwelcome (Sharp 1998). Nevertheless, the case studies reveal that the UK Government did learn from these and earlier experiences. Directives proposed and adopted in the 1970s and 1980s (i.e. the Birds and EIA Directives) produced unintended consequences from the point of view of the DoE and as a result, the government approached subsequent draft directives (i.e. the Habitats and SEA measures) much more warily. The UK Government did achieve a measure of success in shaping the policy more to its liking. However, even after apparently restoring or reclaiming sovereignty with regard to the later directives, the UK Government has still experienced unintended consequences. To conclude, we have detected clear evidence of multi-level governance in a sector and a country where we did not expect to find it. The evidence from our case study, therefore, suggests that although member states (theme five) continue to play a dominant role in the policy process, national executives struggle to predict, let alone fully control, the future course of policy making because of the prevailing conditions.

This takes us neatly on to theme three because clearly both models now need to be subjected to much more detailed testing. We selected environmental policy expecting it to exhibit very different dynamics to structural policy. In fact, there are a number of significant similarities. As summarized above, the policies share common features. This could be a reflection of a set of circumstances which are special to the UK (see Moravcsik 1998: 491–2, fn 19), in which case many other countries should now be tested. Either way, our discovery of multi-level governance in these 'critical' cases, suggests that analysts should now sample cases that lie firmly within the 'home domain' of state-based theories, specifically monetary, foreign, and defence policy.

So, what light does the empirical evidence throw on the explanatory capacity of multi-level governance (theme seven)? Our case study material would appear to confirm several of the criticisms of multi-level governance outlined above.

Crucially, although multi-level governance provides a compelling *description* of EU policy-making processes, it does not explicitly offer any causal motors for the actions of the subnational and supranational actors. It only hints at what might prove to be the reasons (i.e. rewards) for the mobilization of subnational actors. It also overstates the autonomy of subnational and supranational actors: our evidence shows that the state can still be an important shaper of post-decisional politics and a powerful gatekeeper. Multi-level governance also tends to view subnational actors as being relatively passive when our evidence suggests that nationally based interest groups do behave strategically and purposefully to establish direct relations with EU level policy-makers. But perhaps the most telling criticism of multi-level governance is that it overlooks the international drivers of EU policy. Whilst subnational, national, and supranational actors have played an important role in EU (and UK) biodiversity and land use planning policies, the development of UN policy has been an important spur for action, especially in the biodiversity policy area. Although the Commission is actively involved in international negotiations (see above), policy making at a supra-EU level corresponds much more closely to an interstate model of action. That said, multi-level governance can still subsequently creep in when words are turned into action. In this chapter we have illuminated the significant unintended consequences that arose in the United Kingdom when the European Union began to establish measures to implement international agreements within its legal domain.

Our conclusion is therefore very much a provisional one: there is sufficient empirical evidence to suggest that LI is not a general theory of the European Union, nor even a satisfactory theory of specific secondary decisions. Multi-level governance offers a more compelling description of what happens to decisions once they escape the domain of intergovernmental bargaining in the European Union, but is not yet a fully fledged theory. Analysts now need to test multi-level governance in areas of both 'high' and 'low' politics, and in states other than the United Kingdom. In so doing, we may discover whether the common patterns uncovered in EU structural funding and environmental policy are typical or not of the general nature of EU policy-making. Such research might also allow us to determine (or more fully elaborate) the reasons *why* EU policy-making results in the mobilization of subnational actors, is complex, disputed, and unpredictable, produces unexpected outcomes and encourages EU level institutions to behave in an entrepreneurial manner. At the present time much more work needs to be done to covert multi-level governance from a '(dis)ordering framework' (Rosamond 2000: 111), which identifies some important attributes of EU governance (i.e. multiactorness, unpredictability, and complexity) without really explaining them (Benz and Ebelein 1999 : 330), into a comprehensive and exegetical account of the European Union.

10

Multi-level Governance and European Union Regional Policy

IAN BACHE

As noted by other contributors to this volume (George, Chapter 7; Fairbrass and Jordan, Chapter 9), multi-level governance was first developed from a study of EC/EU regional policy[1] and has since been applied in relation to this policy area more than any other (Hooghe 1996; Smith 1997; Bache 1998, 1999; Benz and Eberlein 1998, 1999, 2000). As such, this chapter reflects on the analytical value of multi-level governance on its 'home ground'. Moreover, the discussion here focuses primarily on the implementation stage of EU regional policy making, where multi-level governance is said to be most prominent (Marks et al. 1996: 365). In relation to the themes set out in Chapter 1 of this volume, the main concern here is with how accurately multi-level governance captures developments in this policy field: the findings here suggest considerable variation in this, both across and within states.

The year 1988 marked a watershed in the history of EC/EU regional policy. In the context of enlargement and moves to complete the single market programme, financial allocations to the European Communities poorer regions were doubled and the administration of regional programmes restructured around four principles: additionality, concentration, partnership, programming. The reform was widely seen to reflect Commission preferences rather than those of national governments, with the principles of additionality and partnership in particular presenting a challenge to central government policy control at the implementation stage. This reform, and its subsequent implementation, was central to the development of multi-level governance. This chapter considers the history of the key principles of additionality and partnership

---

[1] More specifically, the initial study by Marks and most of the subsequent examinations of multi-level governance in this sector have focused on the structural funds (not other aspects of regional policy, such as state aids). The structural funds provide the main financial instrument of EU regional policy, the European Regional Development Fund (ERDF). To complete the picture, structural funds and regional policy are sometimes referred to within the broader notion of cohesion policy (e.g. Hooghe 1996). This definition incorporates the Cohesion Fund, which was introduced in 1993 as an additional compensatory measure for the poorer member states (Spain, Portugal, Greece, and Ireland), but which was not governed by the principles of structural policy.

since the 1988 reform and assesses the extent to which multi-level governance captures developments in the sector. It suggests some evidence for multi-level governance in relation to partnership, but little in the case of additionality. Significantly, however, the degree of multi-level governance varies both across and within states.

Partnership and Multi-level Governance

Officially, the partnership principle introduced in the 1988 reform of the structural funds aimed to maximize the effectiveness of EC regional policy interventions by giving subnational actors a formal role in the implementation process for the first time. Unofficially, the notion of partnership advocated by the Commission advanced a particular social and political model in the context of an ideological struggle over the kind of Europe being developed. This struggle between competing models of capitalism has been characterized in a number of ways, but in this context most succinctly by Hooghe (1998) who distinguished between *neoliberalism* and *regulated capitalism*. In essence, the former view emphasizes the minimal state and free markets; the latter seeking to place social concerns alongside market efficiency.

For the Delors Commission, cohesion policy[2] was the 'flagship' of regulated capitalism (Hooghe 1998: 3) and partnership was a key component of this policy. The partnership principle agreed in the 1988 structural fund regulations required: 'close consultation between the Commission, the member states concerned and the competent authorities designated by the latter at national, regional, local or other level, with each party acting as a partner in pursuit of a common goal' (Regulation (EEC) 2052/88).

From January 1989, partnerships were to be established in each assisted region to design, implement, and monitor structural fund programmes. In subsequent structural fund reforms, the partnership principle aimed at the inclusion of social and economic partners (1993) and environmental agencies and other non-governmental agencies (1999).

Partnership and Multi-level Governance across Member States

Before 1989, the implementation of structural policy had been determined by national governments according to national priorities. The first comprehensive assessment of the political implications of the partnership principle for member states was published by Hooghe (1996). This study considered two related questions: whether partnership had led to diverse domestic territorial relations converging; or, whether existing territorial relations within member states had

---

[2] See note 1 for details.

been upheld (Hooghe 1996: 2). In other words, had the partnership principle promoted multi-level governance?

The study demonstrated considerable variation in the degrees of multi-level governance through partnership across member states, in large part shaped by the pre-existing territorial distribution of power. Thus, where a strong national government was determined to retain control over the domestic impact of structural policy, it retained considerable powers to do so. However, in less centralized states there was greater evidence of emerging multi-level governance through the partnership principle.

Later research funded by the European Commission (Kelleher et al. 1999) highlighted continuing differences in the impact of the partnership principle across member states, emphasizing the continuing importance of the pre-existing territorial distribution of power. As with the Hooghe study, Kelleher et al. (1999: viii) found that 'the degree of decentralization and the type of deconcentration occurring in the different member states inevitably shapes the relations between key actors within partnerships and determines the competencies and composition of partnerships'. Central governments generally remained key actors in shaping partnership arrangements: Member States continue to dominate and delimit partnership functioning—through their roles in negotiating programme content and selecting horizontal partners, and through their provision of secretariats and managing authorities (Kelleher et al. 1999: vi).

In addition to governments controlling the input of subnational authorities, the role of social partners was often limited and Non-Governmental Organizations (NGOs) were largely absent from partnerships. Significantly, however, there were instances of some governments increasingly recognizing the benefit of partnership working for their own policy agendas, and voluntarily widening participation. Moreover, in some member states the EC/EU partnership principle had 'kick-started' the operation of partnership forms. In others, it had been seen to reinvigorate partnership 'along more innovatory lines' (Kelleher et al. 1999: viii).

The following themes emerged as common across member states in shaping the impact of the partnership principle:

- the importance of national institutional traditions and the ways accommodation has been sought with Structural Fund programme,
- the importance of prior partnership experience,
- associated 'learning mechanisms' by which the experience is transferred,
- the common tendency towards regionalization/decentralization which is reflected in partnership composition and role, and
- the evolution and sometimes dilution of well-established corporatist models of governance, which can be associated with the withdrawal of existing partners.

(Kelleher et al. 1999: 11–12)

In summary, the evidence suggested that where the EC/EU multi-level partnership model fitted well with domestic institutions and preferences it gave a push to multi-level governance. However, where the model did not fit with domestic institutions and preferences, the partnership principle had little impact on territorial relations unless, primarily through a process of learning, domestic actors chose to embrace it. As discussed subsequently, these findings provide a persuasive explanation for developments in Britain.

Partnership and Multi-level Governance in Britain

While partnership may have been a novel concept in some member states when it was adopted in 1988, it was not new to Britain. The Thatcher governments of the 1980s had embraced the partnership principle for their inner city regeneration policies. Partnership was made a prerequisite for success under the competitive bidding process of the City Challenge programme, and its successor, the Single Regeneration Budget (SRB) programme. However, partnership in this conception differed from that advanced by the Commission.

Partnership for inner city policies in Britain in the 1980s was driven by the neoliberal aim of reducing the role of the public sector, namely local government, and enhancing that of private sector actors. Following this, local authorities were required to develop partnership bids with private sector organizations as a condition of receiving central assistance for urban regeneration. This approach drew on 'an "American" philosophy, culture and ideology that actively seeks to incorporate the business sector into urban regeneration' (Ward 1996: 427). Carley (1990: 32) noted that in 1988, on the eve of a tour of US cities, Mrs Thatcher's 'inner city supremo', Kenneth Clarke, said he believed 'the US is the only country in the world from which Britain has anything to learn about tackling inner city problems (The Independent, 4/11/98)': (for more on this, see Bache 2001).

Thus, the politics of partnership in Britain in the late 1980s and early 1990s were essentially neoliberal. As such, the Commission's partnership model, informed by principles of regulated capitalism, was received with some hostility. The Commission's model sought to empower rather than disempower subnational state actors. Moreover, the EU requirement increasingly placed emphasis on the inclusion within partnerships of the social partners (trade unions and employers representatives) and NGOs. Developed in large part to a rejection of corporatist forms that were seen to have failed in the 1970s, Thatcherite neoliberalism was always likely to react unfavourably to Commission demands for greater horizontal cooperation, particularly where this included the involvement of trade unions.

Over time, however, the British position on structural fund partnerships began to change. While some changes were attributable to the change of governing party in 1997, others began under the Conservatives. While it is not possible to date the moment of change precisely, in broad terms change was observable from the mid-1990s.

1989–1995

This period has been dealt with in detail elsewhere (see Bache et al. 1996), so will be summarized here. Before the 1988 reform of the structural funds, Britain's policy for implementing the structural funds was decided centrally. Subnational authorities were consulted, but central government departments determined policy priorities. Despite the introduction of the partnership principle, the situation in Britain changed little immediately after the principle came into effect in January 1989. Partnerships were established in the assisted regions, but their composition was narrow, limited primarily to central government civil servants and local authority officials. Trade unions were explicitly excluded from representation on structural fund committees. Central government civil servants based in regional offices and territorial ministries chaired and administered the committees to ensure a firm grip on decisions. Local authorities could not be represented by politicians and, in one region, central government actually appointed the local authority officials to serve on structural fund committees. In other words, there may have been multi-level *participation* in the policy process, this was not multi-level *governance* in any meaningful sense: the policy outcomes continued to reflect the preferences of central government (Bache 1999).

The one region in Britain where partnership did mean something more than participation was in Western Scotland. Here, central government (in the form of the Scottish Office) took a relatively 'hands-off' approach to implementation. This was illustrated by the creation of an 'independent secretariat' to administer the funds in 1989, staffed and funded by a range of partners. The European Commission supported this model politically and financially, through co-funding. Before 1997, Western Scotland was the only British structural fund region to operate with this model: this was both a reflection of and reason for relatively dispersed influence within the partnership. That subnational, national, and supranational actors had influence in this region suggested the emergence of multi-level governance.

1995–1999

In the period between 1995 and 1999, central government control over partnership working appeared to relax in other regions of Britain. This was illustrated in a study of South Wales, Western Scotland, the East Midlands, and Yorkshire and Humber: a selection of regions covering different forms of decentralized and deconcentrated institutions (territorial ministries and government regional offices).[3] When this study was conducted, neither the new Scottish Parliament

---

[3] This selection was to allow examination of the importance of different institutional arrangements covering different British regions: the territorial ministries in Scotland and Wales 'integrated' government regional offices in the East Midlands and Yorkshire and Humber. This allowed comparison

nor the Welsh Assembly had any significant role in the implementation process. These new bodies were expected to play a significant role when the new programme period began in 2000.

Western Scotland

> In my experience, the inter-connectedness of the polity in Scotland is extremely different from what I've been involved with and seen elsewhere. There is much more discussion between people from different sectors and localities, there is much more joint partnership project working than in England and this was all well before partnership became the vogue buzz-word. (interview, local authority representative)

The relative cohesiveness of the Western Scotland regional partnership is explained by a combination of particular historical, institutional, and political circumstances.

Partnership working had been a feature of the region since the mid-1970s, when Strathclyde Regional Council introduced the model in its efforts to regenerate the city of Glasgow. As such, the EU partnership principle was relatively easily assimilated into existing practices. The creation of an independent secretariat illustrated the degree of trust developed through prior partnership working between the Scottish Office and other partners. However, this was also an illustration of the relative autonomy of the Scottish Office from Whitehall, compared with other institutions of deconcentrated government at this time. This autonomy reflected not only specific historical features of the place of Scotland within the United Kingdom, but increasing central government sensitivity to popular demands within Scotland for greater autonomy.

Despite the relaxed role played by the Scottish Office on day-to-day structural fund matters, it remained the partner with a 'golden share'. The Scottish Office retained considerable reserve powers, including the right to veto partnership proposals. However, it only used its powers with great reluctance 'because it recognises that to do so undermines the partnership: it pollutes the atmosphere' (interview, voluntary sector partner).

South Wales

> The simple fact is there is no war in Wales any more (interview, local government partner).

Up to the mid-1990s, South Wales was the British region most characterized by conflict over structural fund matters. The Welsh Office was viewed by many

of actor preferences within similar institutional structures: Scottish Office v. Welsh Office; and GOEM v. GOYH and between dissimilar institutional structures (territorial ministries v. regional offices). This research was undertaken jointly with Stephen George. I am grateful to Stephen for allowing me to reproduce some of our interview material here. Interviews were conducted in 1998 and 1999.

partners, particularly those in local government, as being very controlling and highly bureaucratic. Local authorities felt powerless within partnerships.

From around 1996, the political tensions around the structural funds in South Wales began to ease. A number of developments explain this. The starting point, arguably, was the creation of an independent secretariat, agreed by the new Secretary of State for Wales, William Hague. This signalled a thawing in relations between the Welsh Office and the wider partnership that accorded with Conservative party policies of 'open' government in the run up to the 1997 general election, and also cut government administrative costs. In addition, there were personnel changes in the European Affairs Division of the Welsh Office, including the retirement of one senior figure who had a particularly conflictual relationship with local authorities (these findings are consistent with those of the Welsh European Programme Executive, WEPE 1998).

By 1998, relations between the Welsh Office and the other partners had improved considerably from their low point in the early 1990s. As one partner put it, 'it has influence, but has largely played a reasonably "hands-off" role' (interview, local authority official). One illustration of improved partnership relations in South Wales was the establishment of a small team to negotiate the 1997–1999 Single Programme Document (SPD), co-chaired by officials from the Welsh Office and local government, a development unique in Britain. Despite the creation of the independent secretariat, the Welsh Office retained important reserve powers but the extent and nature of its intervention had changed by 1998.

Yorkshire and Humber

> '[T]the whole climate and the environment within which we work in the area of economic development has become much more partnership orientated over the last four or five years . . . people have got used to working together across sectors in a way that simply wasn't the case in the late eighties' (interview, Yorkshire and Humber partner).[4]

As with South Wales, the lack of power felt by local authorities in Yorkshire and Humber resulted in much tension up to the mid-1990s. However, in a relatively short time-span, this region moved from being amongst the most fractured and conflict-ridden British regions to being one of the most cohesive and consensual. Of particular importance to improved partnership relations here was the change in leadership style demonstrated by regional civil servants. This was helped by changes in personnel within the European Secretariat. By mid-1998, Government Office for Yorkshire and Humber (GOYH) was generally seen to be facilitating rather than dominating partnerships.

---

[4] For purposes of anonymity, some interviewees are referred to simply as a 'regional partner', where details of their organization could possibly reveal their identity to other policy-makers.

Again, no one doubted the underlying authority of government officials: GOYH retained the key political administrative functions within the partnerships and did not create an independent secretariat. However, GOYH had chosen to exercise its authority differently, allowing local authorities and other partners more influence. While this change was essentially voluntary, it was also partly a response to dysfunctional partnership relations that hindered policy performance and threatened the region's access to additional structural funding allocated at the Commission's discretion.

East Midlands

> 'The main problem for the East Midlands is that it doesn't have a common identity . . . I think it is one of the peculiar areas that really hasn't got anything that links it altogether' (interview, East Midlands partner).

The findings on the operation of structural fund partnerships confirmed the widely held view of this region as relatively fragmented. Here, Government Office for the East Midlands (GOEM) was closer to Whitehall in its implementation of policy than government departments in the other regions. Civil servants interpreted their role strictly along the lines of directives from Whitehall and in accordance with EU regulations. In this region also, local authorities felt they had little influence over policy making up to the mid-1990s and the partnership was characterized by tension, not least between GOEM officials and the Commission, who saw it as having a 'political agenda with a small "p" . . . It wants to see independent secretariats free from central government control' (regional civil servant, interview).

In policy terms, little changed after Labour's election in 1997: regional programme priorities had been set by then and would not be altered. However, while partners reported an improved change in the tone of exchanges with GOEM officials from around this time, GOEM officials remained less approachable and less innovative in their approach in this period than their counterparts in Yorkshire and Humber. This may have been partly to do with different personnel, but also that the East Midlands region received considerably smaller amounts in structural funding than Yorkshire and Humber. As such, there was less experience of partnership working and less of an onus on making partnerships work in terms of the net impact of the policies on the region.

The Impact of the Labour Government

As suggested above, while some of the changes in partnership relations pre-dated the 1997 general election, a number were directly attributable to the change of government. The Labour government was explicitly more pro-Europe and pro-regional policy than its Conservative predecessor. In party political terms, Labour's election victory, coupled with Labour dominance of local government in the assisted areas, meant for the first time the absence of ideological and party political conflict underpinning the institutional relationships between centre and locality within structural fund partnerships. An improvement in partnership relations was anticipated by the Commission and local authorities.

Despite pressure from the Commission and local authorities for the inclusion of local councillors on partnership bodies, British central government resisted a change of policy until shortly before the general election in May 1997. This change was operationalized by the incoming Labour government. It is unclear what would have happened in the unlikely event of a Conservative victory. This policy change increased the political resources of local government within partnerships and thus improved the prospects for multi-level governance. More generally, the election of a Labour government increased the general levels of confidence of the predominantly Labour-led local authorities in the regions studied. As one local Labour councillor in Yorkshire and Humber (interview) put it: 'I think that subordination is now starting to disappear. Certainly, from our perspective, it's because we've got a Labour government. It's somewhere else to go if we're not happy. Previously there was nowhere else to go'. The same councillor suggested that, without the change of government, 'partnership would have developed but it would have struggled'.

The inclusion of trade unions came only after the 1997 election. As with councillor participation, the Commission had sought to influence British government policy on this for a long period, but without success. Generally, trade union inclusion was seen as a positive step by most partners, not least for practical reasons. Much time had been spent debating the issue during programme committee meetings, rather than planning how to develop programmes. As one regional civil servant (interview) put it: ' A whole load of wasted time has been saved . . . time that was creating a whole adversarial approach when we wanted to build up a more cooperative partnership. Obviously, if you've just spent half an hour arguing about why the social partners aren't there it's quite difficult to say "let's go to the next part of the agenda and have a co-operative discussion about that" '.

Assessment

Cross-EU studies have revealed variation in the implementation of the partnership principle, providing mixed evidence of multi-level governance. In many cases, the composition of partnerships continued to fall short of Commission objectives, particularly in relation to the role played by the social partners and NGOs. However, there was evidence that governments were increasingly receptive to partnership as a general concept, which was leading to fewer conflicts at the implementation stage. Here, the experience of partnership working, and its perceived benefits were seen as important. In addition, research indicated a trend across member states towards regionalization and decentralization that accommodated the principle of multi-level participation (if not governance) more easily. In summary, where multi-level governance is emerging through partnership, it appears to be doing so primarily where this approach fits with domestic practices and preferences. This is clearly the case in Britain.

Up to the mid-1990s, there was little evidence of multi-level governance in Britain through EU regional policy partnerships. The Commission's concept of partnership was resisted both institutionally and politically. Central government departments resisted the transfer of authority both downwards to local authorities and upwards to the European Commission. In addition to this institutional resistance was political resistance. The governing Conservative party was ideologically opposed to aspects of the Commission's partnership concept. Thus, in most British regions, partnership was in name only. The exception to this rule was Western Scotland, which already had a tradition of partnership working within a geographically concentrated policy community pursuing common objectives. From around 1995, the picture began to change with growing evidence of more effective partnership working in England and Wales.

In summary, there are two main conclusions from the study of Britain. First, that different institutional structures in different parts of Britain provide part of the explanation for divergent patterns of implementation. However, at different times, actors within similar institutions adopted a different approach to implementation. Moreover, there is evidence that actor preferences both within regions and centrally changed over time. Clearly, the election of the Labour government signalled some changes in central preferences. However, there were signs before 1997 that actor preferences in some regions were changing through a learning process that led to a re-assessment of the costs and benefits of partnership working. Preferences changed both within the regional civil service and at the centre. Thus, to understand the emergence of multi-level governance within structural fund partnerships requires an actor-centred approach to understanding changing central preferences. The centre retains considerable reserve powers in relation to the implementation of structural policy, but the evidence suggests that in the late 1990s, central government exercised its authority in a way that increasingly facilitated rather than obstructs the operation of multi-level and multi-sectoral partnerships.

Additionality and Multi-level Governance

The additionality principle requires states to spend allocations from EU regional funds in addition to any planned domestic expenditure: a key principle of a genuinely supranational regional policy, but one that state executives interpreted as they saw fit until the requirement was strengthened by the 1988 reform. Beyond this reform, the British government remained the sole obstructer of the additionality principle. This led to a high profile dispute between the Commission and the British government (see Chapter 7 by Stephen George, this volume).

Gary Marks (1993: 403) suggested that: 'Several aspects of the conflict—the way in which local actors were mobilised, their alliance with the Commission, and the effectiveness of their efforts in shifting the government's position—confirm the claim that structural policy has provided subnational governments and the Commission with new political resources and opportunities in an emerging multilevel policy arena'.

The strengthened additionality requirement did provide the Commission and subnational governments with new political resources and opportunities that forced a short-term concession on additionality from the British government. However, in the longer term, the dispute did not undermine the British government's ability to continue to use EU regional funds to substitute for domestic spending (see Bache 1999: 34–5). Indeed, as Stephen George notes in this volume, the main consequence of this dispute was inadvertent: overall spending on regional development may not have increased, but there may have been a reorientation of policy priorities in favour of the Commission. While this consequence may have weakened the position of some government departments in relation to the Commission, it did not strengthen the role of subnational actors within the process and did not, therefore, advance *multi*-level governance.

The case above has been much reported. While it demonstrated the limits to multi-level governance in relation to the financial consequences of regional policy, it must be emphasized that a study of the British Conservative government's response to the additionality requirement represented perhaps the hardest test possible of the 1988 reform. This was a government that not only controlled the strongest and most centralized state apparatus in the EC at the time, but also had a leadership whose political values could not have been less sympathetic to the supranational and redistributive goals of EU regional policy. From 1979, successive Conservative governments advocated market solutions to regional problems and dismantled domestic policies of intervention. EU regional policy represented exactly the kind of 'backdoor socialism' that Conservatives repeatedly warned of coming from Brussels. There was in other words, an institutional conflict over policy control underpinned by ideological conflict between the British governing party and some of the key principles of EU regional policy set out in the 1988 reform.

The Impact of the Labour Government

It is no great secret that New Labour's victory in the 1997 general election was greeted optimistically in Brussels (and in the disadvantaged British regions). For those concerned with securing EU regional funds previously denied, the new government brought new hope. Ideologically, there were no great barriers between the objectives of EU regional policy and the regional goals of Tony Blair's incoming government. Indeed, the government's commitment to political devolution for Scotland, Wales and, in the longer term, the English regions, signalled an unprecedented support for regional autonomy. In the case of the English regions in particular, economic development goals were central to Labour's plans for devolution.

After 1997, Wales was the only British territory covered by newly devolved democratic structures that benefited from an increase in structural funding. A study of additionality in Wales following devolution found evidence that the Labour government had allowed increased public spending in Wales to take into account increased allocations to its eligible regions following the 2000 reform of the structural funds (Bache and Bristow 2003). However, while political devolution had increased the capacity of sub-central actors to scrutinize funding flows from the centre, it was not accompanied by any significant devolution of financial powers. In other words, while Labour demonstrated that it was more sympathetic to regional development, it did not change the mechanisms through which EU funds were processed: the Treasury remained in control. Actors in Wales continued to press for greater financial powers, but without success. This left open the possibility that the additional regional development funds permitted in this period, could feasibly be removed by the Treasury in another, should central government preferences change.

As George notes in Chapter 7, this volume, the determination of the Treasury to control the EU regional policy purse strings may have had inadvertent consequences for the policy control of other British government departments over other aspects of EU regional policy. However, irrespective of what British government negotiators agreed at the EU level, in the post-1997 period the Treasury again demonstrated its gatekeeping powers over the public expenditure implications of EU regional policy at the implementation stage. Moreover, there were indications that, if the government had its way, any inadvertent Europeanization of regional policy priorities resulting from Treasury gatekeeping would only remain if it met with domestic approval.

In the context of debates about the future of EU regional policy for the first post-enlargement programme period (2007–2013), the British government published *A Modern Regional Policy for the United Kingdom (2003)*. While the document was published collectively by the Treasury, the Department of Trade and Industry (DTI) and the Office of the Deputy Prime Minister (ODPM), it was the Chancellor of the Exchequer Gordon Brown who took the lead in launching and publicizing the document. The document acknowledged the need for EU regional policy to focus on the poorest member states post-enlargement and called for an end to financial transfers to the richest member states (i.e. those with greater than 90 per cent of the average EU GNP per capita measured in purchasing power parities). This would reduce the gross contributions to the EU budget of the richer states, who would then use this money for their own regional policy purposes. The preferred approach of the British government was for the English Regional Development Agencies (RDAs) and devolved legislatures of Scotland and Wales to have 'greater power and flexibility to decide

their own priorities . . . the best regional policy is now the most decentralised'
(Gordon Brown 2003: 20).

The British government's proposals would retain an overarching
EU Framework that would retain a supranational dimension to local projects,
but 'Commission regional policy resources would in future be focused on sup-
porting capacity building of institutions and infrastructure in those member
states which need it' (Treasury/DTI/ODPM 2003: 28). While there was a reasonable rationale for the approach of the British government, it was one that
had echoes of previous Conservative governments calls for 'getting our money
back from Brussels'. Institutionally, this view has long characterized the position
of the Treasury in relation to the EU budget generally and the structural funds
specifically. Politically, however, Gordon Brown and other Labour ministers had
different purposes for any reimbursed funds than their Conservative predeces-
sors, who did not value interventionist regional development measures.

This recent development illustrates how even a British government that is generally perceived as pro-EU (at least in relative terms) can advocate policies that
effectively promote European disintegration when there is a clash with domestic
priorities: in this case a different approach to regional policy. However, it is not coin-
cidental that this policy position is underpinned by the Treasury view in relation to
the control of public expenditure: institutionally, the Treasury has never accepted
that EU regional funds were anything other than 'our money' and, as such, should
be disbursed according to domestic priorities and not those of the European Union
(particularly those of the supranationally oriented Commission).

Should the Labour government position win the day, the prospects for multi-
level governance in relation to EU regional policy in Britain are bleak: at least in
the accepted notion of multi-level governance and EU regional policy as bringing together subnational, national, and supranational actors. The role of the
Commission in EU regional policy partnerships within member states reduced
significantly after the 2000 reform: under Labour's proposals, its role in the
domestic arena would disappear altogether.

However, this would not be the end to the prospects for a multi-level regional
policy in Britain. As Bache and Flinders discussed in Chapter 6, Labour's devolution policies have created a new important tier in the British constitutional
configuration. Moreover, while the devolved legislatures and RDAs (and, in
future, the probability of elected regional assemblies in at least some English
regions) will play a key role in regional policy making, the role of local actors
and central government in particular, will not evaporate. It remains significant
that, for all the additional expenditure directed towards the regions and nations
by Labour, and the promise of more under its proposals for the reform of EU
regional policy, the Treasury retains ultimate control of the purse strings. A significant change in this situation is not an immediate prospect. In other words,
EU regional policy in Britain may at some point in the future be characterized
by multi-level governance, but if the Labour government has its way, it is

unlikely to be multi-level governance as we know it: that is, the Commission will be absent.

Conclusion

Multi-level governance has a mixed record in explaining the process of implementing EU regional policy across member states. Moreover, where the evidence of multi-level governance is the strongest it is where it accords with domestic preferences and practices. What has not been explored in any detail here, but is clearly important, is the extent to which domestic preferences are shaped by EU membership. For example, while some British actors changed their view over the Commission partnership model through a process of learning, it is unlikely that the same learning process would have occurred without the EU input. Of course there is an 'uploading' dimension to this: EU policies and governance models are in part shaped by national preferences. This relationship is dynamic and complicated and not the subject of this chapter, but nonetheless deserves acknowledgement.

The picture in Britain is no less complicated. While Britain remained a strongly centralized state led by a Conservative government, the evidence of multi-level governance was limited. With an increasingly devolved and fractured state led by a Labour government, aspects of EU regional policy sit more easily with domestic arrangements and thus the notion of multi-level governance appears to have more resonance. However, even in this changing context, central government is reluctant to release its grip over the key financial channels through which EU funding flows: the financial impact of EU regional funding has remained 'high politics' even under a Labour government committed to political devolution.

Looking to the future, the impact of EU regional policy on the development of multi-level governance in Britain and the other relatively prosperous member states appears set to decline. From 2006, most funding will be redirected to the new member states of Central and Eastern Europe. At the time of writing, all the indications are that the key principles that have sought to advance a multi-level process in EU regional policy to date will apply in the post-2006 period. However, given the findings of research on extant member states on the importance of the pre-existing territorial distribution of power within states, the immediate prospects for multi-level governance in the post-communist states of Central and Eastern Europe would appear to be limited.

11

Multi-level Governance and Economic Policy

JONATHAN PERRATON AND PETER WELLS

The governance of economic policy has been seen as a core function of the nation state since the Second World War. However, economic and political developments, characterized most strongly by forces of globalization, suggest that nation states have less and less control over economic policy. Three general trends can be seen in economic policy making in the last fifty years each of which informs debates on multi-level governance. First, the ceding of power to supranational institutions in the field of economic policy making. This is exemplified by European political integration, as well as the creation of global economic institutions such as the World Trade Organization (WTO). Second, nearly all developed countries have embarked on a programme of political decentralization in the last fifty years through creating new subnational *regional* structures and/or through ceding a range of economic policy-making functions. Pressures for such decentralization and devolution have come from political pressures for greater autonomy from the nation state and a technocratic rationale that subnational government can more effectively meet the needs of citizens. Finally, a more recent development has been the pressure to reduce the size of government and for policy making to take place through new governance and partnership arrangements involving the private sector as well as agents of civil society (notably non-governmental organizations, NGOs).

The aim of this chapter is to explore the relevance of multi-level governance to contemporary economic policy making. The closest corollary to multi-level governance in economics is fiscal federalism and its concern with the optimal allocation of economic policy-making functions to jurisdictional tiers (Musgrave 1959; Oates 1972, 1999). However, in many respects this corollary is a false one, for fiscal federalism's focus is on 'aligning responsibilities and fiscal instruments with the proper levels of government . . . [and] it explores in normative and positive terms, the roles of the different levels of government and the ways in which they relate to each other through such instruments as intergovernmental grants' (Oates 1999: 1120). Fiscal federalism is concerned with issues of income (re)distribution, resource allocation, and growth. This is in contrast to multi-level governance, which is rooted in the methodological approaches of political science and focuses on interpreting and explaining evolving processes of policy making and related policy outcomes. How these two approaches might complement each other is at the heart of this chapter.

It can be argued that the restructuring of economic policy governance and the transforming role of the nation state is due to the contested notion of globalization (for contrasting analyses, see Held et al. 1999; Hirst and Thompson 1999). The elimination of barriers to cross-border economic activity, the qualitative rise in global economic flows, and the emergence of global markets and business organization has transformed the context of economic policy making. Although analysis of economic interdependence dates back at least to the 1960s (e.g. Cooper 1968), it is the globalization processes of the past twenty years that have increased both the impact of external factors on a country's economic performance and the international spillovers from economic policy decisions in any one country (Webb 1995). As governments and their citizens have become embedded in more extensive networks of economic activity and governance, national governments can no longer be regarded as the sole masters of their own or their citizens' fate. This has profound implications for the traditional Westphalian view of the state in relation to economic policy (Held 1995). In some 'hyper-globalist' accounts (see Ohmae 2000) nation states are simply losing power to private market actors, but this is too simplistic both conceptually and empirically.

Globalization acts to undermine the effectiveness of traditional economic policy instruments: spillovers increase and the relationship between policy instruments (expenditure levels, taxation rates, interest rates, etc.) and their ultimate targets (levels of unemployment, inflation, the rate of growth, and the external balance) are weakened. However, globalization is not expected to reduce either the market failures or cycles of economic activity that economic policy is traditionally designed to address, rather the reverse. Moreover, with larger and more competitive global markets, well-designed policy interventions are potentially more effective at boosting national economic performance (Kitson and Michie 1999). Furthermore, while individual governments may lack the capacity to regulate international markets, acting in consort governments may be able to create institutions for international economic governance. The creation of the European Central Bank (ECB) to oversee the European System of Central Banks (ESCB) is clearly an example of such a strategy.

For our purposes, the key point here is that the economic analysis of the appropriate division of functions between national and subnational government is now increasingly used to analyse the appropriate division of functions between national governments and supranational or global bodies. Therefore, from an economic perspective there has been a change of emphasis as scholars have shifted their attention from a consideration of the merits of delegation downwards to subnational actors towards an analysis of delegating functions upwards to supranational actors in the hope of avoiding the negative impacts of globalization.

The remainder of this chapter is made up of four sections. The first section 'Fiscal Federalism'...' outlines the analytical approach of fiscal federalism. In the next section 'Multi-level Governance Problems ...' we consider two case studies to illustrate: the process of decentralization in the transition economies of Eastern and Central Europe and the ceding of monetary policy to the European level by countries in the Euro zone. These case studies will allow us to gauge differences in the structures and processes of multi-level governance across economic policy sectors. The third section 'Towards Global Economic Governance?' reflects on how far economic governance has shifted to the supranational level in response to the globalization of economic activity, and on the implications that such a shift may present to the power, position and role of the nation state. The main themes and implications of this chapter are brought together in the concluding section.

Fiscal Federalism: Scope, New Developments and Limitations

The conceptual framework of fiscal federalism was developed by Wallace Oates (1972) and sits within Musgrave's (1959) theory of public finance. Following Musgrave's work, Oates (1972, 1999) argues that central government should have responsibility for macroeconomic stabilization and income redistribution (such as welfare payments). The main reasons for this are that local economies are highly open and that local government is constrained because it cannot influence monetary policy instruments (primarily, the interest rate and the exchange rate). Any local attempts to use fiscal instruments to boost the local economy would therefore be futile, as benefits would quickly leak away. Indeed this is reflected in the public accounts of all developed countries where, even in federal systems, a high proportion of government revenues are collected through national tax systems, and expenditure is distributed by the central state—although it may be through revenue sharing, block grants and other fiscal transfers to decentralized areas.

Oates suggests the strength of subnational government lies in the provision of goods and services that are consumed locally. The reasoning behind Oates' argument is that as individual preferences for public goods varies, as well as the cost of producing them varying across areas, it is the local level that will provide the most efficient scale at which to produce them. However, if preferences were believed to be less heterogeneous, then the national level would be the most efficient level for producing them. The guiding principles of fiscal federalism are that the central state has imperfect information on individual preferences and that this leads to inefficiency and the suboptimal allocation of public goods, and that political pressures or constitutional issues may constrain governments from providing higher levels of services in some areas than others.

Oates highlights that fiscal federalism is not intended to provide a static analysis of the optimum assignment of fiscal functions but rather should be applied to emerging issues that confront the state in the delivery of public goods. For example, as states have increasingly developed environmental policies, there is evidence that existing jurisdictions may be inappropriate for addressing problems. Many boundaries are located along rivers that in terms of fiscal federalism's pursuit of economic efficiency in the delivery of public goods are the most irrational place for the implementation of water management and pollution policies. Although shared competencies, or other forms of inter-regional governance between bordering jurisdictions may be the solution, unless these can be legally binding or defended constitutionally, then there is an incentive for jurisdictions to act as free riders. Fiscal federalism, therefore, provides a basis for examining the economic efficiency of differing forms of multi-level governance and the two approaches would therefore appear to be complementary. However, a limitation of the traditional fiscal federalism approach is its concern with the assignment of functions for the delivery of *public goods*.

Fiscal federalism has begun to take on developments in other disciplines and within economics itself. This could potentially strengthen its application to the analysis of economic policy making. Oates (1999) suggests two examples. First, the form of governance greatly affects the policy making and the effectiveness of policy implementation. Much of the fiscal federalist literature proposes a trade-off between economic efficiency and political participation: for example, Inman and Rubinfield (1997) argue that greater participation in decentralized systems of government is more likely to reduce economic efficiency. Although there is limited evidence to support or refute this hypothesis, it does appear that the design of political institutions across different jurisdictional tiers, and in particular citizen participation in those institutions, can influence efficiency (de Mello 2000a). This raises an issue of 'trade-off' between democratic notions, such as accountability and participation, and more managerial concerns, such as efficiency and control (Oughton 1995) which has been largely overlooked in the literature on multi-level governance (although see Pierre and Peters, Chapter 5, this volume). Conversely, the adoption of a zero-sum game may be flawed. The introduction of participatory mechanisms in the design stage and scrutiny mechanisms at the implementation stage of new governance structures may produce a positive-sum gain where democratic and managerial concepts become complementary and mutually reinforcing.

The second development in fiscal federalism has been the focus on whether political decentralization preserves and supports growing and productive markets (Oates 1999: 1139). The most provocative development here has been by Weingast in what he terms 'market preserving federalism' (Weingast 1995; Qian and Weingast 1997). For Weingast, a decentralized political system can support the operation of markets if certain conditions are met. These conditions require that: decentralized governments have the primary regulatory responsibility over the economy; the economic system constitutes a common market with no barriers to trade; and that decentralized governments face hard budget constraints. Returning to Musgrave's theory of public finance, this means that local government has no access to the instruments of monetary policy and will not be 'bailed out' by central government. However, local government should have access to capital markets, in particular, for financing long-term infrastructure investment. The rationale underpinning Weingast's approach is that (national and subnational) institutions should be designed in such a way that makes the full costs of public programmes visible to local electorates. Authors in this area have attributed (in part) rising government expenditure and deficits in the past to fiscal decentralization in the absence of hard budget constraints from the centre (von Hagen and Harden 1995). As Oates remarks, Weingast's approach assumes that subnational governments aim to maximize the extraction of tax revenues from the economy (Oates 1999: 1140). If Weingast's three conditions are met, it is possible to reason that the overall size of government expenditure will, *ceteris paribus*, be smaller (cf. Brennan and Buchanan's (1980) 'Leviathan' thesis). There is some evidence that in practice fiscal decentralization in developed countries is associated with lower public expenditure (Moesen and van Cauwenberge 2000).

As to the question of whether political decentralization increases economic performance there is limited evidence one way or the other to support this case. Huther and Shah (1996) drawing on a wide ranging data set (of eighty countries and including measures of governance, political stability, income, income distribution, and public debt) show that there is a significant and positive correlation between increased decentralization and improved economic and political performance. However, this does not prove causation (either way) and any process of decentralization will be part of a wider social, political and economic process. Almost innumerable statistical analyses have found many possible factors in determining economic growth but these often prove to be very sensitive to the sample used (Sala-i-Martin 1997).

A more critical reading of Weingast's approach and that of Brennan and Buchanan (1980) suggests that such a reductionist and libertarian view of government, based on the theory of competitive federalism (Hayek 1979), may create market distorting effects. Predicting whether decentralization encouraging fiscal competition will improve welfare, partly turns on the starting assumption of whether the authorities are attempting to maximize social welfare in their jurisdiction, or are bureaucratic 'Leviathans' pursuing their own interests, or are somewhere in between. However, even under the 'Leviathan' assumption, fiscal competition can lead to suboptimal provision of public goods (Oates 1999, 2001). Rounds of inter-jurisdictional competition may arise in which rival local governments compete for mobile factors of production: in particular capital and highly qualified labour. To do this, local governments are likely to cut business related taxes and income taxes and to increase indirect taxes, particularly value added tax on consumer goods, and property taxes. In the short term, this will result in a shift towards more regressive tax systems, and in the longer term, suboptimal production of public goods. Some empirical findings suggest that in both Europe and the United States, state and local governments are competing actively for mobile capital through financial inducements and the loosening of planning controls. The outcome of such inter-jurisdictional competition is at best a series of zero-sum games (Amin and Malmberg 1992; Dunford 1994; Amin and Tomaney 1995). Moreover, although in principle the European Commission operates strict rules on such state aids to industry, in practice it approves virtually all applications and fails to prevent wasteful competition between authorities to offer inducements (Besley and Seabright 1999).

To restate, multi-level governance and fiscal federalism appear to be complementary methodological approaches, developed in separate academic disciplines, each with quite distinct concerns. Fiscal federalism appears to sharpen the definition of multi-level governance through providing an approach to compare the economic outcomes from different governance arrangements. However, fiscal federalism is weak in explaining the optimum allocation of functions where policies are not bundled together and delivered through a limited number of jurisdictions (what Hooghe and Marks in Chapter 2, of this volume, refer to as Type 1 multi-level governance,). This is the case in many new governance forms such as partnerships that seem to denote the Type II governance characteristics that Hooghe and Marks noted in Part One. Another limitation of fiscal federalism relates to its traditional emphasis on intergovernmental relationships. The concept of governance refers to a much wider range of organizations than those traditionally included within the 'governmental' framework and yet it is unclear how fiscal federalism could accommodate the role of quasi-autonomous agencies, commissions, regulators, private sector actors, and other organizations. Despite these limitations, it is possible to suggest that it still has wide relevance to issues in contemporary economic policy making and can contribute to understanding the nature and development of multi-level governance.

Multi-level Governance Problems in Economic Policy Making

This section draws on the literature of fiscal federalism and public finance to present two case studies of multi-level governance in economic policy making. The case studies are: economic reform and decentralization in (Eastern and Central European) transition economies; and macroeconomic policy coordination in the European Monetary Union. The aim of each case study is to review the governance of each policy area and assess the economic implications of the form of multi-level governance that has emerged. We have chosen these studies for several reasons. First, they are related to the EU's twin objectives of enlargement and monetary union. Second, the study of transition economies highlights the role of international economic agencies in economic governance. Third, it allows us to highlight the wider agenda of fiscal federalism theorists.

Fiscal Decentralization and Transition Economies

The process of economic and political transition in the former communist countries of Eastern and Central Europe since 1989 has demonstrated the multi-level characteristics of economic policy making. Moreover, the policy prescriptions of the IMF, World Bank and Organization for Economic Cooperation and Development (OECD) stress the importance of a well-functioning fiscal system for achieving other reform objectives: macroeconomic stabilization, private sector development, and a social safety net to protect those hurt by transition (Wallich et al. 1995). Furthermore, as an IMF study highlights, 'increased fiscal decentralization in itself, is seen as an important means of increasing democratic participation in the decision making process' (Dabla-Norris and Wade 2002: 3). Given the central importance of macroeconomic stabilization to the transition process, the same authors note that the 'manner in which decentralization is carried out can have a significant impact on macreconomic management and performance' (2002: 3). In line with the public choice arguments made by Weingast, Brennan and Buchanan, the international economic institutions stress the importance of institutional design, the need to combat corruption and the importance of reducing the prevalence of the state in economic and social life.

The World Bank Institute (responsible for managing support programmes for senior policy makers in developing and transition economies) stresses in its Programme for Intergovernmental Fiscal Relations:

The theme that emerges is that a well functioning intergovernmental, or decentralized, system is often integral to the ability to compete globally. Intergovernmental finances affect the degree to which the public sector can mobilize resources and, in turn, promote the allocative efficiency for the nation as a whole. In most economies, intergovernmental finances also influence macro-economic stability, the provision of the social safety net, and the pace and depth of privatization. In countries with a limited tradition of self government, developing effective subnational (e.g., local) fiscal and political institutions is critical for nation building (World Bank Institute 2002).

Although the fiscal decentralization reforms of the transition economies can be interpreted as providing a model for transition that supports democracy and a plurality of public institutions across tiers of government, it is of particular note that the international economic institutions have placed greatest emphasis on a particular model of multi-level governance which creates the basis for reducing the overall size of the (multi-level) state in social and economic life. Although in comparison to the previous command economy this approach can be supported as improving efficiency in the allocation of public goods, it does set in train a process that allows the role of the state to be continually reduced.

Various World Bank, IMF, and OECD studies (Tanzi 1995; de Mello 2000b; OECD 2001a,b) have found that the process of reforming intergovernmental relations since 1989 has been uneven. As Dabla-Norris and Wade (2002: 40) argue the, 'nature and extent of decentralization to date has been shaped in large measure by political, historical, and ethnic realities, and its effectiveness influenced by the institutional design and capacities of the various levels of government'. For example, Dunn and Wetzel (1999) find that 'Hungary, Poland and the Czech Republic are in many respects furthest ahead with decentralization [whilst] . . . in Ukraine and Russia, decentralization has come about through informal mechanisms or unilateral actions by different levels of government responding to an acute fiscal crisis, a political upheaval or vacuum, civil disturbance, or military conflict' (Dunn and Wetzel 1999: 6).

The key point to draw from these country studies is that multi-level governance takes different forms and is shaped by the norms, values and institutions of particular countries. Consequently, the framework of multi-level governance in the economic sector is frequently significantly different to the policy prescriptions that international economic institutions have made for these countries. However, these institutions do not interpret the variance in the transition process as the basis to seek alternative approaches to fiscal decentralization. In many respects, this highlights the contradictions of the model of fiscal decentralization that is being applied in the transition countries. For example, most analyses of regional economic growth stress that an important condition for entrepreneurial activity (leading to higher new firm formation rates) and foreign investment is a stable economic, political, and social environment (Armstrong and Taylor 2000). This line of reasoning is consistent with the critique of the current IMF and past World Bank policies by, amongst others, former World Bank chief economist Joseph Stiglitz (2002).

Fiscal decentralization in transition economies provides an example of multi-level governance in action which is closest to the fiscal federalism of Wallace Oates, but also of the wider public choice and libertarian agenda to use transition as a mechanism to radically reduce the size and remit of the state. Coupled to wider economic reform policies (of privatization and liberalization) it would appear that the goal of short-term macroeconomic stabilization might face the trade-off of greater political and social unrest that jeopardizes the longer-term process of transition. Although the main actors within the framework of multi-level governance in the transition economies are the different tiers of government, their economic agenda, or rules of the game, is set by the international economic institutions and international capital. Thus raising questions about the power and accountability of international economic institutions vis-à-vis nation states and their citizens (Woods and Narlikar 2001).

Macroeconomic Policy Coordination in the European Monetary Union

The design of the EMU institutions and the launch of the Euro in 2001 have shaped the monetary and fiscal policies of both member countries as well as the three EU countries outside EMU. The EMU has a number of unique elements of a multi-level policy-making system. First, the currency is not backed by a single state but, at the time of writing, by a union of twelve members. Moreover, fiscal and monetary powers are separated between the member countries and the ECB, albeit coordinated by the set of rules and procedures laid down by the Maastricht Treaty and the Stability and Growth Pact (SGP). The design of EMU has been held up to be an example of governance and institutional failure, and as a *cause* of the Euro's weakness and decline vis-à-vis the pound and the US dollar (Arestis et al. 2002*a,b*). This section suggests that the multi-level design of EMU governance has fundamental flaws and reviews whether these are best addressed by strengthening the rules for macroeconomic policy coordination or whether more far reaching change is required.

The EMU framework for policy coordination relies on assigning responsibility for the single monetary policy to the ECB, while other economic policies are carried out by governments under the subsidiary principle but subject to the rules laid down in the Maastricht Treaty and the SGP. EMU seeks to combine discipline and flexibility through two requirements of the SGP. First, budgetary position should be close to balance or in surplus over the medium term as required by the SGP and, second, that the general government deficit remains below 3 per cent of GDP unless there are exceptional circumstances. Failure to meet these fiscal targets can result in fines. However, there is still confusion as to how the policy framework should operate. Moreover, as most of the EMU members were already close to the 3 per cent deficit at the launch of the Euro and that they had all cut public expenditure, the 'close to balance' requirement of the SGP has required further fiscal restraint. Countries have also resorted to creative fiscal accounting to meet these targets. At the time of writing sluggish economic performance in the Euro zone has pushed several member countries, including France and Germany, close to the 3 per cent limit. Even the *Economist* (28 September 2002), usually a bastion of fiscal conservatism, has recently asserted that 'Europe's Stability Pact is too rigid' and called for its limits to be loosened to permit greater latitude for counter-cyclical fiscal policy.

The argument for fiscal policy coordination in a monetary union arises because the budgetary policies of individual member countries may affect not only on their own economy but also on the stability of the whole currency area. This may be through intra-currency union area trade flows (which are relatively high within the core EU members), through the area wide interest rate, and through the common external exchange rate. Without policy coordination there could be spillover effects leading to suboptimal policy outcomes. As the Luxembourg Resolution on Economic Policy Coordination of December 1997 argues:

To the extent that national economic developments have an impact on inflation prospects in the Euro area, they will influence monetary conditions in that area. It is for this basic reason that the move to a single currency will require closer Community surveillance and coordination of economic policies (cited in Brunila 2002: 9).

The SGP together with the Broad Economic Policy Guidelines (BEPGs) form the basic devices for fiscal policy coordination at the EU level. Coordination of fiscal policies can take many forms highlighting the complex governance arrangements of EMU (including the use of information exchange, multilateral surveillance of common rules and procedures and peer pressure). The responsibility for policy coordination is shared across the European Commission, ECOFIN Council, the Euro group, the Economic and Financial Committee, and the Economic Policy Committee. While the European Commission undertakes monitoring and surveillance activities, the main responsibilities rest with the Council. As Brunila (2002: 9) comments, 'it [the Council] endorses BEPGs, makes formal decisions on recommendations, gives opinion on Stability Programmes, decides on the existence of excessive deficit and the application of sanctions'.

The question arising from the institutional design and coordination procedures surrounding EMU is whether they support or undermine economic stability? Moreover, as others have argued (Budd 2000; Arestis et al. 2002a,b) do they also weaken the policy credibility of the EMU as indicated in the performance of the Euro? Most analysis of currency unions accept that there is a need for supranational fiscal rules to prevent political distortions (such as deficit bias, moral hazard, and free riding) and which in turn could 'result in negative financial market spillovers and erode the credibility of the common monetary policy' (Buiter et al. 1993; Beetsma and Uhlig 1999; Brunila 2002: 10). Nevertheless, even here the limits of the SGP appear excessively stringent: evidence from US states indicates that excessive spending by one state has limited impact on interest rates for others (Eichengreen and Wyplosz 1998).

How policy coordination is achieved in EMU—in terms of institutional design, rules and instruments—remains contested. The seminal work of Mundell (1961) on Optimum Currency Area theory and reflected in the Keynesian view of the MacDougall report (European Commission 1977) is that adjustment to asymmetric shocks affecting regions with a common currency works most effectively where there is a central or federal government collecting taxes from and paying taxes to these regions. The critical question for the European Commission is not whether such a system should be established but what level of fiscal transfers are required. The approach advocated by MacDougall and Delors clearly requires a reordering of the governance of European economic policy. In the context of EMU, it would give the European Union institutions much greater influence in both monetary and fiscal policy. However, Fatas (1998) argues that the stabilizing effect of the Federal budget in the US is overestimated in the studies cited above and that national governments can still stabilize their economies using fiscal policy; this does, though, also point towards relaxing the provisions of the SGP.

Otmar Issing (2002: 345), a Member of the Executive Board of the ECB, argues that 'there are no convincing arguments in favour of attempts to coordinate macroeconomic policies *ex ante* in order to achieve an overall policy favourable to growth and employment'. In contrast to Brunila's (2002) argument for harder and deeper forms of coordination, Issing argues that attempts which 'extend beyond the informational exchange of views and information give rise to the risk of confusing specific roles, mandates and responsibilities of the policies in question' (Issing 2002: 345). Issing therefore suggests that whilst national governments and social partners (in wage bargaining) should bear in mind the Maastricht framework and the SGP they should be left to govern the policies for which they are responsible. However, Issing argues that if governments and social partners take seriously the ECB's commitment to maintaining price stability (the primary objective being the setting of interest rates) then this will lead to '*implicitly* coordinated policy outcomes *ex post*, while at the same time limiting policy conflicts and overall economic uncertainty' (italics in original, Issing 2002: 346).

The case for the relaxation of *explicit* and *ex ante* policy coordination is based on the rejection of the notion that welfare gains can be achieved through negotiated and bargained equilibrium. Issing and others suggest three main reasons for the rejection of the bargained and coordinated approach. First, that empirical estimates suggest that the gains from coordination are small. Second, that coordination involves time lags because it is difficult for policy makers to identify the scale and scope of asymmetric shocks. Finally, policy coordination among several actors can distort their individual incentives to take action. In the worst cases, attempts to coordinate policy across jurisdictions can lead to 'free riding' behaviour and the attendant problems of enforcement. Therefore, the argument of the ECB is that its responsibility is to maintain overall price stability in the medium term through interest rates and for national governments to contribute to economic stability through their control of fiscal policy.

The divergent views here reflect differing assumptions over the nature of the shocks likely to hit the Euro zone economies, the economic impact of those shocks, and the efficacy of government macroeconomic policy (individually or coordinated) in response. Nevertheless, under demand-side shocks not only are unemployment and output losses likely, but the SGP is likely to aggravate the impact of such shocks by limiting governments' ability to use counter-cyclical fiscal policy (cf. Eichengreen and Wyplosz 1998; Creel 2002). Under some simulations at least, coordinated fiscal policy would raise welfare under these circumstances (Neck et al. 2002).

Significantly, the ECB and commentators such as Kletzer and von Hagen (2000) do not deny that there will be asymmetric shocks in a monetary union. However, following the arguments of Sala-i-Martin and others (Barro and Sala-i-Martin 1990; Sala-i-Martin and Sachs 1992) these will not cause persistent and structural imbalances between regions if labour markets are flexible and all barriers to trade are removed. This logic is reflected in the conclusions of March 2000 Lisbon European Council, which agreed a wide ranging strategy for improving employment, investment and growth prospects in the European Union (European Council 2000).

Arestis et al. (2002*a*,*b*) and Budd (2000) take issue with the institutional design and coordination framework of EMU. They argue that the governance failure of EMU and the SGP coordination procedures is because they have not only taken insufficient note of the persistent structural imbalances between regions (which mean that asymmetric shocks may have consequences into the medium term) but have also reduced the credibility of EMU and hence undermined the position of the Euro. Although Arestis et al. (2002*a*) accept the need for clarity in the roles and instruments of the different institutions (as per Issing); they reject the argument that there is little need for *ex ante* and *explicit* coordination of policy between member countries and the EMU institutions.

Arestis et al. (2002*a*,*b*) argue that the EU economy remains extremely heterogeneous and that there has been little observed convergence between the economies in the last 20 years. This analysis is based both on indicators such as employment, income and the state of national government finances (borrowing requirements and long-term debt). Critically, the authors find limited evidence of convergence in the business cycles between EMU members. Without a trend towards convergence, asymmetric shocks will remain severe. Moreover, and based on these real observations, it can be argued that Maastricht criteria and SGP rules for coordination may exacerbate regional disparities. Policies advanced by the Lisbon Council to increase labour market flexibility therefore appear to rest on weak assumptions and critically the capacity for labour market flexibility (and inter regional mobility) to approach the level of the United States.

In conclusion, EMU has not previously been the subject of extensive analysis for scholars of multi-level governance. However, it is clear that the EMU, and in particular the SGP and the role of the ECB, suggest that formal and informal processes of multi-level governance are in operation. The governance provisions of EMU are very rigid with clearly defined roles for different tiers of government. Therefore, in this policy sector multi-level governance is hierarchical. However, this raises two interesting governance issues. First, what effect do the policy coordination mechanisms (whether implicit or explicit) have on policy outcomes? Despite the formal prescriptions of EMU, governance and political action would still appear to matter. Second, the strongest explanations of the governance of EMU appear to rest on the role of institutions (the ECB) and states and the mobilization of their interests through intergovernmental and supranational institutions. The role of other policy actors (e.g. from wider civil society and NGOs) is largely peripheral. This would appear to conflict with much of the literature on multi-level governance which downplays the role of powerful state and institutional actors.

Towards Global Economic Governance?

Although we have noted trends towards globalization of economic activity, thus far we have said little about global economic governance, although we have noted the role of international agencies in transition economies. This is partly because the principles of fiscal federalism have few applications here: the budgets of international agencies are small and dependent on national government contributions. The United Nations and associated agencies do not have effective resources to promote global public goods or tax global public 'bads', such as pollution, overuse of the seas, etc. (Mendez 1992). More fundamentally, we suggest that there are few genuine institutions of global economic governance.

There have been many proposals for governance of global economic architecture, particularly reform of the international financial system after the late 1990s crises, but there has been little tangible reform. Although governments do regularly exchange information through meetings of the G5, G7, G8, etc., this does not amount to formal policy coordination in the terms discussed above in relation to EMU. In part, this may reflect limited potential gains from coordination, as with the EMU case examined above. However, it also reflects governments' reluctance to cede autonomy over macroeconomic policy which is compounded by governments having limited powers over their own central banks as these have increasingly become independent of political authorities (Elgie 1998, 2001; McNamara 2002). After potential crisis episodes, notably the October 1987 global stock market crash and the 1997–1998 currency crises, the US Federal Reserve aggressively cut interest rates to prevent global recession and other central banks largely followed suit. This leadership by the Federal Reserve, rather than negotiated policy coordination, partly reflects the continued economic hegemony of the US. However, recently this has also been attributable to the policy conservatism of the ECB as it tries to establish its credibility and to the ineffectiveness of the Bank of Japan in the face of persistent deflation. It is debatable how far the absence of global regulatory authorities reflects technical difficulties of regulating global markets and how far it simply reflects a failure of political will (Held et al. 1999; Hirst and Thompson 1999).

We have already noted the role of international agencies, notably the IMF and World Bank, in the transition economies. At any time, around 70–90 developing and transition economies are operating under IMF programmes. As the roles of the IMF and World Bank have become blurred, both have become heavily involved in economic policy making across a range of countries. Moreover, both have often been seen as promulgating the 'Washington Consensus', a policy package of liberalizing markets (particularly the trade regime and financial system), privatizing state-owned enterprises, reducing government expenditure and restoring fiscal balance, and tight monetary policy to control inflation. The IMF has been heavily involved in the aftermath of late 1990s financial crises, although its interventions were widely criticized and often claimed to have aggravated the situation (e.g. Stiglitz 2002).

Nevertheless, it is important to recognize the limits of these institutions as global governance mechanisms. They do not have power over international economic activity: the IMF is not an international 'lender of last resort' and neither it nor the World Bank has regulatory powers. In this respect, the IMF's powers have diminished since it functioned as regulator of the Bretton Woods fixed exchange rate system. Formally, these institutions cannot impose policies: notwithstanding the power asymmetries involved, IMF and World Bank programmes must be agreed with the national government concerned, and there remains some space for bargaining and negotiation (Mosely et al. 1995). Further, criticisms of the IMF from inside the World Bank (Stiglitz 2002) and beyond have led the latter to move towards a 'post Washington Consensus' that pays more attention to the historical and institutional specificities of each country and a less doctrinaire approach to liberalization (see Fine et al. 2001 for a critical assessment).

The one major institution of global economic governance is the WTO. The WTO does have considerable regulatory powers over national governments. Whilst the preceding GATT regime had limited powers and was largely concerned with reducing tariffs on manufacturing goods amongst developed countries, the WTO is a truly global institution, with equal voting rights. This is unlike the IMF and World Bank, where voting rights reflect shareholdings. Indeed, a major cause of the failure of the 1999 Seattle WTO negotiations was developing countries' unwillingness to accept the deal presented to them. In practice, though, developing countries often lack access to specialist legal and technical support during WTO negotiations and dispute settlements. The WTO has moved beyond trade in goods to cover a range of policy areas, including investment measures, intellectual property rights, and services. The General Agreement on Trade in Services may be particularly significant, since some authorities argue its provisions could be used to open up public sector service providers to market competition. Further, by a two-thirds majority the WTO can vote to bring any new subject into its ambit. The more invasive nature of the WTO regime and its shift to deeper harmonization than the GATT regime is indicated by references to dispute panels: while there was around 120 references to the GATT disputes panel over 1948–1990, since 1995 there have been 268 references to the WTO disputes panel (October 2002 figure). The WTO effectively prohibits many of the policy instruments to promote domestic industry used by currently developed countries during their industrialization and, more recently, by newly industrializing countries like Korea and Taiwan during their postwar development (Chang 2002; Perraton 2004).

Overall, despite the globalization of economic activity, governments have been unwilling to cede power over the provision of public goods or over macroeconomic policy to supranational bodies, or to coordinate their policy responses to economic fluctuations. To a considerable degree, national authorities (and markets) have put their faith in the US Federal Reserve offering effective policy leadership. The key institutional development here is EMU, but this is in part a defensive *regional* response to globalization. Thus, whilst the efficacy of the key functions of government expenditure highlighted by the fiscal federalist literature may have been undermined by globalization processes, this has not led to a political will emerging to coordinate economic policy. International economic agencies continue to promote balanced budgets, often in the context of reducing government expenditure, and strongly anti-inflationary monetary policy amongst developing and transitional countries. Arguably, though, the most significant development is not in the areas of government expenditure and revenue-raising but in microeconomic policy: the WTO places significant limits on government intervention and contains the potential at least for more invasive moves towards harmonization.

Conclusions

To date, there have been few attempts to incorporate the insights of multi-level governance into areas such as economic transition in central and eastern European countries or EMU. Moreover, the approach has not been used by economists in research considering issues of growth, stability, and redistribution. Despite this, different configurations of multi-level governance can be held, a priori, to have an effect on economic policy outcomes although the evidence is not clear as to the scale and direction of its effect. Theoretical approaches embodied in fiscal federalism and empirical studies on EMU and transition economies do not provide conclusive evidence one way or the other of its effect.

It is clear that structures and processes of multi-level governance vary across different areas of economic policy making. However, in the areas reviewed here, including the consideration of global economic governance, the role of states and the bargaining structures they create play a dominant role in explaining policy outcomes. This suggests that although multi-level governance does offer insights into these policy sectors, there are also rival and competing explanations that should not be discounted.

The policy areas we have explored have tended to be those that have neat hierarchical tiers. The exception to this is that of global economic governance where non-state actors, such as companies and NGOs, have been able to influence policy outcomes. The mechanisms through which this has occurred have typically been horizontal and multilateral and separate to the traditional jurisdictional tiers applied to state and federal systems. However, a common concern of economists and political scientists with economic policy has been the continued role of the national state and in particular the competing analyses of globalization. Multi-level governance clearly offers some insights here in relation to defensive reactions to managing globalization. This is a worrisome conclusion, but one that is reflected in the emergence and growth of the WTO as the only genuine institution of global governance.

In conclusion, it appears that multi-level governance has much to offer in the explanation of economic policy outcomes and would complement economic analyses, such as fiscal federalism. However, there are risks in extending this too far: partly because it is easy to find hierarchical relationships in a myriad of economic policy domains, but also because multi-level governance downplays explanations centred on the relationship between states and markets.

12

Conclusions and Implications

IAN BACHE AND MATTHEW FLINDERS

One thing is clear from this collection, that multi-level governance is used in different ways and for different purposes. Crucially, there is a need to distinguish between multi-level governance as an analytical model and multi-level governance as a normative concept. Our central task in this volume has been to evaluate multi-level governance as an analytical model: to assess how it captures the changing nature of decision making in the context of complexity. This task, guided by the themes set out in Chapter 1, is addressed below. However, such is the attention given by contributors to this volume in relation to multi-level governance as a normative concept, we discuss this issue first.

Multi-level Governance as a Normative Concept

For a number of contributors, multi-level governance is emerging as a normatively superior mode of allocating authority. Moreover, multi-level governance has been assimilated into the discourse of practitioners to describe developments in the European Union, notably by European Commission officials (COM 428 2001). As Hooghe and Marks (Chapter 2) suggest, its main advantage lies in its 'scale flexibility' in that it 'allows jurisdictions to be custom-designed in response to externalities, economies of scale, ecological niches, and preferences' (p.29). However, beyond this appreciation is dispute about how multi-level governance should be organized to maximize its advantages (e.g. efficiency) and minimize its costs (e.g. accountability). Here, the distinction between Type I and Type II developed by Hooghe and Marks is helpful in highlighting the differing qualities of different types of multi-level governance (p.17). Type I multi-level governance creates *general-purpose jurisdictions* with non-intersecting memberships, with jurisdictions at lower tiers nested into higher ones; it is oriented towards intrinsic communities and suited to the articulation and resolution of conflict. By contrast, Type II consists of *special-purpose jurisdictions* focused around particular policy problems and is more suited to Pareto-optimality.

Yet, on the value of multi-level governance as a mode of organizing authority there are dissenting voices. Jessop is keen to emphasize that governance, like markets and hierarchies, is prone to failure. This is in part because governance theories are closely associated with problem solving and crisis management in relation to specific issues, when issues of *metagovernance* (the 'ground rules' for governance) may be more pertinent. In the context of the European Union, this leads to the relative neglect of 'questions of the relative compatibility or incompatibility of different governance regimes and their implications for the overall unity of the European project and European statehood' (p.61). Welch and Kennedy-Pipe (Chapter 8) raise a related issue, citing the work of Paul Cammack, which chimes with the notion of metagovernance. This is the role of the World Bank's Comprehensive Development Framework as a 'management tool' for monitoring government policies, which Cammack suggests reflects the Bank's aspiration to be 'the mother of all governments'.

This discussion raises two issues that are worthy of further investigation. The first is whether there is anything intrinsic to multi-level governance as an analytical framework that would exclude a simultaneous focus on both metagovernance and governance issues as Jessop defines them: the case might be made that such a focus is at least an aspiration of the concept. The second, for those concerned with issues of institutional and/or policy efficiency, is how we measure the impact or outcomes of multi-level governance processes. There are claims and counterclaims about the efficiency or otherwise of different governance structures, but little agreement about the appropriate methodological tools for investigation and measurement. The suggestion by Perraton and Wells (Chapter 10) that fiscal federalism might be a valuable complement to multi-level governance in this respect is one worth pursuing for those concerned with issues of efficiency. We return to some of these issues in the final section, but now we turn to the seven themes outlined in the opening chapter of this volume that largely addresses the issue of multi-level governance as an analytical concept.

How Should Multi-level Governance be Defined?

In Orwell's (1946) 'Politics and the English Language' he lamented the often purposive use of conceptual imprecision in order to justify certain actions, decisions or viewpoints, suggesting that 'political language has to consist largely of euphemism, question-begging and sheer cloudy vagueness' (1946: 153). Gallie (1955) developed this line of argument in his work on the 'essentially contested' nature of concepts. In this view, concepts become so permeated and surrounded by values that scholars may argue interminably without ever reaching agreement on their meaning and implications (Birch 1993: 8). While it is possible to criticize Gallie's position (Ball 1988), it usefully underpins the nature of the debate on multi-level governance as we seek to assess its value from different perspectives.

Throughout the volume, contributors have discussed the need for conceptual clarity in relation to the related notions of governance and multi-level governance. As concepts become more widely applied, they can become devoid of meaning. By bringing together diverse contributions on a common theme, we have sought to identify common understandings and applications of the concept. Four common strands have emerged. First, that decision making at various territorial levels is characterized by the increased participation of non-state actors. Second, that the identification of discrete or nested territorial levels of decision making is becoming more difficult in the context of complex overlapping networks. Third, that in this changing context the role of the state is being transformed as state actors develop new strategies of coordination, steering, and networking to protect and, in some cases, enhance state autonomy. Fourth, that in this changing context, the nature of democratic accountability has been challenged and need to be rethought or at least reviewed. These common strands provide the basis for a parsimonious definition of multi-level governance that raise clear hypotheses for future research.

How is Multi-level Governance utilized by Scholars Working in Different Disciplinary Traditions?

Here we draw specifically on contributions to Part Two of this volume, in which the authors utilize multi-level governance in the traditionally separate academic (sub)disciplines of British Politics, European Studies and International Relations. More general observations on the different interpretations and applications of multi-level governance are contained under the various headings of this chapter.

Given its origins, it is unsurprising that the application and maturity of multi-level governance is most advanced in the field of EU studies. In this field, George suggests, it is an established theory of EU policy making, which generates clear expectations that draw on neo-functionalist antecedents. Crucially, multi-level governance suggests an emerging dynamic in the context of European integration that pulls authority away from national governments and empowers subnational and supranational actors. The consequence of this is that governments will be taken further along the road of diffused authority than they originally intended.

As the concept has travelled to different areas of study, it is been applied in varying ways. In its application to British politics, Bache and Flinders (Chapter 6) suggest the concept has potential as an organizing perspective: a map of how things (inter)relate that leads to a set of research questions. The theoretical dimension to multi-level *governance* here is strengthened in this context by incorporation of hypotheses from the differentiated polity model, which posits aspects of a fragmented versus centralized executive. The multi-level component of the concept is useful in this case for highlighting the changing nature of vertical relationships in the context of devolution and, within this new context, the changing state strategies aimed at maximizing control and coordination.

In applying multi-level governance to international relations, Welch and Kennedy-Pipe use it as a contrastive concept alongside the more commonly applied notion of governance. The contrast is made with the notion of government, in a tradition where government refers to 'the political control of a centralized state' and (multi-level) governance 'denotes the coordination of social relations in the absence of a unifying authority'. Alongside this contrastive application, is the use of governance as a generic term similar to authority or coordination. This strategy is necessary in the context of the international realm, where the absence of discrete policy areas suggests that the application of multi-level governance to individual case studies, as is the case with the European Union, is not possible. Instead, the authors take a synoptic view to investigate issue areas of international relations where the question of the distribution of authority arises: governance in the generic sense. While the generic use of governance guides the choice of issue areas, the contrastive concept is used to address a number of questions in these areas relating to the nature of power and authority.

How do the Structures and Processes of Multi-level Governance Differ Across Policy Sectors and how Can these Differences be Explained?

Here, we consider the application of multi-level governance to the policy sectors in Part three of the book: environmental policy, EU regional policy and economic policy. Each of these policies has a strong EU dimension, which reflects both the advanced use of multi-level governance in this area of study and the development of discrete EU policy competences in these sectors. The three sectoral studies provided a mix of 'easy' and 'hard' tests for multi-level governance. Conventionally, environmental and regional policies are considered 'low politics' areas for national governments, while economic policy is generally recognized as 'high politics' (Hoffmann 1966, 1982). The structures and processes of multi-level governance differed across the case studies. The case of regional policy highlights the effective formalization and promotion of multi-level governance relations through the partnership principle, the case of environmental policy suggests multi-level interactions that were less formalized but nonetheless evident, while the case of economic policy highlights more formal layering of authority and less evidence of non-state and multi-level interaction. However, despite the differences in structures and processes of multi-level governance, there were some commonalities in terms of outcomes.

Fairbrass and Jordan's study (Chapter 9) of EU environmental (biodiversity and land use planning) policy making and the implementation of these policies in the United Kingdom presents a 'critical test' for multi-level governance. This study takes a policy area characterized by dispersed decision-making competences and the involvement of state and non-state actors, that would seem to make it 'an excellent vehicle' for analysing multi-level governance. However, the United Kingdom provides a 'hard case', in terms of its likely response to multi-level governance pressures emerging from the European Union, because of its history of centralized authority and its sceptical approach to the European Union. The study revealed mixed evidence for multi-level governance. Fairbrass and Jordan argue that the proliferation of actors with competing policy objectives led to unintended consequences. There was 'clear evidence' of the national executive struggling to predict, let alone fully control the course of policy making. Despite this, the study showed that 'the state can still be an important shaper of post-decisional politics and a powerful gatekeeper'.

Similar conclusions emerged from Bache's discussion of EU regional policy, another policy area where multi-level governance could be expected to be prominent. This chapter suggested that there was some evidence of multi-level governance in some territories and in relation to some issues, but also evidence of effective gatekeeping powers at the implementation stage in the United Kingdom.

Perraton and Wells looked at economic policy, an area where expectations for evidence of multi-level governance would not necessarily be high. They found that structures and processes of multi-level governance varied across different areas of economic policy making. In their cases, European Monetary Union (EMU) and the transition of former communist countries, tended to demonstrate decisional authority at a number of levels, but little evidence of wide non-governmental participation. They conclude that 'this would appear to conflict with much of the literature on multi-level governance which downplays the role of powerful state and institutional actors'.

It would be inappropriate to draw too many conclusions from three studies about how and why multi-level governance structures, processes and outcomes vary across policy sectors. However, we can sketch out a number of findings that at least point the direction for future research. First, the distinction between 'high' and 'low' politics issue areas is important. The argument from this follows that multi-level governance is likely to be more prominent in areas that state actors deem less important to their interests. This distinction is a crude one and we do not suggest here that policies and issues cannot travel from one end of the high-low spectrum to another over time. However, the studies confirm that multi-level governance is most likely to be prominent in sectors or issues deemed 'low politics' by national governments. Second, multi-level governance has overstated the prospects for diminishing central control at the implementation and post-decisional stage. The evidence from environmental and regional policies is that determined state executives can be effective gatekeepers in relation to the impact of EU policies within the domestic arena. However, we note here that the studies looked at implementation in the 'hard' case of the United Kingdom (see above). Third, while state executives remain pivotal actors, there is evidence of unintended consequences arising from multi-level governance that are beyond state control and this is true even in the case of the United Kingdom.

Does Multi-level Governance Connote Hierarchy? If so, is This a Weakness in the Approach?

Our contributors suggest that the answer to this question is highly dependent on the conceptual lens through which individuals view the notion of multi-level governance. Some read the concept as clearly hierarchical, suggesting vertically layered tiers of authority, making it 'misleading and imprisoning' (Rosenau, Chapter 3). It is for this reason that Rosenau prefers the term 'spheres of authority', while others suggest that the 'multi-level' aspect of the concept is unnecessary and the notion of 'governance' is itself enough (Welch and Kennedy-Pipe, Chapter 8). The counterview is that multi-level governance 'sets up an alternative hypothesis that the hierarchy of levels of governance is being eroded' (George, Chapter 7). These contending views on multi-level governance reinforce our earlier point that, to date, the concept has lacked clarity. However, Hooghe and Marks's development of Types I and II multi-level governance provides more clarity in this respect by suggesting that these different typologies describe different circumstances captured by either orderly or disorderly processes and either the presence or absence of vertical layering of authority. Rosenau's argument reflects an understanding of Type I multi-level governance; Type II is explicitly characterized by 'specialized, territorially overlapping jurisdictions in a relatively flexible, *non-tiered* system with a large number of jurisdictions' (emphasis added).

Where multi-level governance is described as connoting hierarchy, this is usually intended as a criticism, suggesting that it overemphasizes vertical relationships to the detriment of horizontal coordination. The distinction between Types I and II multi-level governance provides a useful heuristic tool for deconstructing and refining arguments in this area. While Type I eschews tiering of authority, Type II directs attention to relationships between actors organized at distinct and different territorial levels, which in some circumstances may be appropriate and advantageous. Chapter 6, on Britain, provides an example of the heuristic value of Type I multi-level governance, in which attention is placed on the newly devolved governmental framework around which broader networks and processes in the United Kingdom are largely structured. The case of the United Kingdom is, to paraphrase Jessop, an illustration of multi-level governance in the shadow of governmental hierarchy: but a hierarchy where authority is being vertically layered.

What Implications does Multi-level Governance Have for the Power, Position and Role of the Nation state?

This question has been central to the debate around multi-level governance and is addressed throughout the contributions to this volume. We did not expect an easy consensus in response to this question, and we did not find one. State power remains important, but how it is exercised is increasingly complex.

Theories of governance and multi-level governance are closely associated with predictions of the demise of the nation state. Yet, this appears to be a parody of multi-level governance. None of the 'governance' theorists contributing to this collection deny the continued importance of nation states at various territorial levels and throughout the policy process. There is broad recognition that state executives possess both legitimacy and nodality, which ensures that they are at least 'first among equals' in the context of governance.

There is also a growing recognition of the role of states in shaping and regulating governance: what Jessop (Chapter 4) describes as 'metagovernance'. It is possible that much of the misunderstanding in relation to governance and the nation state stems from the work of hyperglobalists (e.g. Ohmae 1990, 1996) who, while disagreeing about the risks and opportunities of globalization, all emphasize the demise of the nation state. As Welch and Kennedy-Pipe argued, the relationship between globalization and governance has frequently been opaque. While the two concepts raise a large number of related issues, the nature of the relationship between these processes is often assumed rather than demonstrated. Moreover, the variance between the two concepts is arguably stark in relation to the nation state. A common theme running throughout the chapters in this book has been the transformation or reconfiguration of the state to protect and, some would argue enhance, its continuing centrality within evolving structures of multi-level governance.

Consequently, a number of arguments emerge from this collection in relation to how states respond to the changing context of governance to retain or enhance state power. First is the role of states in metagovernance, that is in providing the ground rules for governance. Second, state executives have some control over what powers are transferred upwards, downwards and sideways and may exercise this control to pass on some responsibilities while concentrating resources on issues and projects deemed more important (see Jessop). Third, state executives may mobilize and draw on the resources of supportive non-state actors to achieve specific objectives and outcomes. However, as George's discussion of the additionality dispute demonstrates, this strategy is also available to supranational organizations as well as national state executives. Fourth, state executives have illustrated the importance of the implementation stage in shaping the outcomes of policy decisions taken in a more pluralistic arena (see Bache, Chapter 10; Fairbrass and Jordan, Chapter 9). Fifth, states can introduce institutional reforms with the aim of increasing their vertical and horizontal strategic capacity while also augmenting their 'gatekeeping' capacity. The creation of the Regional Coordination Unit within the Cabinet Office in the United Kingdom can be identified as an example of this strategy. Finally, states can re-scale state powers as a response to subnational and supranational pressures in ways that may increase state capacity in some areas at least (see Bache and Flinders, Chapter 1).

Of course, listing the possibilities for state action in the context of multi-level governance does not imply success in each instance. The collection has demonstrated evidence of limited state executive rationality and of the unintended consequences of governance processes. In context of complexity and rapid change, states will face increasing pressures to reinvent themselves and develop new strategies: popular legitimacy secured through free elections will continue to provide states with the right to exercise authority, but not with the means.

What are the Implications of Multi-level Governance for Democratic Accountability?

Until now the implications of multi-level governance for democratic accountability have been relatively neglected. Yet this normative debate emerged as a theme concerning a number of contributors to this collection. The issue is discussed in some detail by Peters and Pierre (Chapter 5), but is a feature of other chapters also. Peters and Pierre ask whether problem-solving capacity and outcomes has taken precedence over democratic input and accountability. Similarly, Perraton and Wells raise the question of a 'trade-off between democratic notions, such as accountability and participation, and more managerial concerns, such as efficiency and control'.

As the nation state has become more enmeshed in complex networks, responsibility for certain functions is increasingly blurred (Flinders 2001). In this context, the important question is whether governance can be democratic. The inevitable answer is this depends on how democracy is defined and understood. For those attached to liberal democratic notions of democracy, the rise of multi-level governance should be accompanied by the extension of the basic framework of representative democracy to the relevant territorial levels. An alternative view suggests the creation of new mechanisms of control and accountability that draw on the principles of self-governing communities. What both these top-down and bottom-up approaches to democracy seek is a way to 'save our souls from the Faustian bargain' to ensure frameworks of accountability that do not diminish the independence and operational efficiency of these bodies. However, as the work of Bellone and Goerl (1992), Moe (1994), Oughton (1995) and Roth (1996) suggests, achieving a synthesis between accountability and efficiency is difficult. We return to this issue in the final section.

What are the Strengths and Weaknesses of Multi-level Governance as an Analytical Framework?

Jessop (p.61) suggests that work on governance-centred approaches 'largely remains at a pre-theoretical stage'. Similarly, Fairbrass and Jordan prefer to avoid calling multi-level governance a 'fully-fledged theory', but suggest that it provides a 'compelling description' of what happens to decisions once they escape the domain of intergovernmental bargaining in the European Union. Peters and Pierre (p.88) also suggest that 'multi-level governance appears incapable of providing clear predictions or even explanations (other than the most general) of outcomes in the governance process'. George rejects this position, suggesting that multi-level governance is a theory that generates the hypothesis that the European Union is a system not dominated by national governments. Further hypotheses come from this, relating to the role of other actors, particularly supranational and subnational institutions. As discussed above, we suggest that whether multi-level governance is accepted as a theory, an organizing perspective or a contrastive concept, it can be used in a number of ways that contribute to our understanding of the changing nature of policy making. The use of multi-level governance as a contrastive concept by Welch and Kennedy-Pipe illustrates this well.

Welch and Kennedy-Pipe suggest that analytically, the emphasis of multi-level governance on the effect of international civil society upon states appears unproblematic, but the empirical evidence suggests considerable variation of this effect. More firmly, they conclude that this is an 'exceptionally unpropitious time to be suggesting, as the concept of multi-level governance does, a general trend of the eclipse of the government of the nation state'. Yet, the advantage of multi-level governance here is in acting as a counterpoint to the state-centric approaches that have dominated analysis of international relations: in this case, multi-level governance raises questions about the role of non-state actors and highlights variation in different patterns of participation and influence in different cases that state-centric approaches may well overlook.

Final Thoughts and Future Directions

In this book we have assembled and analysed critical perspectives on multi-level governance in order to clarify some conceptual confusion and to assess the value of the concept. It is clear that, whatever perspective is taken, multi-level governance (and related notions of governance) is a concept with an appeal that demands attention. In other words, it may not always be liked, but it is very difficult to ignore. We hope the book has contributed to understanding on multi-level governance—its uses, misuses, and limitations—but recognize that there is much more that ought to be done if the potential of the concept is to be fully developed. We would suggest that the concept deserves further testing and analyses in relation to both the outstanding analytical and normative issues, which we discuss here in turn.

It is both a strength and a weakness of multi-level governance as an analytical framework that it can be applied in a wide range of circumstances: it is careful to avoid strong claims about the demise of the state and the influence of non-state actors, but this means that its theoretical content is weak. As Jessop suggests, there are 'marked ambiguities in the referents of multi-level governance'. A particular problem is the emphasis on the increased mobilization and participation of 'new' (subnational and non-state) actors in policy processes rather than a focus on how this change affects policy outcomes. Put another way, a distinction must be drawn between multi-level *governance* and multi-level *participation*, where the latter notion signals greater involvement without effective influence for at least some types of new actors (the role of UK trade unions in EU regional policy provides an example of this, see Bache and George 1999). Pursuing this line of reasoning, it is possible to suggest that multi-level governance incorporates a weakness of neo-pluralist assumptions in relation to the location and fluidity of power that fail to address the continuing existence of structural inequalities (Marsh et al. 2003).

If multi-level governance is going to overcome this weakness, and in general terms move from being generally viewed as a 'proto-theory' to one that is 'fully fledged', it needs to generate clearer expectations in relation to the *influence* of subnational and non-state actors, as well as highlighting their mobilization and participation. Similarly, it might more clearly hypothesize the behaviour of state actors in response to the different challenges posed by different types of multi-level governance in different spatial, temporal, and policy context and, in particular, on how central control is maintained in some states and sectors rather than in others. We note here the potential dangers highlighted by Sartori's distinction between 'conceptual travelling' and 'conceptual stretching'. The first of these notions refers to the effective application of a concept to new cases, while the second involves the distortion of a concept where it does not fit new cases. *Travelling* is valid and proper, *stretching* is problematic in that 'gains in extensional coverage tend to be matched by losses in connotative precision' and that 'we can cover more—in travelling terms—only by saying less, and by saying less in a far less precise manner' (Sartori 1970: 1035). Only when multi-level governance has travelled further in hostile academic and policy territories will we know if the concept is being overstretched.

In normative terms, multi-level governance is seen by its advocates to present a number of advantages. However, as Jessop suggests, it is wrong to think that multi-level governance can solve old problems without creating new ones. Here, we suggest, the critical problem is that of legitimacy in the context of multi-level governance. While multi-level governance in its different forms may add to the legitimacy of public policy making through increased efficiency, it may reduce legitimacy in the form of democratic accountability unless new means are found to connect citizens more effectively with the shifting locations of power. The electoral legitimacy of national governments ensures them a pivotal role in this changing context, but the diffusion of competencies and the changing patterns of participation demand additional mechanisms of accountability beyond those provided by representative institutions. This does not only mean democratizing supranational and global processes, but also revisiting and revising the mechanisms of democracy within the state, at both national and subnational level. The increasingly fragmented nature of governing processes is a feature of politics within and without the nation state driven by related processes (hence 'fragmegration'), and, as such, demands a response that takes this as its starting point. Our view is that the evolving structures of multi-level governance are likely to necessitate new forms and models of accountability that seek to build new and innovative conduits between the public and the institutions involved in complex networks. In essence, this may involve a fundamental reappraisal of the meaning of democracy and the role of representative institutions within nation states.

However, the very developments that some see as potential threats to legitimate authority, others suggest might be part of the democratic solution. Thus, while on the one hand, complex multi-level governance may be seen to reduce transparency and accountability, on the other, the proliferation of actors involved may be seen to provide 'safety in numbers' by limiting the power of any single actor or type of actor (see Rosenau, Chapter 3). Yet, while 'safety in numbers' through increased participation may provide part of the answer to the challenges of democracy, this cannot be taken for granted. Participation does not equate to power and the emergence of multi-level governance does not necessarily enhance the position of weaker social groups and may indeed concentrate power more in the hands of those groups and actors with the necessary resources to operate most effectively in the context of complexity. In the words of Peters and Pierre (p.89), multi-level governance that is 'embedded in a regulatory setting which enables weaker actors to define a legal basis for their action might be the best strategy to escape the Faustian bargain and to cheat the darker powers.' In one view, this may involve granting 'special rights' to groups who are disadvantaged within this new context (Young 1997).

Following this argument, we would suggest that the next phase of research on multi-level governance pays particular attention to the implications for democracy of empirical developments and, related to this, to the design of frameworks of accountability that adopt a positive-sum gain in relation to the accountability versus efficiency debate (see Jessop 1998: p. 42). We would not expect a 'one size fits all' solution to this challenge: it is likely that in the context of different types of multi-level governance, different types of democratic arrangements will be needed to ensure popular consent.

Already, there are indications that this research agenda is being taken forward. Olsson (2003) has recently considered three models of democracy in the context of theorizing multi-level governance and the EU regional policy: the parliamentary model, the pluralistic model, and the elite-democratic model. In a similar vein, Pollack (2003: 14) has characterized the three options for enhancing democracy in the EU's complex polity as parliamentarization, deliberation and constitutionalization. Another alternative would be to increase state regulation of governance: an echo of Jessop's work on metagovernance. However, as Olsson and others acknowledge, democratic renewal and efficient policy making in the context of emerging multi-level governance cannot be easily legislated for. Public cynicism towards politics and politicians has increased, rather than diminished, as elected leaders have experimented with new forms of governance to meet heightened public demands characterized by the desire for better public policies alongside lower taxes. As this pressure and other processes accelerate complexity and obscure accountability, meeting the challenges presented by multi-level governance in both analytical and normative terms will become ever more urgent.

References

ABRAHAMSEN, R. (2000). *Disciplining Democracy: Development Discourse and Good Governance in Africa* (London and New York: Zed Books).

ALESINA, A. and WACZIARG, R. (1999). 'Has European Integration Gone too Far?', NBER Working Paper No. 6883.

AMIN, A. and MALMBERG, A. (1992). 'Competing Structural and Institutional Influences on the Geography of Production in Europe', *Environment and Planning A*, 24: 401–16.

AMIN, A. and TOMANEY, J. (1999). 'The Regional Dilemma in a Neo-liberal Europe', *European Urban and Regional Studies*, 2/2: 171–88.

ANDERSON, J. (1990). 'Skeptical Reflections on a Europe of Regions: Britain, Germany, and the ERDF', *Journal of Public Policy*, 10: 417–47.

—— (1996). 'Germany and the Structural Funds: Unification Leads to Bifurcation', in L. Hooghe (ed.), *Cohesion Policy and European Integration: Building Multi-level Governance* (Oxford: Clarendon Press).

ANSELL, C., PARSONS, C., and DARDEN, K. (1997). 'Dual Networks in European Regional Development Policy', *Journal of Common Market Studies*, 35/3: 347–75.

—— (2000). 'The Networked Polity: Regional Development in Western Europe', *Governance*, 12: 303–33.

ARATO, A. (1981). 'Civil Society Against the State: Poland 1980–81', *Telos*, 47: 23–47.

ARQUILLA, J. and RONFELDT, D. (1997). 'A New Epoch—and Spectrum—of Conflict', in J. Arquilla and D. Ronfeldt (eds), *In Athena's Camp: Preparing for Conflict in the Information Age* (Santa Monica: RAND).

ARESTIS, P., BIEFANG-FRISANCHO MARISCAL, I., BROWN, M., and SAWYER, M. (2002a). 'Explaining the Euro's Initial Decline', *Eastern Economic Journal*, 28/1: 71–88.

ARESTIS, P., BROWN, A., MOURATIDIS, K., and SAWYER, M. (2002b). 'The Euro: Reflections on the First Three Years', *International Review of Applied Economics*, 16/1: 1–17.

ARKSEY, H. and KNIGHT, P. (1999). *Interviewing for Social Scientists: An Introductory Resource with Examples* (London: Sage Publications).

ARMSTRONG, H. and TAYLOR, J. (2000). *Regional Economics and Policy*, 3rd edn (Oxford: Blackwell).

ASHFORD, D. (ed) (1990). *Discretionary Politics: Intergovernmental Social Transfers in Eight Countries* (Greenwich, CT: JAI Press).

BACHE, I. (1998). *The Politics of European Union Regional Policy: Multi-level Governance or Flexible Gatekeeping?* (Sheffield: Sheffield Academic Press/University Association for Contemporary European Studies).

—— (1999). 'The Extended Gatekeeper: Central Government and the Implementation of EC Regional Policy in Britain', *Journal of European Public Policy*, 6/1: 28–45.

—— (2000). 'Government Within Governance: Steering Economic Regeneration Policy Networks in Yorkshire and Humberside', *Public Administration*, 78/3: 575–92.

—— (2001). 'Different Seeds in the Same Plot? Competing Models of Capitalism and the Incomplete Contracts of Partnership Design', *Public Administration*, 79/2: 337–59.

BACHE, I. and BRISTOW, G. (2003). 'Devolution and the Gatekeeping Role of the Core Executive: The Struggle for European Funds', *British Journal of Politics and International Relations*, 5/3: 405–28

—— and GEORGE, S. (1999). 'Towards Inclusion: UK Trade Union Participation in EU Structural Fund Partnerships', *Report for the TUC's of Scotland, Wales, East Midlands and Yorkshire and Humberside* (Sheffield: University of Sheffield), March.

BACHE, I. and GEORGE, S. (2001). Europeanization and Regional Policy: Paper presented to the UACES Annual Conference, Bristol, September 3–5.

—— and OLSSON, J. (2001). 'Legitimacy through Partnership? EU Policy Diffusion in Britain and Sweden', *Scandinavian Political Studies*, 24/3: 215–37.

——, GEORGE, S., and RHODES, R. (1996). 'The European Union, Cohesion Policy, and Subnational Authorities in the United Kingdom', in L. Hooghe (ed.), *Cohesion Policy and European Integration: Building Multi-level Governance* (Oxford: Oxford University Press).

BALL, S. (1997). 'Has the UK Government Implemented the Habitats Directive Properly?', in J. Holden (ed.), *The Impact of EC Environmental Law in the United Kingdom* (Chichester: John Wiley).

BALL, T. (1988). Transforming Political Discourse (Oxford: Blackwell).

BALME, R. and CHABANET, D. (2002). 'Introduction: Action collective et Gouvernance de l'Union Européenne', in R. Balme, D. Chabanet, and V. Wright (eds), *L'Action Collective en Europe* (Paris: Presses de Sciences Politiques).

BARRO, R. and SALA-I-MARTIN, X. (1990). 'Convergence across States and Regions', *Brookings Papers on Economic Activity*, 1: 107–82.

BARRY, A. (2001). *Political Machines: Governing a Technological Society* (London: Athlone).

BATLEY, R. 'Comparisons and Lessons', in R. Batley and G. Stoker (eds), *Local Government in Europe. Trends and Developments* (London: MacMillan).

BEAUREGARD, R. A. and PIERRE, J. (2000). 'Disputing the Global: A Skeptical View of Locality-based International Initiatives', *Policy and Politics*, 28: 465–78.

BEETSMA, R. and UHLIG, H. (1999). 'An Analysis of the Stability Pact', *Economic Journal*, 109: 546–71.

BELLONE, C. and GOERL, G. (1992). 'Reconciling Public Entrepreneurship and Democracy', *Public Administrative Review*, 52/2: 130–34.

BENNETT, D. (1995). 'The Process of Harmonization Under NAFTA', *New Solutions*, 6: 91–5.

BENNEY, M. GRAY, A. and PEAR, R. (1956). *How People Vote* (London: Routledge and Kegan Paul).

BENZ, A. and EBERLEIN, T. (1999). 'The Europeanization of Regional Policies: Patterns of Multi-level Governance', *Journal of European Public Policy*, 6/2: 329–48.

—— and EBERLEIN, B. (1998). 'Regions in European Governance: The Logic of Multi-level Interaction', EUI, RSC Working Paper No. 98/31 (Florence).

BERG, B. (1998). *Qualitative Research Methods for the Social Sciences*, 3rd edn (Boston and London: Allyn and Bacon).

BERTRAM, E. and SPENCER, B. (2000). Democratic Dilemmas in the U.S. War on Drugs in Latin America, Carnegie Council on Ethics and International Affairs, Case Study No. 21.

BESLEY, T. and SEABRIGHT, P. (1999). 'The Effects and Policy Implications of State Aids to Industry', *Economic Policy*, 28: 13–42.

—— and COATES, S. (1999). 'Centralized versus Decentralized Provision of Local Public Goods: A Political Economy Analysis', NBER Working Paper No. 7084.

BIRCH, A. (1984). 'Overload, Ungovernability and Delegitimation: The Theories of the British Case', *British Journal of Political Science*, 14: 135–60.

BIRD, R. and VAILLANCOURT, F. (eds) (1998). *Fiscal Decentralization in Developing Countries* (Cambridge: Cambridge University Press).

Birdlife International (2000). Interview with J. Fairbrass Brussels, 23 August.

BLACKHURST, R. (1998). 'The Capacity of the WTO to Fulfill Its Mandate', in A. O. Krueger (ed.), *The WTO as an International Organization* (Chicago and London: University of Chicago Press).

BLAIR, T. (2003). *The Right Values for Today at Home and Abroad*, 28 February. Speech at the 'Welsh Labour Party Conference', Swansea, www.labour.org.uk/tbswansea/, accessed 16 March 2003.

BLATTER, J. (2001). 'Debordering the World of States. Towards a Multi-level System in Europe and a Multi-Polity System in North America? Insights from Border Regions', *European Journal of International Relations*, 7/2: 175–210.

BOLI, J. (1999). 'Conclusion: World Authority Structures and Legitimations', in J. Boli and G. Thomas (eds), *Constructing World Culture: International Nongovernmental Organisations Since 1875* (Stanford: Stanford University Press).

BOMBERG, E. and PETERSON, J. (1998). 'European Union Decision Making: The Role of Sub-national Authorities', *Political Studies*, 46/2: 219–35.

BÖRZEL, T. (2001). *Nations and Regions in Europe* (Cambridge: Cambridge University Press).

—— and RISSE, T. (2000). 'When Europe Hits Home: Europeanization and Domestic Change', *EIoP*, 4/15: http://eiop.or.at/eiop/texte/2000-015a.htm, accessed 15 July 2002.

—— and RISSE, T. (2000a). 'Who is Afraid of a European Federation? How to Constitutionalize a Multi-level Governance System?', in C. Jörges, Y. Mény, and J. Weiler (eds), *What Kind of Constitution for What Kind of Polity? Responses to Joschka Fischer* (Florence: European University Institute).

—— and RISSE, T. (2000b). 'Private–Public Partnerships: Effective and Legitimate Tools of International Governance?' (Unpublished).

BRANCH, A. P. and ØHRGAARD, J. C. (1999). 'Trapped in the Supranational–Intergovernmental Dichotomy: A Response to Stonesweet and Sandholtz', *Journal of European Public Policy*, 6: 123–43.

BRAND, J. and MITCHELL, J. (1997). 'Home Rule in Scotland: The Politics and Bases of a Movement', in J. Bradbury and J. Mawson (eds), *British Regionalism and Devolution: The Challenges of State Reform and European Integration* (London: Jessica Kingsley Publishers).

BRENNAN, G. and BUCHANAN, J. (1980). *The Power to Tax: Analytical Foundations of a Fiscal Constitution* (Cambridge: Cambridge University Press).

—— (2000). 'How the Parliament Works', in G. Hassan (ed.), *The New Scottish Politics: The First Year of the Scottish Parliament* (Edinburgh: The Stationery Office).

BROWN, G. (2003). 'As the EU Expands, We Must Repatriate Some of the Power from Brussels', *The Times*, 6th March.

BRUNILA, A. (2002). 'Fiscal Policy: Coordination, Discipline and Stabilisation', *Bank of Finland Discussion Papers*, 7 (Helsinki: Bank of Finland).

BUDD, L.C. (2000). 'Cohesive Divergence in Euroland: The Regional Implications of a Single Currency Dimension', Conference Paper for 'Regional Studies Association International Conference', Aix-en-Provence, 14–15 September.

BUITER, W., CORSETTI, G. and ROUBINI, N. (1993). 'Excessive Deficits: Sense and Nonsense in the Treaty of Maastricht', *Economic Policy*, 16: 57–100.
—— (1997). 'The Politics of the Third Level', in C. Jeffery (ed.), *The Regional Dimension of the European Union: Towards a Third Level in Europe?* (London: Frank Cass).
BULMER, S. (1993). 'The Governance of the European Union: A New Institutionalist Approach', *Journal of Public Policy*, 13: 351–80.
—— et al. (2001). 'European Policy-making Under Devolution: Britain's New Multi-level Governance', ERPU Research Paper 1/01 (Manchester: University of Manchester).
BURCH, M. and HOLLIDAY, I. (2000). 'New Labour and the constitution', in D. Coates and P. Lawler (eds), *New Labour in Power* (Manchester: Manchester University Press).
BUREAU, D. and CHAMPSAUR, P. (1992). 'Fiscal Federalism and European Economic Unification', *American Economic Review*, 82: 88–92.
BURGESS, M. (2000). *Federalism and European Union: The Building of Europe, 1950–2000* (New York: Routledge).
BUTT, P. (1999). 'Regionalism in the United Kingdom', in P. Wagstaff (ed.), *Regionalism in the European Union* (Exeter: Intellect Books).
BUZAN, B., WÆVER, O., and DE WILDE, J. (1998). *Security: A New Framework for Analysis* (Boulder, CO and London: Lynne Rienner).
Cabinet Office (2000). *Reaching Out: The Role of Central Government at Regional and Local Level* (London: Performance and Innovation Unit).
CAFRUNY, A. and ROSENTHAL, G. (eds) (1993). *The State of the European Community Vol. 2: The Maastricht Debates and Beyond* (Boulder: Lynne Riener/Harlow: Longman).
CAMMACK, P. (2002). 'The Mother of All Governments: The World Bank's Matrix for Global Governance', in R. Wilkinson and S. Hughes (eds), *Global Governance: Critical Perspectives* (London and New York: Routledge).
CAPORASO, J. (2000). 'Changes in the Westphalian Order: Territory, Public Authority, and Sovereignty', *International Studies Review*, 2: 1–28.
CARLEY, M. (1990). *Housing and Neighbourhood Renewal—Britain's New Urban Challenge*, Policy Studies Institute (London: Pinter).
CARPENTER, T. G. (ed.) (2000). *NATO's Empty Victory: A Postmortem on the Balkan War* (Washington: Cato Institute).
CASELLA, A. and FREY, B. (1992). 'Federalism and Clubs. Towards An Economic Theory of Overlapping Political Jurisdictions', *European Economic Review*, 36: 639–46.
—— and WEINGAST, B. (1995). 'Elements of a Theory of Jurisdictional Change', in B. Eichengreen, J. Frieden and J. von Hagen (eds), *Politics and Institutions in an Integrated Europe* (New York/Heidelberg: Springer Verlag).
CASTELLS, M. (2000). *End of Millennium*, 2nd edn (Oxford: Blackwell).
CHANDLER, D. (1999). *Bosnia: Faking Democracy After Dayton* (London and Sterling: Pluto Press).
CHANG, H.-J. (2002). *Kicking Away the Ladder: Development Strategy in Historical Perspective* (London: Anthem Press).
CHOMSKY, N. (1999). *The New Military Humanism: Lessons from Kosovo* (London: Pluto Press).
CM 4806 (2000). *Memorandum of Understanding and Supplementary Agreements* (London: HMSO).

COKER, C. (2002). *Globalisation and Insecurity in the Twenty-first Century: NATO and the Management of Risk. Adelphi Paper No. 345* (Oxford and New York: Oxford University Press for the Royal Institute of Strategic Studies).

COLLINGE, C. (1999). 'Self-organization of Society by Scale: A Spatial Reworking of Regulation Theory', *Environment and Planning D: Society and Space*, 17/5: 557–74.

COLLINSON, S. (1999). ' "Issue Systems", "Multi-level Games" and the Analysis of the EU's External Commercial and Associated Policies: A Research Agenda', *Journal of European Public Policy*, 6: 206–24.

COM (2001). *428 White Paper on European Governance: A White Paper.*

COOMBES, D. (1970). *Politics and Bureacracy in the European Community* (London: Allen and Unwin).

COOPER, R. N. (1968). *The Economics of Interdependence* (New York: McGraw Hill).

COURCHENE, T. J. (1995). 'Celebrating Flexibility: An Interpretive Essay on the Evolution of Canadian Federalism', Benefactors Lecture, *C.D. Howe Institute*, Montreal, October 16.

COX, R. W. (1986). 'Social Forces, States and World Orders: Beyond International Relations Theory', in R. O. Keohane (ed.), *Neorealism and Its Critics* (New York: Columbia University Press) 204–54.

CREEL, J. (2002). 'The European Stability Pact and Feedback Policy Effects', *Journal of Economic Integration*, 17/3: 570–95.

CROZIER, M. HUNTINGTON, S. and WATANUKI, J. (1975). *The Crisis of Democracy.* (New York: New York University Press).

DABLA-NORRIS, E. and WADE, P. (2002). 'The Challenge of Fiscal Decentralization in Transition Economies', IMF Working Paper WP/02/103 (Washington: IMF).

DE MELLO, L. (2000a). 'Can Fiscal Decentralization Strengthen Social Capital?', IMF Working Paper WP/00/129 (Washington: IMF).

—— (2000b). 'Fiscal decentralization and Intergovernmental Fiscal Relations: A Cross Country Analysis', *World Development*, 28: 365–80.

Department of the Environment (2000). Transport and the Regions, Interview with J. Fairbrass, Bristol, 4 July.

DIXON, J. (1998). 'Nature Conservation', in P. Lowe and S. Ward (eds), *British Environmental Policy and Europe* (London: Routledge).

DOWDING, K., JOHN, P. and BIGGS, S. (1994). 'Tiebout: A Survey of the Empirical Literature', *Urban Studies*, 31: 767–97.

DOWNING, B. M. (1992). *The Military Revolution and Political Change: Origins of Democracy and Autocracy in Early Modern Europe* (Princeton, NJ: Princeton University Press).

DUNFORD, M. (1994). 'Winners and Losers. The New Map of Economic Inequality in the European Union', *European Urban and Regional Studies*, 1/2: 95–114.

DUNN, J. and WETZEL, D. (1999). Fiscal Decentralization in former Socialist Economies: Progress and Prospects (Washington: World Bank Institute).

DUNSIRE, A. (1996). 'Tipping the Balance: Autopoiesis and Governance', *Administration and Society*, 28/3: 299–334.

EICHENGREEN, B. and WYPLOSZ, C. (1998). 'The Stability Pact: More than a Minor Nuisance?', *Economic Policy*, 26: 65–104.

ELAZAR, DANIEL J. (1987). *Exploring Federalism* (Tuscaloosa: University of Alabama Press).

ELAZAR, DANIEL J. (1991). *Federal Systems of the World: A Handbook of Federal, Confederal and Autonomy Arrangements* (London: Longman).

—— and KINCAID, J. (eds) (2000). *The Covenant Connection: From Federal Theology to Modern Federalism* (Lanham: Lexington Books).

ELGIE, R. (1998). 'Democratic Accountability and Central Bank Independence', *West European Politics*, 21/3: 53–76.

—— (2001). 'Democratic Accountability and Central Bank Independence: A Reply to Various Critics', *West European Politics*, 24/1: 217–21.

ENDS (2001). 'Accord Reached on EU Strategic Assessment Rules', ENDS Daily, 3 May.

European Commission (1977). Report of the Strategy Group on the Role of Public Finance in European Integration. (Brussels: European Commission).

European Commission (2001). *European Governance. A Whitepaper* COM, 428 final, Brussels 27th July.

European Council (2000). *Lisbon European Council, Presidency Conclusions*, 23–4 March, http://europa.eu.int/council/off/conclu/.

European Parliament (2002). *The Eight Scottish MEPs and the European Parliament Office in Scotland: Contact Details and Role and Functions* (Edinburgh: European Parliament Office in Scotland).

—— (1988). *Committee on the Environment, Public Health and Consumer Protection, 'First Working Document on the Application of the Birds Directive in the EC*, Council Directive of 2 April 1979 on the Conservation of Wild Birds 79/409/EEC, March 1998.

EVANS, PETER (1997). 'The Eclipse of the State? Reflections on Stateness in an Era of Globalization', *World Politics*, 50: 62–87.

FAIRBRASS, J. (2002). 'Business Interests: Strategic Engagement with the EU Policy Process', Ph.D. thesis (University of Essex).

—— and JORDAN, A. (2001). 'European Union Environmental Policy and the UK Government: A Passive Observer or Strategic Manager?', *Environmental Politics*, 10/2: 1–21.

—— and JORDAN, A. (2002). 'The Europeanisation of Interest Representation: The Case of UK Environment Policy', in A. Warleigh and J. Fairbrass (eds), *Integrating Interests in the European Union: The New Politics of Persuasion, Advocacy and Influence* (London: Europa).

FATAS, A. (1998). 'Does EMU Need a Fiscal Federation?', *Economic Policy*, 26: 163–92.

FIELDER, N. (2000). 'The Origins of the Single Market', in V. Bornschier (ed.), *State-building in Europe: The Revitalization of Western European Integration* (Cambridge: Cambridge University Press).

FINE, B., LAPAVITSAS, C., and PINCUS, J. (eds) (2001). *Development Policy in the Twenty-First Century: Beyond the Post-Washington Consensus* (London: Routledge).

FLINDERS, M. (2001). *The Politics of Accountability in the Modern State* (London: Ashgate).

—— (2002). 'Governance in Whitehall', *Public Administration*, 80/1: 51–75.

—— (2003). Delegated Governance in Britain. Mimeo. Department of Politics, University of Sheffield.

FOSTER, KATHRYN A. (1997). *The Political Economy of Special-Purpose Government* (Washington: Georgetown University Press).

FREESTONE, D. (1996). 'The Enforcement of the Wild Birds Directive: A Case Study', in H. Somsen (ed.), *Protecting the European Environment: Enforcing EC Environmental Law* (London: Blackstone Press).

FREY, BRUNO, and EICHENBERGER, REINER (1999). *The New Democratic Federalism for Europe. Functional, Overlapping, and Competing Jurisdictions* (Cheltenham: Edward Elgar).

FRY, E. H. (1998). *The Expanding Role of State and Local Governments in U.S. Foreign Affairs* (New York: Council on Foreign Relations Press).

GALLIE, W. (1955). 'Essentially Contested Concepts', Proceedings of the Aristotelian Society, 56: 167–98.

GAMBLE, A. PAYNE, A. HOOGRELT, A. DIETRICH, M. and KENNY, M. (1996). 'Editorial: New Political Economy' *New Political Economy*, 1/1: 5–11.

GAMBLE, A. (1990). 'Theories of British Politics', *Political Studies*, 38/3: 404–20.

—— (2000). 'Policy Agendas in a Multi-level Polity', in A. Gamble et al. (eds), *Developments in British Politics 6* (London : Macmillan).

GARMAN, C., HAGGARD, S., and WILLIS, E. (2001). 'Fiscal Decentralization: A Political Theory with Latin American Cases', *World Politics*, 53: 205–36.

GARMISE, S. (1997). 'The Impact of European Regional Policy on the Development of the Regional Tier in the UK', *Regional and Federal Studies*, 7: 1–24.

GARRETT, G. (1992). 'International Co-operation and Institutional Choice: The European Community's Internal Market', *International Organisation*, 46: 533–60.

GEORGE, S. and BACHE, I. (2001). *Politics in the European Union* (Oxford: Oxford University Press).

GIDDENS, A. (1985). *The Nation-State and Violence: Volume Two of a Contemporary Critique of Historical Materialism* (Oxford: Polity).

GIDDENS, A. and PIERSON, CHRISTOPHER (1988). *Conversations with Anthony Giddens: Making Sense of Modernity* (Cambridge: Polity Press).

GILL, S. (2000). 'Toward a Postmodern Prince? The Battle in Seattle as a Moment in the New Politics of Globalisation', *Millennium*, 29: 131–40.

—— (2001). 'Constitutionalising Capital: EMU and Disciplinary Neo-liberalism', in A. Bieling and A. D. Morton (eds), *Social Forces in the Making of the New Europe* (Basingstoke: MacMillan).

GOLDSMITH, M. J. F and KLAUSEN, K. K. (1997). *European Integration and Local Government.* (Cheltenham: Edward Elgar).

GOLUB, J. (1995). 'The Politics of Judicial Discretion', *West European Politics*, 19/2: 360–85.

GRAMSCI, A. (1971). *Selections from the Prison Notebooks* (London: Lawrence & Wishart).

GRANDE, E. (2000). 'Charisma und Komplexität. Verhandlungsdemokratie, Mediendemokratie und der Funktionswandel politischer Eliten', *Leviathan*, 28/1: 122–41.

—— (2001). Die neue Unregierbarkeit. Globalisierung und die Grenzen des Regierens jenseits des Nationalstaats (Munich: Technische Universität München).

GRAY, VIRGINIA (1973). 'Innovation in the States: A Diffusion Study', *American Political Science Review*, 67: 1174–85.

GREENLEAF, W. (1983). *The British Political Tradition Vol. 1: The Rise of Collectivism* (London: Methuen).

GREWAL, S.S. (2001). Book Review of Hooghe and Marks, *Political Studies*, 50: 413.

GUSTAFSSON, G. (1987). *Decentralisering av Politisk Makt* [Decentralization of Political Power] (Stockholm: Carlssons).

HAAHR, J. H. (2002). 'Open Methods of Coordination as Advanced Liberal Government', Paper prepared for the 'ECPR 1st Pan-European Conference on European Union Politics', Bordeaux, 26–8 September.

HAAS, E. B. (1970). 'The Study of Regional Integration: Reflections on the Joy and Anguish of Pretheorizing', *International Organization*, 24: 607–46.

—— (1958). *The Uniting of Europe: Political, Social and Economic Forces 1950–57* (London: Library of World Affairs).

HAIGH, N. (1983). 'The EEC Environmental Assessment Directive', paper for the 'International Land Reclamation Conference', Grays, Essex, 26–9 April.

—— (1997). *Manual of Environmental Policy* (London: Cartermill).

HARDING, A. and LE GALES, P. (1998). 'Cities and States in Europe', *West European Politics*, 21/3: 120–45.

—— (2002). 'A Case Study of Scottish Labour: Devolution and the Politics of Multi-level Governance', *The Political Quarterly*, 73/2: 144–57.

—— and LYNCH, PETER (2001). *The Almanac of Scottish Politics* (London: Politico's Publishing).

—— WARHURST, CHRIS (2001). 'New Scotland? Policy, Parties and Institutions', *The Political Quarterly*, 72/2: 213–26.

HAY, C. (2002). *British Politics Today* (London: Polity).

HAYEK, F.A. (1979). *The Political Order of a Free People, Law, Legislation, and Liberty, Vol. 3* (Chicago: University of Chicago Press).

HAZELL, ROBERT (1999). 'The New Constitutional Settlement', in Hazell, Robert (ed.), *Constitutional Futures: A History of the Next Ten Years* (Oxford: The Constitution Unit, Oxford University Press).

HC 209 Quangos (1998/1999). *Sixth Report of the Public Administration* (London: HMSO), Session 1998/1999.

HC 367 (2000/2001). Mapping the Quango State, Fifth Report of the Public Administration Committee (London: HMSO), Session 2000/2001.

HELD, D. (1995). *Democracy and the Global Order* (Cambridge: Polity Press).

—— McGREW, A., GOLDBLATT, D., and PERRATON, J. (1999). *Global Transformations: Politics, Economics and Culture* (Cambridge: Polity Press).

—— and McGREW, A. (2002). *Governing Globalization: Power, Authority and Global Governance* (London: Polity).

HENDERSON, VERNON (2000). 'The Effects of Urban Concentration on Economic Growth', NBER Working Paper W7503.

HETTNE, B. (1997). 'A New Europe in the Changing Global System', in R. Falk and T. Szentes (eds), *A New Europe in the Changing Global System* (Tokyo: United Nations University Press).

HIRST, P. and THOMPSON, G. (1999). *Globalization in Question: The International Economy and the Possibilities of Governance* (Cambridge: Polity Press).

HIX, S. (1994). 'The Study of the European Community: The Challenge to Comparative Politics', *West European Politics*, 17: 1–30.

HL 28 (2002). 'Devolution: Inter-Institutional Relations in the United Kingdom; Select Committee on the Constitution, 2nd Report Session 2002–03.

HOCK, DEE. (1999). *Birth of the Chaordic Age* (San Francisco: Berret-Koehler Publishers).

HOCKING, BRIAN (1999). 'Patrolling the 'Frontier': Globalization, Localization, and the 'Actorness' of Non-central Governments', *Regional and Federal Studies*, 9: 17–39.

HOFFMANN, S. (1964). 'The European Process at Atlantic Cross purposes', *Journal of Common Market Studies*, 3: 85–101.

—— (1966). 'Obstinate or Obsolete? The Fate of the Nation State and the Case of Western Europe', *Daedalus*, 95/3: 862–915.

—— (1982). 'Reflections on the Nation State in Western Europe Today', *Journal of Common Market Studies*, 21/2: 21–37.

—— (1995). *The European Sisyphus. Essays on Europe 1964–1994* (Boulder: Wesview Press).

HOLLIDAY, I. (2000). 'Is the British State Hollowing Out?', *The Political Quarterly*, 71/2: 167–77.

HOLT, E. (2001). Presentation Paper SP Paper 341 in 'Scottish Parliament (2001): Scotland and Europe. A European Seminar', February, pp. 13–18.

HOOD, C. (1991). 'A Public Management for all Seasons?', *Public Administration*, 69/2: 3–19.

HOOGHE, L. (1995). 'Subnational Mobilisation in the European Union', *West European Politics*, 18/3: 175–98.

—— (1996). 'Building a Europe with the Regions: The Changing Role of the European Commission', in L. Hooghe (ed.), *Cohesion Policy and European Integration: Building Multi-level Governance* (Oxford: Oxford University Press).

—— (1996). *Cohesion Policy and European Integration: Building Multi-level Governance.* (Oxford: Oxford University Press).

—— (1998). 'EU Cohesion Policy and Competing Models of Capitalism', *Journal of Common Market Studies*, 36/4: 457–77.

HOOGHE, L. and MARKS, G. (1996). 'Contending Models of Governance in the EU', in A. Cafruny and C. Lankowski (eds), *Europe's Ambiguous Unity* (Boulder, CO: Lynne Rienner).

—— (2001a). 'Types of Multi-level Governance', *EIoP*, 5/11: http://eiop.or.at/eiop/texte/2001-011a.htm, accessed 15/07/02.

—— (2001b) *Multi-level Governance and European Integration* (Maryland, USA and Oxford: Rowman & Littlefield Publishers).

—— (2003). 'Unravelling the Central State, But How? Types of Multi-level Governance', *American Political Science Review*, 97/2: 233–43.

HOOGLAND, R. D., LOWERY, D., and LYONS, W. E. (1990). 'Citizen Satisfaction with Local Government: A Test of Individual, Jurisdictional, and City Specific Explanations', *Journal of Politics*, 52: 807–37.

HORWITZ, R. B. (1986). 'Understanding Deregulation', *Theory and Society*, 15: 139–74.

HUEGLIN, T.O. (1999a). *Early Modern Concepts for a Late Modern World: Althusius on Community and Federalism* (Waterloo, Ont.: Wilfrid Laurier Press).

HUEGLIN, T. O. (1999b). 'Government, Governance, Governmentality: Understanding the EU as a Project of Universalism', in B. Kohler-Koch and R. Eising, (eds), *The Transformation of Governance in the European Union* (London and New York: Routledge).

HUTHER, J. and SHAH, A. (1996). *A Simple Measure of Good Governance and Its Application to the Debate on the Appropriate Level of Fiscal Decentralization* (Washington: World Bank).

Independent International Commission on Kosovo (2000). *The Kosovo Report: Conflict, International Response, Lessons Learned* (Oxford and New York: Oxford University Press).

INMAN, R. and RUBINFELD, D. (1997). 'The Political Economy of Federalism', in D. Mueller, (ed.), *Perspectives on Public Choice: A Handbook* (Cambridge: Cambridge University Press).

INMAN, R. and RUBINFELD, D. (1992). 'Fiscal Federalism in Europe: Lessons from the United States Experience', *European Economic Review*, 36: 654–60.

ISSING, O. (2002). 'On Macroeconomic Policy Co-ordination in EMU', *Journal of Common Market Studies*, 40/2: 345–58.

JEFFERY, C. (1997). 'Conclusions: Sub-national Authorities and "European Domestic Policy"', in C. Jeffery (ed.), *The Regional Dimension of the European Union: Towards a Third Level in Europe?* (London: Frank Cass).

—— (1998). *Multi-layer Democracy in Germany* (London: Constitution Unit).

—— (2000a). 'Sub-national Mobilization and European Integration: Does it Make Any Difference?', *Journal of Common Market Studies*, 38: 1–23.

—— (2000b). *Devolution and Subsidiarity: Relationships Between Central and Next-Lower Levels of National Government* Ditchley Foundation, Conference Report No. D00/03.

JENNINGS, I. (1966). *The British Constitution* (Cambridge: Cambridge University Press).

JESSOP, B. (1995). 'The Regulation Approach, Governance and Post-Fordism: Alternative Perspectives on Economic and Political Change?', *Economy and Society*, 24/3: 307–33.

—— (1990). *State Theory: Putting the Capitalist State in its Place* (Cambridge: Polity).

—— (1998). 'The Rise of Governance and the Risk of Failure', *International Social Science Journal*, 50/155: 29–45.

—— (1999). 'Governance Failure', in G. Stoker (ed.), *The New Politics of British Local Governance* (London: MacMillan).

—— (2002a). 'Governance and Metagovernance in the Face of Complexity: On the Roles of Requisite Variety, Reflexive Observation, and Romantic Irony in Participatory Governance', in P. Getimis and G. Kafkalas (eds), *Participatory Governance and Multi-Level Governance* (Opladen: Leske and Budrich).

—— (2002b). *The Future of the Capitalist State* (Cambridge: Polity).

JOHN, P. (1996). 'Europeanisation in a Centralising State', in C. Jeffery (ed.), *The Regional Dimension of the EU* (London: Frank Cass).

—— (2000). 'The Europeanisation of Sub-national Governance', *Urban Studies*, 37/5–6: 877–94.

—— (2001). *Local Governance in Western Europe* (London: Sage Publications).

JORDAN, A. J. (1997). "Overcoming the Divide Between International Relations and Comparative Politics Approaches to the EC: What Role for 'Post-decisional' Politics?', *West European Politics*, 20/4: 43–70.

—— (2001a). 'National Environmental Ministries: Managers or Ciphers of European Environmental Policy?', *Public Administration*, 79/3: 643–63.

—— (2001b). 'The European Union: An Evolving System of Multi-level Governance ... or Government?', *Policy & Politics*, 29/2: 193–208.

—— (2002a). *Environmental Policy in the European Union* (London: Earthscan).

—— (2002b). *The Europeanization of British Environmental Policy* (London: Palgrave).

—— and LENSCHOW, A. (2000). 'Greening' the European Union: What can be Learned From the Leaders of EU Environmental Policy?', *European Environment*, 10/3: 109–20.

JUDGE, D. (1993). *The Parliamentary State* (London: Sage).

KAGAN, R. (2002). 'Power and Weakness', *Policy Review Online*, 113: www.policyreview.org/JUN02/kagan.htm, accessed 10 March 2003.

KAHLER, M. and LAKE, D. (2003). 'Globalization and Governance: Definition, Variation, and Explanation', in M. Kahler and D. Lake (eds), *Governance in a Global Economy: Political Authority in Transition* (Princeton: Princeton University Press).

KASSIM, H., PETERS, B., and WRIGHT, V. (eds) (2000). *European Union Policy Coordination: The National Dimension* (Oxford: Oxford University Press).

KATZENSTEIN, P. J. (ed.) (1996). *The Culture of National Security: Norms and Identity in World Politics* (New York: Columbia University Press).

KAUFMAN, H. (1976). *Are Government Organizations Immortal?* (Washington: Brookings Institution).

KEATING, M. (1998). *The New Regionalism in Western Europe: Territorial Restructuring and Political Change* (Cheltenham: Edward Elgar).

—— (2001). 'The Politics of the European Union Regional Policy: Multi-level Governance or Flexible Gatekeeping?', *Common Market Law Review*, 38: 1326–7.

KELLEHER, J., BATTERBURY, S. and STERN, E. (1999). *The Thematic Evaluation of the Partnership Principle: Final Synthesis Report* (London: The Tavistock Institute Evaluation Development and Review Unit).

KENNEDY-PIPE, C. and JONES, C. (2000). *International Security in a Global Age* (London: Frank Cass).

KEOHANE, R. and OSTROM, E. (eds) (1995). *Local Commons and Global Interdependence. Heterogeneity and Cooperation in Two Domains* (London: Sage).

—— and NYE, J., Jr. (2000). 'Introduction' in J. Nye and J. Donahue (eds) *Governance in a Globalizing World* (Washington: Brookings Institution).

KING, A. (1975). 'Overload: problems of governing in the 1970s', *Political Studies*, 23: 289–96.

KITSON, M. and MICHIE, J. (1999). 'The Political Economy of Globalisation', in D. Archibugi, et al. (eds), *Innovation Policy in a Global Economy* (Cambridge: CUP).

KLETZER, K. and VON HAGEN, J. (2000). 'Monetary Union and Fiscal Federalism', Centre for European Integration Studies Working Papers, 2000-B1 (Bonn: Rheinische-Fiedrich-Wilhelms-Universität).

KOHLER-KOCH, B. (1996). 'Catching-up with Change: The Transformation of Governance in the EU', *Journal of European Public Policy*, 3: 359–81.

—— (ed.) (1998). *Interaktive Politik in Europa: Regionen im Netzwerk der Integration* (Opladen: Leske and Budrich).

KOOIMAN, J. (ed.) (1993). 'Social–Political Governance: Introduction', in J. Kooiman (ed), *Modern Governance: New Government–Society Interactions* (Newbury Park and London: Sage).

KOREY, W. (1998). *NGOs and the Universal Declaration of Human Rights: 'A Curious Grapevine'* (New York: St Martin's Press).

KRAHMANN, E. (2001). *The Emergence of Security Governance in Post-Cold War Europe*, ESRC 'One Europe or Several?', Programme, Working Paper 36/01.

KRASNER, S. (ed.) (1983). *International Regimes* (Ithaca: Cornell University Press).

—— (1999). *Sovereignty: Organized Hypocrisy* (Princeton: Princeton University Press).

KRÄTKE, M. (1984). *Kritik der Staatsfinanzen. Zur politischen Ökonomie des Steuerstaats* (Hamburg: VSA Verlag).

Labour Party (1997). 'New Labour Because Britain Deserves Better, General Election Manifesto 1997' (London). www.labour.org.uk, accessed 24/3/01

LADEUR, K. H. (1997). 'Towards a Legal Theory of Supranationality—the Viability of the Network Concept', *European Law Journal*, 3/3: 33–54.

LAFFIN, M., THOMAS, A., and WEBB, A. (2000). 'Intergovernmental Relations after Devolution: The National Assembly for Wales', *The Political Quarterly*, 71/2: 223–33.

LARNER, W. and WALLACE, W. (2002). 'The Political Rationality of "New Regionalism": Toward a Genealogy of the Region', *Theory and Society*, 31/3: 391–432.

LE GALES, P. (2002). *European Cities: Social Conflicts and Governance* (London: Oxford University Press).

—— and HARDING, A. (1998). 'Cities and States in Europe', *West European Politics*, 21: 120–45.

—— and LEQUESNE, C. (eds) (1997). *Les paradoxes des régions en Europe* (Paris: Editions La Découverte).

—— —— (eds) (1998). *Regions in Europe* (London: Routledge).

LEDOUX, L., CROOKS, S., JORDAN, A., and TURNER, R. (2000). 'Implementing EU Biodiversity Policy: A UK Case Study', CSERGE Working Paper GEC 2000–03.

LEE, N. and WOOD, C. (1978). 'EIA of Projects in EEC Countries', *Environmental Management*, 21: 271–86.

LEFTWICH, A. (1993). 'Governance, Democracy and Development in the Third World', *Third World Quarterly*, 14: 605–23.

LEICESTER, G. (1998). 'Devolution and Europe: Britain's Double Constitutional Problem, in H. Elcock and M. Keating (eds), *Remaking the Union. Devolution and British Politics in the 1990s* (London: Frank Cass).

—— (1999). 'Scottish and Welsh Devolution', in R. Blackburn and R. Plant (eds), *Constitutional Reform: The Labour Government's Constitutional Reform Agenda*, (London and New York: Longman).

LEWIS, J. (2000). 'The Methods of Community in EU Decision-making and Administrative Rivalry in the Council's Infrastructure', *Journal of European Public Policy*, 7: 261–89.

LINDBERG, L. (1963). *The Political Dynamics of European Economic Integration* (Stanford: Stanford University Press, and London: Oxford University Press).

LOWERY, D., LYONS, W., HOOGLAND DEHOOG, R., TESKE, P., SCHNEIDER, M., MINTROM, M., and BEST, S. (1995). 'The Empirical Evidence for Citizen Information and a Local Market for Public Goods', *American Political Science Review*, 89: 705–9.

LOWI, T. (1964). 'Four Systems of Policy, Politics and Choice', *Public Administration Review*, 32: 298–310.

LOYA, T. and BOLI, J. (1999). 'Standardisation in the World Polity: Technical Rationality over Power', in J. Boli and G. Thomas (eds), *Constructing World Culture: International Nongovernmental Organisations Since 1875* (Stanford: Stanford University Press).

MACKINTOSH, J. (1977). *The Politics and Government of Britain* (London: Hutchinson).

MAJONE, G. (1997). 'From the Positive to the Regulatory State: Causes and Consequences in the Mode of Governance', *Journal of Public Policy*, 17/2: 139–67.

—— (1998). 'Europe's 'Democratic Deficit': The Question of Standards', *European Law Journal*, 4: 5–28.

—— (2002). 'The New European Agencies: Regulation by Information?', *Journal of European Public Policy*, 4/2: 262–75.

MANOR, J. *The Political Economy of Democratic Decentralization* (Washington: The International Bank for Reconstruction and Development/The World Bank).

MARCH, J. and OLSEN, J. (1989). *Rediscovering Institutions: The Organizational Basis of Politics* (New York: Free Press).

—— —— (1995). *Democratic Governance* (New York: Free Press).

MARKS, G. (1992). 'Structural Policy in the European Community', in A. Sbragia (ed.), *Europolitics: Institutions and Policymaking in the "New" European Community* (Washington: The Brookings Institute).

—— (1993). 'Structural Policy and Multilevel Governance in the EC', in A. Cafruny and G. Rosenthal (eds), *The State of the European Community Vol. 2: The Maastricht Debates and Beyond* (Boulder, CO: Lynne Riener, and Harlow: Longman).

—— (1996). 'An Actor-centred Approach to Multi-level governance', in C. Jeffery (ed.), *The Regional Dimension of the EU* (London: Frank Cass).

—— (1996). 'Exploring and Explaining Variation in EU Cohesion Policy', in L. Hooghe (ed.), *Cohesion Policy and European Integration: Building Multi-level Governance* (Oxford: Clarendon Press).

—— and HOOGHE, L. (2000). 'Optimality and Authority: A Critique of Neo-classical Theory', *Journal of Common Market Studies*, 38: 795–816.

—— and McADAM, D. (1996). 'Social Movements and the Changing Structure of Political Opportunity in the EU', *West European Politics*, 19/2: 249–78.

—— ——, and BLANK, K. (1995). 'European Integration and the State', EUI Working Paper RSC No. 95/7, Badia Fiesolana, San Domenico, Italy.

—— —— —— (1996). 'European Integration from the 1980s: State Centric v Multi-level Governance', *Journal of Common Market Studies*, 34/3: 341–78.

——, NIELSEN, F., RAY, L., and SALK, J. (1996). 'Competencies, Cracks and Conflicts: Regional Mobilization in the European Union', in G. Marks, F. Scharpf, P. Schmitter, and W. Streeck (eds), *Governance in the European Union* (London: Sage).

—— et al. (1996). 'Competencies, Cracks and Conflicts—Regional Mobilization in the European Union', *Comparative Political Studies*, 29: 164–92.

MARQUETTE, H. (2001). 'Corruption, Democracy and the World Bank', *Crime, Law and Social Change*, 36: 395–407.

MARSH, D. (2002). 'Pluralism and the Study of British Politics' in C. Hay (ed.), *British Politics Today* (London: Polity).

—— and FURLONG, P. (2002). 'A Skin Not a Sweater: Ontology and Epistemology in Political Science', in D. Marsh and G. Stoker (eds), *Theory and Methods in Political Science* (London: Palgrave).

—— and STOKER, G. (eds), *Theory and Methods in Political Science* (Basingstoke: Palgrave).

——, RICHARDS, D., and SMITH, M. (2003). Unequal Plurality: Towards an Asymmetric Power Model of the British Polity, *Government and Opposition*, 38/3: 306–32.

—— et al. (1999). 'Studying British Politics', *British Journal of Politics and International Relations*, 1/1: 1–11.

MAYNTZ, R. (2001). 'Zur Selektivität der steuerungstheoretischen Perspektive', Working Paper 01/2 (Köln: Max Planck Institut für Gesellschaftsforschung).

McCORMICK, J. (2001). *Environmental Policy in the European Union* (Basingstoke: Palgrave).

McGinnis, M. (ed.) (1999). *Polycentric Governance and Development. Readings from the Workshop in Political Theory and Policy Analysis* (Michigan: University of Michigan Press).

McNamara, K. (2002). 'Rational Fictions: Central Bank Independence and the Social Logic of Delegation', *West European Politics*, 25 / 1: 47–76.

Mendez, R. (1992). *International Public Finance* (Oxford: OUP).

Metcalfe, L. (1994). 'International Policy Co-ordination and Public Management Reform', *International Review of Administrative Sciences*, 60: 271–90.

Milward, A. (1984). *The Reconstruction of Western Europe, 1945–51* (London: Routledge).

—— (1992). *The European Rescue of the Nation State* (London: Routledge).

Mittag, J. (2000). Ausschuss der Regionen', in W. Weidenfeld and W. Wessels (eds), *Europa von A bis Z. Taschenbuch der europäischen Integration* (Bonn: Bundeszentrale für politische Bildung).

Moe, R. (1994). 'The "Reinventing Government" Exercise', *Public Administration Review*, 54 / 2: 111–22.

Moesen, W. and van Cauwenberge, P. (2000). 'The Status of the Budget Constraint, Federalism and the Relative Size of Government', *Public Choice*, 104: 207–24.

Moravcsik, A. (1991a). 'Negotiating the Single European Act', *International Organization*, 45: 19–56.

—— (1993). 'Preferences and Power in the European Community: A Liberal Intergovernmentalist Approach', *Journal of Common Market Studies*, 31: 473–524.

—— (1994). 'Why the EC Strengthens the State: Domestic Politics and International Cooperation', Centre for European Studies Working Paper 52 (Cambridge, MA: Department of Government, University of Harvard).

—— (1997). 'Taking Preferences Seriously: A Liberal Theory of International Politics', *International Organization*, 51: 538–41.

—— (1998). *The Choice for Europe: Social Purpose and State Power from Rome to Maastricht* (Ithaca, NY: Cornell University Press).

Mosley, P., Harrigan, J., and Toye, J. (1995). *Aid And Power: The World Bank and Policy-based Lending* (London: Routledge).

Mundell, R. (1961). 'A Theory of Optimum Currency Areas', *American Economic Review*, 51: 657–75.

Musgrave, R. (1959). *The Theory of Public Finance* (New York: McGraw-Hill).

Nairn, T. (2000a). 'UKania under Blair', *New Left Review*, 1: 69–103.

National Security Strategy of the United States of America, 17 September 2002, www.whitehouse.gov / nsc / nss.html, accessed 9 March 2003.

Neck, R, Haber, G., and McKibbin, W. (2002). 'Monetary and Fiscal Policy-makers in the European Economic and Monetary Union', *Empirica*, 29: 225–44.

Neocleous, M. (2000). *The Fabrication of Social Order: A Critical Theory of Police Power* (London: Pluto).

Nicolaidis, K. (2001). 'Conclusion: The Federal Vision Beyond the State', in K. Nicolaidis and R. Howse (eds), *The Federal Vision: Legitimacy and Levels of Governance in the United States and the European Union* (Oxford: Oxford University Press).

Nitschke, P. (ed.) (1999). *Die Europäische Union der Regionen—Subpolity und Politiken der Dritten Ebene* (Opladen: Leske and Budrich).

NORTON, A. (1991). 'Western European Local Government in Comparative Perspective', in R. Batley and G. Stoker (eds) *Local Government in Europe: Trends and Developments* (London: MacMillan).

O'BRIEN, R. et al. (2000). *Contesting Global Governance: Multilateral Economic Institutions and Global Social Movements* (Cambridge: Cambridge University Press).

OATES, W. (1972). *Fiscal Federalism* (New York: Harcourt Brace Javonavich).

—— (1999). 'An Essay on Fiscal Federalism', *Journal of Economic Literature*, 37: 1120–49.

OATES, W. (2001). 'Fiscal Competition and European Union', *Regional Science and Urban Economics*, 31: 133–45.

OECD (2001a). *Distributed Public Governance: Agencies, Authorities and other Autonomous Bodies* (London: OECD).

—— (2001b). *Fiscal Design Across Levels of Government Year 2000 Surveys* (Paris: Directorate for Financial, Fiscal and Enterprise Affairs, OECD).

OHMAE, K. (1990). The Borderless World (London: Harper Collins).

OHMAE, K. (1996). The End of the Nation State (London: Wiley).

OHMAE, K. (2000). *The Invisible Continent* (London: Brearley).

OLSSON, J. (2003). 'Democracy Paradoxes in Multi-level Governance', *Journal of European Public Policy*, 10(2): 283–300.

Oswell, G. (1946). 'Politics and the English Language', *Horizon*, April.

OSTROM, E. (1990). *Governing the Commons: The Evolution of Institutions for Collective Action* (Cambridge: Cambridge University Press).

OSTROM, E. and WALKER, J. (1997). 'Neither Markets nor States: Linking Transformation Processes in Collective Action Arenas', in D. Mueller (ed.), *Perspectives on Public Choice: A Handbook* (Cambridge: Cambridge University Press).

OSTROM, V. (1999). 'Polycentricity (Part II)', in M. McGinnis (ed.), *Polycentricity and Local Public Economies. Readings from the Workshop in Political Theory and Policy Analysis* (University of Michigan Press).

—— and JANSSEN, M. (2002). 'Beliefs, Multi-level Governance, and Development', Paper presented at the Annual Meeting of the American Political Science Association (Boston, August 29–September 1).

—— and OSTROM, E. (1999). 'Public Goods and Public Choices', in M. McGINNIS (ed.), *Polycentricity and Local Public Economies. Readings from the Workshop in Political Theory and Policy Analysis* (Michigen: University of Michigan Press). (originally published in 1977).

OSTROM, V., TIEBOUT, C., and WARREN, R. (1961). 'The Organization of Government in Metropolitan Areas: A Theoretical Inquiry', *American Political Science Review*, 55: 831–42.

OUGHTON, D. (1995). 'Accountability versus Control—Rust never Sleeps', *Public Sector*, 17/3: 2–6.

PAGE, E. and GOLDSMITH, M. (eds) (1987). *Central and Local Government Relations: A Comparative Analysis of West European Unitary States* (London: Sage).

PANIZZA, U. (1999). 'On the Determinants of Fiscal Centralization', *Journal of Public Economics*, 74: 97–139.

PAYNE, A. (2004). 'The Study of Governance in a Global Political Economy,' in N. PHILLIPS (ed.), *The Globalisation of International Political Economy* (London: Palgrave).

PERKMANN, M. (1999). 'Building Governance Institutions Across European Borders', *Regional Studies*, 33: 657–67.

PERRATON, J. (2004). 'What's left of "State Capacity"? The Developmental State after Globalisation and the East Asian Crisis', in G. HARRISON (ed.), Global Encounters: International Political Economy, *Development and Globalisation* (Basingstoke: Palgrave).

PETERS, B. (1999). 'Managing Horizontal Government: The Politics of Networks', *Public Administration*, 76: 295–312.

—— (2000). 'Governance and Comparative Politics', in J. Pierre (ed.), *Debating Governance: Authority, Steering, and Democracy* (Oxford: Oxford University Press).

—— and PIERRE, J. (2000). 'Is there a Governance Theory?', Paper presented to Conference 'International Political Science Association', Quebec City, August.

—— —— (2001*a*). 'Developments in Intergovernmental Relations: Towards Multi-level Governance', *Policy and Politics*, 29/2: 131–5.

—— —— (2001*b*). 'Multi-Level Governance: A Faustian Bargain?', Paper presented to Conference 'Multi-level Governance: Interdisciplinary Perspectives', University of Sheffield, 28–30 June.

—— —— (2000). 'Developments in Intergovernmental Relations: Towards Multi-level Governance', *Policy and Politics*, 29: 131–35.

PETERSON, J. (1997). 'States, Societies and the EU', *West European Politics*, 20/4: 1–23.

PETRAS, J. and VIEUX, S. (1996). 'Bosnia and the Revival of US Hegemony', *New Left Review*, 218: 3–25.

PIERRE, J. (2000). *Debating Governance: Authority, Steering and Democracy* (Oxford: Oxford University Press).

—— and PETERS, B. (2000). *Governance, Politics and the State* (London: Macmillan).

—— and STOKER, G. (2000). 'Towards Multi-level Governance' in P. Dunleavy, A. Gamble, I. Holliday, and G. Peele (eds), *Developments in British Politics*, 6th edn (London: MacMillan).

PIERSON, P. (1998). 'The Path of European Integration: A Historical Institutionalist Analysis', in W. Sandholtz and A. Stonesweet (eds), *European Integration and Supranational Governance* (Oxford: Oxford University Press).

PINDER, J. (1991). *European Community: The Building of a Union* (Oxford: Oxford University Press).

PITSCHAS, G. (1995). 'Europäische Integration als Netzwerkkoordination komplexer Staatsaufgaben', in T. Ellwein, D. Grimm, J. J. Hesse, and G. F. Schuppert (eds), *Jahrbuch zur Staats- und Verwaltungswissehschaft. Band 8* (Baden-Baden: Nomos Verlag).

POLLACK, M. (1994). 'Creeping Competence: The Expanding Agenda of the European Community', *Journal of Public Policy*, 14/2: 95–145.

—— (1995). 'Regional Players in an Inter-governmental Play', in C. Rhodes and S. Mazey (eds), *The State of the EU, Volume 3* (Harlow: Longman).

POLLACK, M. (1997). 'Delegation, Agency and Agenda Setting in the European Community', *International Organization*, 51: 99–134.

Pollack, M. The Engines of European Integration: Delegation, Agency and Agenda Setting in the European Union (Oxford: Oxford University Press, 2003).

POULANTZAS, N. (1979). *State, Power, Socialism* (London: Verso).

PRINS, G. (2002). *The Heart of War: On Power, Conflict and Obligation in the Twenty-first Century* (London and New York: Routledge).

PRUD'HOMME, R. (1995). 'The Dangers of Decentralization', *The World Bank Research Observer*, 10: 201–26.

PUCHALA, D. (1972). 'Of Blind Men, Elephants and International Integration', *Journal of Common Market Studies*, 10: 267–84.

PUTNAM, R. D. (2000). *Bowling Alone: The Collapse and Revival of American Community* (New York: Simon & Schuster).

QIAN, Y. and WEINGAST, B. (1997). 'Federalism as a Commitment to Reserving Market Incentives', *Journal of Economic Perspectives*, 11/4: 83–92.

REINER, R. (2000). *The Politics of the Police*, 3rd edn (Oxford and New York: Oxford University Press).

REINICKE, W. (1999–2000). 'The Other World Wide Web: Global Policy Networks', *Foreign Policy*, 7 (July).

RHODES, R. (1981). *Control and Power in Central-Local Relations* (Farnborough: Gower).

—— (1986). 'The New Governance: Governing Without Governance', *Political Studies*, 44: 652–67.

—— (1994). 'The Hollowing Out of the State', *Political Quarterly*, 65: 138–51.

—— (1997). *Understanding Governance: Policy Networks, Governance, Reflexivity and Accountability* (Buckingham: Open University Press).

RHODES, R. A. W. (1986). *The National World of Local Government* (London: Allen & Unwin).

RHODES, R. A. W. (1988). Beyond Westminster and Whitehall (London: Urwin-Hyman).

——, BACHE, I., and GEORGE, S. (1996). 'Policy Networks and Policy-making in the European Union: A Critical Appraisal', in L. Hooghe (ed.), *Cohesion Policy and European Integration: Building Multi-level Governance* (Oxford: Oxford University Press).

RICHARDS, D. (1996). 'Elite Interviewing: Approaches and Pitfalls', *Politics*, 16: 199–204.

—— (2001). 'New Labour, the Constitution and Reforming the State', in S. Ludlam and M. Smith (eds), *New Labour in Government* (Basingstoke: MacMillan Press).

—— and SMITH, M. (2002). *Governance and Public Policy in the United Kingdom* (Oxford: Oxford University Press).

RICHARDSON, J. (2001). *European Union: Power and Policy-making*, 2nd edn (London: Routledge).

RIKER, W. (1964). *Federalism: Origin, Operation, Significance* (Boston: Little, Brown, and Co).

RODDEN, J. (forthcoming). 'Comparative Federalism and Decentralization: On Meaning and Measurement', *Comparative Politics*.

—— and ROSE-ACKERMAN, S. (1992). 'Does Federalism Preserve Markets?', *University of Virginia Law Review*, 83: 1521–72.

ROSAMOND, B. (2000). *Theories of European Integration* (Basingstoke: MacMillan).

ROSE, R. and PETERS, G. (1978). *Can Government go Bankrupt?* (New York: Basic Books).

ROSENAU, J. (1990). *Turbulence in World Politics: A Theory of Change and Continuity* (Princeton: Princeton University Press).

—— (1997). *Along the Domestic-Foreign Frontier. Exploring Governance in a Turbulent World* (Cambridge: Cambridge University Press).

ROSENAU, J. (2000). 'The Globalization of Globalization', a Paper presented for 'International Studies Association', Los Angeles, March 16.

—— (2001). 'Strong Demand, Huge Supply: Governance in an Emergent Epoch', Paper prepared for Conference 'Multi-level Governance: Interdisciplinary Perspectives', University of Sheffield, 28–30 June.

—— (2003). *Distant Proximities: Dynamics Beyond Globalization* (Princeton: Princeton University Press).

ROSENAU, J. N. and SINGH, J. P. (2002). *Information Technologies and Global Politics: The Changing Scope of Power and Governance* (New York: State University of New York Press).

Roth, D. (1996). 'Finding the Balance: Achieving a Synthesis between Improved performance and enhanced accountability', in OECD Performance Auditing and the Modernisation of Government (Paris: OECD).

RSPB Interview with J. Fairbrass, 1 June, Sandy, Beds. (2000).

RSPB/WWF Joint Campaigner Interview with J. Fairbrass, 18 July, Redgrave, Norfolk. (2000).

RUGGIE, J. (1993). 'Territoriality and Beyond: Problematizing Modernity in International Relations', *International Organization*, 46: 139–74.

RUIGROK, W. and VAN TULDER, R. (1996). 'The Price of Diversity: Rival Concepts of Control as a Barrier to an EU Industrial Strategy', in P. Devine, Y. Katsoulacos, and R. Sugder (eds), *Competitiveness, Subsidiarity, and Industrial Policy* (London: Routledge).

RUSSELL, M. and HAZELL, R. (2000). 'Devolution and Westminster: Tentative Steps Towards a More Federal Parliament', in R. Hazell (ed.), *The State and the Nations: The First Year of Devolution in the United Kingdom* (Thorverton: Imprint Academic).

SALA-I-MARTIN, X. (1997). 'I Just Ran Two Million Regressions', *American Economic Review*, 87/2: 178–83.

—— and SACHS, J. (1992). 'Fiscal Federalism and Optimum Currency Areas: Evidence from Europe and the United States', in M. Canzoneri, V. Grilli, and P. Masson (eds), *Establishing a Central Bank: Issues in Europe and Lessons from the US* (Cambridge: Cambridge University Press).

SALMON, T. (2000). 'An Oxymoron: The Scottish Parliament and Foreign Relations?', in A. Wright (ed.), *Scotland: The Challenge of Devolution* (Aldershot: Ashgate).

SANDHOLTZ, W. and ZYSMAN, J. (1989). '1992: Recasting the European Bargain', *World Politics*, 42: 95–128.

—— and STONESWEET, A. (1998). *European Integration and Supranational Governance* (Oxford: Oxford University Press).

—— and STONESWEET, A. (1999). 'European Integration and Supranational Governance Revisited: Rejoinder to Branch and Øhrgaard', *Journal of European Public Policy*, 6: 144–54.

SARTORI, G. (1970). 'Concept Misformation in Comparative Politics', *American Political Science Review*, 64/4: 1033–53.

SBRAGIA, A. (1992). 'Thinking about the European Future: The Uses of Comparison', in A. Sbragia (ed.), *Euro-Politics: Institutions and Policymaking in the 'New' European Community* (Washington: Brookings Institution).

—— (1993). 'The European Community: A Balancing Act', *Publius*, 23: 23–38.

—— (2000). 'The European Union as Coxswain: Governance by Steering', in J. Pierre (ed.), *Debating Governance: Authority, Steering, and Democracy* (Oxford: Oxford University Press).

SCHARPF, F. (1988). 'The Joint Decision Trap: Lessons from German Federalism and European Integration', *Public Administration*, 66: 239–78.

—— (1994a). 'Community and Autonomy: Multi-Level Policy-making in the European Union', *Journal of European Public Policy*, 1: 219–42.

—— (1994b). 'Games Real Actors could Play: Positive and Negative Coordination in Embedded Negotiations', *Journal of Theoretical Politics*, 6/1: 27–53.

—— (1994c). 'Community and Autonomy. Multilevel Policy-Making in the European Union', EUI Working Paper RSC No. 94/1 (Florence: European University Institute).

—— (1997). 'Introduction: The Problem-solving Capacity of Multi-level Governance', *Journal of European Public Policy*, 4: 520–38.

—— (1998). *Governing in Europe: Effective and Democratic?* (Oxford: Oxford University Press).

—— (2001). 'Notes Towards a Theory of Multilevel Governing in Europe', *Scandinavian Political Studies*, 24/1: 1–26.

SCHMITTER, P. (1970). 'A Revised Theory of Regional Integration'. *International Organization*, 24: 836–68.

—— (1992). 'Representation and the Future Euro-Polity', *Staatswissen-schaften und Staatspraxis*, 3(3): 379–405.

—— (2000). *How to Democratize the European Union . . . And Why Bother?* (Boulder, Col.: Rowman and Littlefield).

SCHOLTE, JAN ART. (2000). *Globalization: A Critical Introduction* (London: MacMillan Press).

SCOTT, J. and TRUBEK, D. M. (2002). 'Mind the Gap: Law and New Approaches to Governance in the European Union', *European Law Journal*, 8/1: 1–18.

—— (2000b). 'Scotland House 1999–2000—One Year On, Scottish Executive EU Office', www.scotland.gov.uk/euoffice/shr2000.asp, accessed 18 March 2002.

—— (2002c). 'Scotland and the European Union', Scottish Executive EU Office, www.scotland.gov.uk, accessed 11 September 2002.

SHANKS, C., JACOBSON, H. and KAPLAN, J. (1996). 'Inertia and Change in IGOs, 1981–1992', *International Organisation*, 50: 593–627.

SHARPE, L. (1998). 'The Growth and Decentralisation of the Modern State', *European Journal of Political Research*, 16: 365–80.

SHARPE, R. (1998). 'Responding to Europeanisation. A Governmental Perspective', in P. Lowe and S. Ward (eds), *British Environmental Policy and Europe. Politics and Policy in Transition* (Routledge: London).

SHAW, M. (2000). *Theory of the Global State. Globality as an Unfinished Revolution* (Cambridge: Cambridge University Press).

SHEATE, W. (1997). 'From EIA to SEA: Sustainability and Decision Making' in J. HOLDER (ed.), *The Impact of EC Environmental Law in the UK* (Chichester: John Wiley).

SKELCHER, C. (1998). *The Appointed State* (Milton Keynes: Open University Press).

SLOAT, A. (2001c). 'Scotland and the European Union: Contribution to EU Governance Debates', in 'Scottish Parliament (2001): Report on the Governance of the European Union and the Future of Europe: What Role for Scotland?', European

Committee Report, 9th Report 2001, SP Paper 466, Session 1, www.scottish. parliament.uk/official_report/cttee/europe-01/eur01-09-vol01-01.htm, accessed 28 January 2002.

SMITH, M. J. (1995). 'Pluralism', in Marsh, D. and Stoker, G. (eds.), *Theory and Methods in Political Science* (Basingstoke: Macmillan) pp. 209–27.

SMITH, M. (1997). 'Studying Multi-level Governance: Examples from French Translations of the Structural Funds', *Public Administration*, 20: 711–29.

SMITH, M. (1999). *The Core Executive* (London : MacMillan).

SMOUTS, M. (1998). 'The Proper use of Governance in International Relations', *International Social Science Journal*, 50: 81–101.

SMYRL, M. E. (1997). 'Does European Community Regional Policy Empower the Regions?', *Governance: An International Journal of Policy and Administration*, 10: 287–309.

SØRENSEN, G. (2001). *Changes in Statehood. The Transformation of International Relations* (Basingstoke: Palgrave).

STIGLITZ, J. (2002). *Globalization and its Discontents* (London: The Penguin Press).

STOKER, G. (1998). 'Governance as Theory: Five Propositions', *International Social Science Journal*, 155: 17–28.

—— (2000). 'Urban Political Science and the Challenge of Urban Governance', in J. PIERRE (ed.), *Debating Governance: Authority, Steering, and Democracy* (Oxford: Oxford University Press).

STONE SWEET, A. and Sandholtz, W. (1998). 'Integration, Supranational Governance and the Institutionalization of the European Polity' in Sandholtz, W. and Zysman, J. (eds.), *European Integration and Supranational Governance*. (Oxford: Oxford University Press) pp. 1–26.

TANZI, V. (1995). 'Fiscal Federalism and Decentralization: A Review of Some Efficiency and Macroeconomic Aspects', in *Proceedings of the Annual World Bank Conference on Development Economics*.

TAYLOR, A. (2000). 'Hollowing Out or Filling In? Taskforces and the Management of Cross-cutting Issues in British Government', *British Journal of Politics and International Relations*, 2/1: 46–71.

TAYLOR, P. (1975). 'The Politics of the European Communities: The Confederal Phase', *World Politics*, 27/4: 336–60.

TELÒ, M. (2002). 'Governance and Government in the European Union: the Open Method of Coordination', in M. Rodrigues (ed.), *The New Knowledge Economy in Europe* (Cheltenham: Edward Elgar).

The Ditchley Foundations (2000). 'Devolution and Subsidiarity: Relationships Between Central and Next-Lower Levels of National Government', News No. 06, Note by the Director, Ditchley 00/3, www.ditchley.co.uk/news/devolution00-3.htm, accessed 24 May 2002.

THERIVEL, R., WILSON, E., THOMPSON, S., HEANEY, D. and PRITCHARD, D. (eds) (1992). *Strategic Environmental Assessment* (London: Earthscan).

THIELEMANN, E. R. (1999). 'Institutional limits of a "Europe with the Regions": EC state-aid control meets German federalism', *Journal of European Public Policy*, 6: 399–418.

TIEBOUT, C. (1956). 'A Pure Theory of Local Expenditures', *Journal of Political Economy*, 64: 416–24.

TILLY, C. (ed.) (1975). *The Formation of National States in Western Europe* (Princeton, NJ: Princeton University Press).

TINDALE, S. (1996). 'Introduction: The State and the Nations', in S. Tindale (ed.), *The State and the Nations: The Politics of Devolution* (IPPR).

TOMANEY, J. (2000*a*). 'The Regional Governance of England' in R. Hazell, (ed.), *The State and the Nations* (Thorverton : Imprint).

—— (2000*b*). 'End of the Empire State? New Labour and Devolution in the United Kingdom', *International Journal of Urban and Regional Research*, 24/3: 675–88.

TREISMAN, D. (1999). 'Political Decentralization and Economic Reform: A Game-theoretic Analysis', *American Journal of Political Science*, 43: 488–517.

Treasury/DTI/ODPM (2003). *A Modern Regional Policy for the United Kingdom* (London: HMSO).

TRENCH, A. (2001). 'Intergovernmental Relations a Year On: Whitehall still Rules UK', in A. TRENCH (ed.), *The State of the Nations 2001: The Second Year of Devolution in the United Kingdom* (The Constitution Unit, Imprint Academic, Thorverton).

—— (2001). 'Introduction: Devolution's Second Year: But Mountains Left to Climb?', in A. TRENCH (ed.), *The State of the Nations 2001: The Second Year of Devolution in the United Kingdom* (The Constitution Unit, Imprint Academic, Thorverton).

—— (ed.) (2001). *The State of the Nations 2001: The Second Year of Devolution in the United Kingdom* (The Constitution Unit, Imprint Academic, Thorverton).

US Bureau of the Census (1999). *1999 Census of Governments GC97(1)-1. Volume I, Government Organization* (Washington: US Government Printing Office).

—— (2002). *2002 Census of Governments GC02–1(P). Preliminary Report* Issued July 2002 (Washington: US Government Printing Office).

VAN APELDOORN, B. (2002). *Transnational Capitalism and the Struggle over European Integration* (London: Routledge).

VAN DER PIJL, K. (1984). *The Making of an Atlantic Ruling Class* (London: New Left Books).

VAUBEL, R. (1994). 'The Political Economy of Centralization and the European Community', *Public Choice*, 81: 151–90.

VELASCO CRUZ, J. L. (1999). *El Debate Actual Sobre el Federalismo Mexicano* (Mexico DF: Instituto Mora).

VON HAGEN, J. and HARDEN, I. (1995). 'Budget Processes and Commitment to Fiscal Discipline', *European Economic Review*, 39/3: 771–79.

WALKER, D. (1999). *The Future of Federalism*, 3rd edn (New York: Chatham House).

WALKER, J. L., Jr (1991). *Mobilizing Interest Groups in America: Patrons, Professions, and Social Movements* (Ann Arbor: University of Michigan Press).

WALKER, N. (2000). 'Flexibility within a Metaconstitutional Frame: Reflexions on the Future of Legal Authority', in G. Búrca and J. Scott (eds), *Constitutional Change in the EU: from Uniformity to Flexibility?* (Oxford: Hart).

WALLACE, H. (1995). 'Britain Out on a Limb?', *Political Studies*, 66/1: 46–58.

—— (1997). 'At Odds with Europe', *Political Studies*, XLV: 677–88.

WALLICH, C., BIRD, R., and EBEL, R. (eds) (1995). *Decentralization of the Socialist State: Intergovernmental Finance in Transition Economies* (Washington: World Bank).

WANG, H. and ROSENAU, J. (2001). 'Transparency International and Corruption as an Issue of Global Governance', *Global Governance*, 7: 25–49.

WARD, K. (1996). 'Rereading Urban Regime Theory: a Sympathetic Critique', *Geoforum* (Elsevier Science Ltd), 27/4: 427–38.

WARLEIGH, A. (1999). *The Committee of the Regions: Institutionalising Multi-level Governance?* (London European Research Centre, London: Kogan Page).

WEALE, A. *et al.* (2000). *Environmental Governance in Europe* (Oxford: Oxford University Press).

WEARER, R. and ROCKMAN, B. (1993). *Do Institutions Matter?* (Washington D.C.: The Brookings Institution).

WEBB, M. (1995). *The Political Economy of Policy Coordination* (Ithaca: Cornell University Press).

WEILER, J. (1981). 'The Community System: the Dual Character of Supranationalism', *Yearbook of European Law*, 1: 268–306.

WEILER, J. (2000). 'Federalism and Constitutionalism: Europe's Sonderweg' (Unpublished paper).

—— and WESSELS, A. (1988a). 'EPC and the Challenge of Theory', in A. Pijpers, E. Regelsberger, and W. Wessels, (eds), *European Political cooperation in the 1980s: A Common Foreign Policy for Western Europe?* (Dordrecht: Martinus Nijhoff).

—— —— (1998b). 'EPC and the Challenge of Theory', in A. Pijpers, E. Regelsberger, and W. Wessels (eds), *European Political cooperation in the 1980s: A Common Foreign Policy for Western Europe?* (Dordrecht: Martinus Nijhoff).

WEINGAST, B. (1995). 'The Economic Role of Political Institutions: Market Preserving Federalism and Economic Development', *Journal of Law, Economics and Organization*, 11: 1–31.

WELCH, S. (2001). 'Ethical–Political Dimensions of Police Intervention: Domestic and International Contexts Compared', *Civil Wars*, 4: 104–24.

WENDT, A. (1999). *Social Theory of International Politics* (Cambridge: Cambridge University Press).

WEPE (1998). *Welsh European Programme Executive: Business Plan 1998–99* (Mountain Ash/Machynlleth: Welsh European Programme Executive).

WEYAND, S. (1999). 'Inter-regional Associations and the European Integration Process', *Regional and Federal Studies*, 6: 166–82.

WHEARE, K. (1953). *Federal Government* (New York: Oxford University Press).

WILLKE, H. (1992). *Ironie des Staates* (Frankfurt: Suhrkamp).

WILKINSON, R. (2002). 'The Contours of Courtship: The WTO and Civil Society', in R. Wilkinson and S. Hughes (eds), *Global Governance: Critical Perspectives* (London and New York: Routledge).

WILS, J. (1994). 'The Birds Directive 15 Years Later', *Journal of Environmental Law*, 6/2: 219–42.

WILSON, R. 'The Civil Service in the new Millenium', Speech given at City University, London, 5 May 1999.

WILSON, D. (2003). 'Unravelling Control Greatly: Redefining Central-local Government Relations', *British Journal of Politics and International Relations*, 5/3: 317–47.

WINCOTT, D. (1995). 'Institutional Interaction and European Integration: Towards an Everyday Critique of Liberal Intergovernmentalism', *Journal of Common Market Studies*, 33/4: 597–609.

WOOD, C. (1995). *Environmental Impact Assessment*, (Harlow: Longman).

WOOD, C. and JONES, C. (1991). *Monitoring Environmental Assessment and Planning* (London: HMSO).

WOODS, N. and NARLIKAR, A. (2001). 'Governance and the Limits of Accountability: The World Trade Organisation, the International Monetary Fund and the World Bank', *International Social Science Journal*, 53/170: 569–83.

World Bank Institute (2002). Overview to WBI Program on Intergovernmental Fiscal Relations, www.worldbank.org/wbi/publicfinance/decentralization/about.html

WRIGHT, D. (1989). *Intergovernmental Relations in the United States*, 3rd edn (Monterey, CA: Brooks/Cole).

YOUNG, I. M. (1997). 'Polity and Group Difference: A Politics of Ideas or a Politics of Presence?', in R. E. Gooden and P. Pettit (eds), *Contemporary Political Philosophy* (Oxford: Blackwell), 256–72.

YOUNG, O. (ed.) (1999). *The Effectiveness of International Environmental Regimes: Causal Connections and Behavioral Mechanisms* (Cambridge: MIT Press).

ZILTENER, P. (1999). *Strukturwandel der europäischen Integration. Die Europäischer Union und die Veränderung von Staatlichkeit* (Münster: Westfälisches Dampfboot).

Index

Cats Rule!

Cat.

Raintree is an imprint of Capstone Global Library Limited, a company incorporated in England and Wales having its registered office at 264 Banbury Road, Oxford, OX2 7DY – Registered company number: 6695582

www.raintree.co.uk
myorders@raintree.co.uk

Edited by Carrie Sheely, Alesha Halvorson
Designed by Philippa Jenkins
Illustrated by HL Studios p. 6, Jeff Edwards p. 14, Bridge Creative Services p. 26
Original illustrations © Capstone Global Library Limited 2016
Picture research by Svetlana Zhurkin
Production by Steve Walker
Originated by Capstone Global Library Limited
Printed and bound in China

ISBN 978 1 4747 1290 3 (hardback)
19 18 17 16 15
10 9 8 7 6 5 4 3 2 1

ISBN 978 1 4747 1722 9 (paperback)
20 19 18 17 16
10 9 8 7 6 5 4 3 2 1

British Library Cataloguing in Publication Data
A full catalogue record for this book is available from the British Library.

Acknowledgements
We would like to thank the following for permission to reproduce photographs: Alamy: Gari Wyn Williams, 25, Steven Roe, 21; Capstone Press: Philippa Jenkins, back cover and throughout; Dreamstime: Olga Volodina, 6; Granger, NYC, 15; Newscom: Zuma Press/Greg Sorber, 27, Zuma Press/Michael Holahan, 10; Shutterstock: Andrey Degtyaryov, 14, Anton Gvozdikov, 7, 8, 9, 26, Eric Isselee, 28, Konstantin Gushcha, 18, KWJPhotoArt, 5 (inset), Linn Currie, cover, 5, 12, 17 (bottom), Lubava, 11, Marten_House, 19, photo_master2000, 20, se media, 23, VGstockstudio, 17 (top), Ysbrand Cosijn, 13

The author would like to thank Laurie Patton, Regional Director, TICA Southeast, for her invaluable help in the preparation of this book.

Some words are shown in bold, **like this**. You can find out what they mean by looking in the glossary.